Praise for Previous Editions

"This is an essential handbook for anyone interested in a career in acting. No matter if you are in the US, UK, Australia, the EU or any other market where a person can have a career as an actor, this new book should be on top of your list." Alan Nusbaum, *Founder and CEO of TVI Actors Studio*

"An invaluable labor... [which] may well prevent the profession from breaking many young hearts...[Its] tone is tough but strangely conspiratorial with the reader, and it may well send a wave of young actors into show business at once resolved and cynical, at once principled and skeptical, and it is hard to imagine a better state of mind than that." Austin Pendleton, *Yale Theatre*

"An excellent book... [which] will help steer you in the right direction with its pragmatic advice and realistic picture of showbiz survival." Thomas Mills, *Back Stage West*

"The much-praised book is as successful and valuable as ever... [and] fully exposes the aspiring actor to the 'raw facts' of the business." Jeffrey Scott Elwell, *Theatre Journal*

"*Acting Professionally* is a must for those who want to understand the biz." Davi Napoleon, *Theatre Week*

"The most straightforward, accurate, and honest description of what the acting business is like in the United States and what it takes to break into it. An absolute must for any student-actor seriously contemplating the possibility of entering this dismal and indescribably wonderful profession." Roger Ellis, *An Audition Handbook for Student Actors*

"A magnificent service both to aspiring actors and to the theatre by presenting the profession of acting in its myriad, unadorned aspects." Eric Forsythe, *Dartmouth Alumni Magazine*

Other books by Robert Cohen

Acting One
Acting Two
Acting in Shakespeare
Theatre
Acting Power: the 21st Century Edition
Working Together in Theatre: Leadership and Collaboration
Shakespeare on Theatre: A Critical Look
Falling Into Theatre – and Finding Myself
More Power to You (essays)
Creative Play Direction (with John Harrop)
Giraudoux: Three Faces of Destiny
Eight Plays for Theatre (anthology)
Twelve Plays for Theatre (anthology)

Acting Professionally

Raw Facts about Careers in Acting

8th edition

Robert Cohen and James Calleri

macmillan
education

palgrave

First edition published 1972 by
National Press Books

Second edition published 1975 by
Mayfield Publishing Company

Third edition published 1981 by
Mayfield Publishing Company

Fourth edition published 1989 by
Mayfield Publishing Company

Fifth edition published 1997 by
Mayfield Publishing Company

Sixth edition published 2003 by
McGraw-Hill Companies Inc.

Seventh edition published 2009
by Palgrave Macmillan

Eighth edition published 2017 by
PALGRAVE

Palgrave in the UK is an imprint of Macmillan Publishers Limited, registered in England, company number 785998, of 4 Crinan Street, London, N1 9XW.

Palgrave is a global imprint of the above companies and is represented throughout the world.

Palgrave® and Macmillan® are registered trademarks in the United States, the United Kingdom, Europe and other countries.

ISBN 978–1–137–60586–3 paperback

This book is printed on paper suitable for recycling and made from fully managed and sustained forest sources. Logging, pulping and manufacturing processes are expected to conform to the environmental regulations of the country of origin.

A catalogue record for this book is available from the British Library.

A catalog record for this book is available from the Library of Congress.

Printed and bound by CPI Group (UK) Ltd, Croydon, CR0 4YY

Contents

About the Authors

Robert Cohen (see www.robertcohendrama.com) is an acclaimed professional and academic stage director, and has served fifty years as the founding Chair of Drama at the University of California, Irvine. The author of twenty-four books on theatre, several obtaining multiple and translated editions, his major awards include a Claire Trevor Professorship, the UCI Medal, Romania's Honoris Causa Medal, Poland's Medal of Honor, the ATHE (Association for Theatre in Higher Education) Award for Career Achievement, and UCI's 2015 Award for Distinguished Professor of Research.

James Calleri (see http://www.callericasting.com) is an acclaimed casting director in New York City and an Associate Professor and Head of Acting at the Columbia University School of the Arts Graduate Acting Program.
Along with his partners Paul Davis and Erica Jensen, he has won over a
dozen Artios Awards for Outstanding Achievement in Casting. James has
led the casting on Broadway of *The Elephant Man, Hedwig and the Angry
Inch, Of Mice and Men, and A Raisin in the Sun*, among others. His films
have appeared at Sundance and Cannes, and he has cast the television
shows The Path, Monk, Lipstick Jungle, Ed to name a few. James has lec-
tured and taught acting all over the country and as far as Shanghai, China.
He is a proud member of the Casting Society of America where he serves
on the Board.

1 The Way It Is

Let's face it. Acting is fun. Millions of people do it for free, and millions more want to make their living from it. And why not? Who wouldn't want to take home $20 million for six weeks of work? Add to this the great travel to exotic shooting locations, the fabulous parties, the global fame, and the effortless sexual, romantic, and marital opportunities thrust into your lap from every corner of the world.

Just imagine the amazement and envy of your friends as you go head to head with Stephen Colbert or Jimmy Fallon, sharing juicy gossip from the set, expounding your political opinions, and suavely putting down your rivals and enemies (including the former professor who said you'd never make it) with a toothy grin and a wry riposte. And don't forget the world tours, fawning politicians, and ardent groupies, or running down the aisle to pick up your Tony or Oscar in front of millions of cheering viewers around the world. You might even—why not?—head a national association as Charlton Heston did, address a national political convention as Eva Longoria and Kal Penn did, or deliver the annual State of the Union address as President (and actor) Ronald Reagan did.

As the late Jimmy Durante used to say, "Everybody wants to get into the act!" No wonder, especially when dozens of books and hundreds of acting teachers tell you that all you need to learn in order to do this is simply to "be yourself!" Forget college, medical school, or mastering the split-fingered fastball. Act!

Well, you're right, of course. At the summit, acting is one of the most sublime activities of the human species. Playing Hamlet or Hecuba or Alexander Hamilton may not only give you an income, it may make you feel like a God.

And—again at the top—acting can be extremely lucrative, particularly in Hollywood. For men, the sky seems to be the limit. Leonardo DiCaprio, Matt Damon, Robert Downey Jr., and Denzel Washington routinely earn more than $20 million for a single film, often plus profit bonuses. And Sandra Bullock is also in that category, making—after including additional bonuses from the film's revenues—an astonishing $70 million for *Gravity*. Other members of the $20-plus million per film club are Johnny Depp, Brad

Pitt, Will Ferrell, Tom Hanks, Daniel Radcliffe, Jennifer Aniston, and Jennifer Lopez, among many others.

These figures are for film, the money pot for superstars, but top pay in other entertainment media isn't too shabby. On TV's *The Big Bang Theory*, Jim Parsons earned a reported $29 million in the 2014–15 season, with Ashton Kutcher receiving $20 million for *Two and a Half Men*, Ray Romano picking up $15 million, and the *Modern Family* major players earning from $10.5 to $11.5 million dollars annually.

No matter how you look at it, there is big money at stake. The late James Gandolfini, who ended his reign on *The Sopranos* at a reported million dollars per episode, summed it up best: "All I can say," he quipped, "is they wouldn't pay it if they ain't makin' it."

The income in legitimate (live) theatre is admittedly less, but certainly more than respectable at the top. Nathan Lane and Matthew Broderick each garnered $100,000 a week for reprising their Broadway roles in *The Producers* back in 2001. Since then, Idina Menzel and Kristin Chenoweth each collected a reported weekly pay of $25,000–$30,000 to star in *Wicked*, Julia Roberts earned $35,000 (plus a box office percentage that more than doubled this amount) for starring in *Three Days of Rain*, while Kevin Spacey earned as much as $60,000 a week ($25,000 plus 10% of the weekly gross ticket income) for his Broadway turn in the Eugene O'Neill classic, *A Moon for the Misbegotten*.

So, why not get into the act? Children do it. Models do it. Ex-athletes and ex-cons do it. Even dogs do it. Let's do it—let's act!

But *not for the money*! One thing must be said at the outset of this book: *acting is a lousy way to make a living*. On this score, at least, your parents were right.

Let's face the facts. Each year, tens, maybe hundreds of thousands, of people find their way on stage or before a camera, and some of them even get paid for it, but the number who actually *make a living* from it is ridiculously small. By "making a living" we mean receiving paid employment sufficient to provide you with a regular annual income, permitting you to rent a decent apartment or home in a big city, to marry or develop a solid personal relationship, to eat three meals a day and go out once in a while, and even to have children and take vacations if you want to. The number of people who actually become fully self-supporting through acting alone for, say, ten years in a row is probably no larger than those holding a seat in the U.S. Congress. Yes, SAG-AFTRA (the actors' union that in 2012 merged the Screen Actors Guild with the American Federation of Television and Radio Artists) now covers both film and TV actors, and boasts about 160,000 professionals in these fields. And another 50,000 professional actors—many of whom are also in SAG-AFTRA—are in America's Actors Equity Association (AEA), which covers, and sets wages for, all professional stage productions. But fewer than *half* of these actors, though professionals, will earn an income *higher than the national poverty level in any given year*, which in 2016 was only $11,770. And far fewer than half of *them* will earn that amount for ten years in a row!

To put it in even clearer perspective: there are far more self-supporting acting *teachers* in the United States than self-supporting actors.

So, not only is acting one of the toughest businesses in the world to break into; it is, even more so, one of the toughest to build a lifetime career in. Maybe it's *the* toughest. For the vast majority of acting hopefuls who try out don't even get a foot in the door, and the vast majority who do get a foot in the door don't keep it there for very long. You may hate us for saying this, but you must face it nonetheless: the vast majority of America's professional actors are, at any given time, "between jobs." And for most of them, "between" is simply a euphemism for "without."

Acting is therefore a boutique profession, like being a U.S. Senator or a network anchorperson. Only a handful make it into the boutique. This wouldn't be quite so bad except for the fact that acting is often treated (and marketed) as if it were a mass occupation. Nearly 200 graduate actor-training programs are offered in the nation's 1,000-plus college and university theatre and drama departments, and another 1,000 private acting schools and studios claim to train professional actors. Just how many Master of Fine Arts (MFA) programs or private schools do you think are out there offering professional training for aspiring U.S. Senators or network anchorpersons? A good guess would be none. And for this reason acting enjoys a lot more competition than most boutique professions; and it certainly has more disappointed aspirants.

But do not despair utterly. If you've got the goods and the smarts and the opportunities—and the luck—you have as good a crack at it as anyone. Our book will give you some solid pointers in that direction.

You're going to have to really work at it, though, and that's the most fundamental point underlying these pages. Wanting success isn't enough, studying for it isn't enough, and no amount of dedication or commitment will, on its own, get you into the casting office. Being "discovered" at a drugstore soda fountain is, and always has been, a fan magazine myth. No, you're going to have to work harder than you ever have on your acting, and to work even harder on learning how to *present* yourself—and *represent* yourself—in the job market. Yes, you're going to have to *market* yourself.

In the context of the "raw facts" that constitute the acting market, that is what the rest of this book is about. So, let's get started.

you—the "dreadful pudder o'er our heads," as King Lear says—but they're there. They, their policies and influence, will determine much of what goes on in your professional life. As Hollywood casting director Francine Witkin makes clear, "Actors must understand this is a business and treat it as a business. They're a product. Most people don't think of themselves as human beings with fantasies and dreams. They've got to realize what this business is and what the politics are."

Art and industry

If acting is part of an industry, is it still an art? Well, of course. Indeed, one of the problems of acting professionally is that it's an art within an industry, within a world in which "the gross" and "box office revenue (B.O.)" are both fiscal realities and cultural metaphors.

When young actors first read a trade paper like *Variety*, they might be excused if they think they've ended up with *Gross Magazine* or *The Journal of Dental Hygiene*. "Grosses" and "B.O." hold the main attention, page after page. "*Amazing Grace* Grosses" headlined *Variety* when the film by that name had an "amazing gross" income at its weekend premiere. "B.O. flags in August sag" trumpeted a *Variety* column when one year's late-summer blockbusters tanked at the ticket office—and the trade wasn't talking about damp underarms.

The gross (income) and B.O. (box office revenue) are the bottom line of the accountant's report. But grossness (in the sense of crassness) and the odor of mendacity—as Tennessee Williams might have said—often pervade the entertainment industries as well. Hollywood, of course, comes in for most of the disdain. Films about films as old as Charlie Chaplin's 1916 *Behind the Screen* to David Cronenberg's 2014 *Maps to the Stars* and Olivier Assayas' 2015 *Clouds of Sils Maria* show us the seamy, commercial side of tinseltown (aka Hollywood), where (we are told) lying, stealing, nepotism, lawsuits, and sexual politics are the order of the day. But films about the so-called legitimate theatre, such as the 2014 *Birdman* (subtitled *The Unexpected Value of Ignorance*), show that it isn't all that superlegit either, winning the Academy Award for Best Picture by showing the catastrophic horrors of Broadway rehearsals. For David Mamet's *Speed the Plow*, the (nonprofit) Lincoln Center Theatre production company cast Madonna as the female lead—not, one must imagine, wholly for her thespian talents (though they are considerable) but for the potential contribution to the gross receipts that such a sometime sex symbol and rock star might generate. The aroma of B.O., it is clear, knows no geographical boundaries in the entertainment business.

So, where do actors fit into the gross? The "suits" (that is, the executives) are at the top, as in every industry. As for the actors, Samuel Beckett put it best in his *Waiting for Godot*:

> *Estragon*: Where do we come in?
> *Vladimir*: Come in? Come in? On our hands and knees!

The most fundamental law of economics, as you probably know, is the law of supply and demand. In part, this means that the more of something there is, the less anyone has to pay for it. Well, there are an awful lot of actors willing to work out there—a fact not lost on theatre and film producers. In addition to the roughly 200,000 stage, film, and TV actors currently in the AEA and/or SAG-AFTRA unions, over 1000 college drama departments are turning out new actors every year, and an even greater number of high school drama programs, private acting schools, conservatories, and private teachers are sending young men and women to New York and Hollywood with plans to "break into" the field. Thousands more simply head into one of those towns, and others make it to Chicago or Seattle or other "acting mini-centers" of their own choice. The supply of actors, in other words, vastly exceeds the demand—and the economics of acting reflect this.

Yet while everyone in the Western world must know by now that a star can make a lifetime income performing in a single film, few are aware that the star's fee will vacuum up half or more of the entire cost of making that movie, which means that the rest of the actors (together with the several hundred other people involved in making it—from the director to the set dressers to the caterers) can only divide the other half, and that after the producer has also tapped into that same pot for the scenery, costumes, rentals, royalties, and what-not.

The point is that today actor salaries, other than the star's, are a stunningly *minor* part of the entertainment industry budget. As the "Secret Agent Man" in a *Backstage* column said, "You're either getting millions or you're getting scale," which means that those film and TV pros who are *not* stars are working for SAG-AFTRA's minimum daily wage of $859. And actors in low-budget films will receive even less, under a recently approved "SAG-AFTRA Modified Low Budget Theatrical Wage" of $335 per day as of 2016. Yes, that may be more than you're making now—but remember that, if hired, you'll probably be making that for only *one day*—which could turn out to be the only day that year.

We want you to think about this. Young actors are often very idealistic about this inescapable reality of the business. Many are quick to point out that they don't have any desire to become "stars" but are simply seeking steady acting work, say in an acting position at a modest repertory company in a medium-size town. They will, they may then proclaim, happily trade fame and riches for "just" a position that offers creative opportunities and artistic respectability. They don't need a lot of money, they assert, "just enough to live on." OK, but please beware of the "just." Having "just enough to live on" is the big problem! Surprise! Merely rejecting Broadway and Hollywood does not magically get you into the Denver Theatre Center, any more than rejecting an unoffered Mercedes Benz will put a bicycle in your driveway. The simple fact is that it is *desperately difficult* for a beginner to get *any* professional acting job. At *any* theatre. In *any* city.

At a statistical level, your chances for getting a professional (i.e. paid) role after any *single* application or group audition are no more than one in a hundred—one in a hundred *literally*, and maybe one in a thousand if the truth be known. That's the law of supply and demand working, and in acting the supply is all but unlimited. The fact is that you should no more expect to get a paid acting job because of your undergraduate drama degree than your sister can expect to become a U.S. Senator on the basis of her BA in political science. You can *hope*, of course, but not *expect*. "Listen," says a prominent and hardworking casting director (and most theatre professionals will give you the same advice), "if you can think of anything you can possibly do instead of acting, do it! Get out now! Save yourself the heartache and the pain—and save me the time."

Developing a mature viewpoint

The previous paragraphs contain some hard lessons, but they are basic adult realities—and they are lessons worth learning. If you're going to pursue an acting career, you're going to have to deal with adult reality. And you're going to have to *be* an adult—while retaining enough of the childlike innocence required of any artist.

What does being an adult mean? It means, basically, that you—not your parents or teachers—will be taking the initiative in your own life. You will be making (and responding to) your own assignments, as it were. The biggest difference between life as a student and life after graduation is that after graduation *nobody assigns you anything*. Nobody tells you what to do next. Nobody *cares* what you do next. And you receive no grades. As wonderful as this may seem, it can lead to life's first great agonies: What do I do now? How good am I? Am I going to make it? Why doesn't anybody care about me?

No one in the adult world will answer those questions for you—unless you pay them to (in which case they are not unbiased) or unless they love you (in which case they are *definitely* not unbiased)!

Moreover, you have no *automatic* community to rely on. Think of it: from kindergarten to college or graduate school, you have been thrown in with dozens of people (at close range) and hundreds more (at extended range) close to your age and with parallel aspirations. They're now gone—or at least they're not showing up in your life in the way they once showed up at your nine o'clock class. To have a community, you must re-find your old friends and, more important, find some new ones. Modern technology comes to your aid here: Facebook and other social networking sites are among the greatest inventions of the twenty-first century and among the most useful innovations of modern professional life. Online contacts with people you know can become a terrific way to discover people you *don't* know—but will be delighted to meet, for both social and professional reasons.

But along with maintaining and developing a community, you still must assume leadership of your own life. And this is harder: you are now wholly responsible for your decisions and accountable for your actions. Your life is now about working, not whining; striving, not complaining; staying focused, not being buffeted by the winds of gossip, empty promises, or false praise.

And yes, one thing you need to get out of your system right away—if you want to be an actor—is your incessant craving for praise.

Praise

Praise is so easily given and so inexpensive to part with as to be functionally meaningless (and cruelly misleading) in the adult world, where it is mainly a soothing balm in the often abrasive world of doing business. It costs nothing (and therefore means nothing) for casting directors to say "Oh, you're very talented, I loved your audition!" It's simply the easiest (and safest) way for the casting director to turn you down and get you out of the room. In the words of Pauline Kael, "Hollywood is the only place where you can die of encouragement." Nothing is more depressing than to hear actors coming back from an audition exclaiming enthusiastically "I didn't get the part, but I could tell that they liked me!" It's depressing because professional actors don't audition to be liked; they audition to be hired.

Acting professionally is a business. What difference does it make whether they like you if they never hire you? And *do* they like you? Maybe they're just trying to get rid of you. Some actors hang around for years subsisting on such dollops of empty praise.

Praise is an incentive to children; it's the A+ or the gold star or the pat on the back that induces good study habits and good behavior. But praise is mainly a lubricant in an adult business, and it can generate enormous friction and despair among its participants. Praise is doled out by worldly-wise producers mainly to keep you from seeking retaliation. They may give you praise when you seem to need it, but they will give you a job only when *they* need it—and that's where you have to learn to fit in.

Here's to you

If you've read this far—and haven't yet thrown the book against the wall—you might just have a chance. If you suspect that the discussion on the past few pages has been designed to alarm you, your suspicions are indeed correct. There are much pleasanter things to say about acting as a profession, however, and there is much more positive advice to be given. The rest of the book will move in this direction.

Of course, acting is one of the most thrilling and wonderful things you can do with your life. If the raw facts of the entertainment industry don't frighten you off altogether, if you have a passion for acting and for the theatrical arts, if you think you have the gifts and the drive and the emotional stability to begin and sustain a career—well, you could surely do worse than give it your best shot. The challenge is daunting, but the quest will teach you more about yourself—and more about life—than almost any other. You will find the pursuit demanding, sometimes depressing, but much of the time exhilarating as well. You're undertaking a high-stakes adventure. The rest of this book, like an adventure, might even be fun.

Always know, however, that you're going to be in the competition of your life. Don't settle for half measures. This is a business of champions. Your competitors are every bit as dedicated as you are. They too have their dreams and their fantasies and their hometown reviews from the *Fresno Bee* and the *Keokuk Gazette*. They've read this book—or others like it. But realize also that they're no more likely to make it than you are—at least at this point. The path, though desperately narrow, is not altogether blocked. By all means, go for it if you want to—but go for it all the way.

2 What You Will Need

As we said, the rest of this book is about getting work. "Doing the job is easy as hell," says Brian Dennehy, who's starred in long-running Broadway revivals of *Death of a Salesman, Long Day's Journey into Night, Inherit the Wind,* and *Love Letters,* and performed in over 170 films and TV series. "It's fun, it's simple, and we're lucky to be able to do it," he continues, but *"getting the job* is the hard part."

Well, if you are going to tackle the hard part—not just to get a job but to make a living as an actor—you must possess *at least* the following:

- Talent
- A charming/fascinating/interesting/likable/hateful/definable *personality*
- Looks
- Training
- Experience
- Contacts
- Commitment and a massive will to succeed
- A healthy attitude and a capacity for psychological adjustment
- Freedom from entanglements and inhibitions
- Good information, advice, and help
- Luck

You might want to rebel against some of these items, such as "contacts," "looks," or "freedom from inhibitions." But these requirements should not be understood in a negative sense. You do not have to be the son of a film editor or a Miss Georgia contestant to succeed as an actor—and you certainly do not have to sleep with the casting director. Developing contacts, becoming flexible in your acting, and caring for your personal health, however, are extremely important to career success. Each requirement listed is a basic ingredient of professional work, and each deserves a full discussion.

Talent

The first requirement for professional success, and this should be no surprise, is acting talent. Talent is the *sine qua non* of a performer: without it, you have nothing. While there are certainly those who make a brief professional appearance without it, a lasting career comes only to those who have it. But what *is* it? And do *you* have it? Well, these are questions on which neuroses are based.

"Talent: I can't define it, but I know it when I see it." Almost everyone says this, one way or another, and it makes perfectly good sense. Talent is essentially an extraordinary skill—or gift—in the art of *communication*. And because it is mostly nonverbal, it is not defined so much as it is recognized. "Magnetism," "electricity," stage "presence"—these are the metaphors we use to discuss talent. They describe those qualities that make people communicate a highly compelling personality without simply pushing themselves on us.

Talent is a *two-way exchange* with the audience—whether alive on stage or mediated through film or video. It's not simply something you have within you; it's something you give and something you take. Your ability to interact with an audience is what makes them think they "know" you—the real you—through your stage or film performance. We, the audience, will define your talent as much as you, the actor, will reveal it.

Personal magnetism or "electricity" (think of it as "alternating current") is the ability to draw others to you, to inspire them, and to lead them with your words, your body, and your eyes. It is the ability to establish rapport and set up mutual vibrations, both intellectually and emotionally. It is the ability to enter into mutual feedback with other actors as well as with an audience.

Confidence is central to talent. In fact, some say talent is *only* confidence. Confidence is the power you have over your own personality. It is what allows you to be unafraid in your own persona, to stand tall and easy on your own feet, to accept criticism freely—and at the same time to rise above it. *You* have to develop this confidence. Think of it as a test of your talent rather than as subservience to your critics.

Talent allows you to believe in yourself—in the reality of your performance and in the reality of your "being an actor"—even when no one else does. You may have substantial doubts about your potential for long-term career success, but you can never doubt that you are an actor. That belief must be in your bones, sustaining itself through every interview and every audition, so that it shows even though you make no effort to show it. Such belief gives you a power that lets you galvanize every aspect of your personality, training, and experience into an exciting, apparently artless performance or audition. It gives you the freedom to be authentic—even as you sail off on the most exotic dramatic adventures.

So, do *you* have talent? How can you tell? You can't rely on mere compliments, good grades, or the old devil-word *praise*. Rather, ask yourself this:

as a performer, are you *getting cast*? In college or in neighborhood plays, you should be auditioning for—*and getting*—significant roles, or at least being regularly considered for them. If, after two or three years of training as an actor, you are still unsuccessful at getting such key roles in college or community theatre productions—and if those roles are going to people you think are less than terrific (presuming your bad casting is not being hampered by gender or appearance or racial prejudice or favoritism beyond your control)—you might want to reconsider your career goals. This is tough advice, but better now than later.

"Significant" roles, of course, are not just defined by the size of the part. They are the roles you *want* to play, the roles you think you *ought* to play, and the roles that convey at least a few interesting impressions or ideas to the audience. While it may be perfectly true that "there are no small roles, only small actors," the fact remains that only a *significant* role will fully expand and test your abilities. The size of a role is not always of primary consequence; rather, the depth, breadth, wit, passion, individuality, and "electricity" of the role are the characteristics that determine whether it provides this sort of talent test.

In general, the actors who rise to successful careers and even stardom are recognized as *very talented* from the very beginning. Craft and experience can be acquired along the way, but talent, where it exists, shows up almost immediately.

However, extraordinary talent does not mean perfection of performance—or anything close to it. Extraordinarily talented people have been known to sink in one disaster after another. They perform badly, they cannot be heard, they aren't believable, they do the same thing over and over, they get too fat or too thin, they're always committing some terrible error or other, and they frequently reap the derision of their peers, teachers, and even their directors.

ASIDE FROM ROBERT: I remember four acting students at the Yale Drama School in the mid-1960s who were always being criticized by their fellow students. Even their teachers regularly despaired of their "bad habits" and frequent "lapses." Their names were Stacy Keach, Sam Waterston, Daniel Travanti, and Joan Van Ark. All, of course, went on to create brilliant careers on stage and screen—and we all knew that would happen. Why? Because come audition time, the four of them were *always cast*. Directors (such as myself) fought like wildcats over them. The proof here is in the "putting"—of names on cast lists. Most of the "despair" was merely envy.

Talent means all that we have discussed, and more. It *can* mean, in addition, that:

- A person can communicate nuances clearly yet subtly, varying inflection and timing with both assurance and consistency so as to communicate what a director wants without excessive coaching or reworking. Whether the actor does this from technique or instinct is not the concern of this book, but everyone agrees that the actor must be *able* to do it and do it rapidly, particularly during an audition.
- A person can take direction, make quick adjustments when asked, and remain flexible for a director without apparent effort or discomfort— while still maintaining a sense of self and unique point of view.
- A person has a flexible, mobile, and infinitely expressive voice and body. These are the actor's basic tools. For stage work, the voice dominates: a voice that communicates what is between the lines, and that convincingly connotes feelings, ideas, hopes, and personal authenticity—well beyond the mere content of the words spoken. But body language is almost equally important on stage, and often more important in film: in both media, the talented performer communicates both by movement and repose. Great actors naturally assume interesting positions and postures, and are—yes—attractive to look at while doing so. Sex appeal is obviously related to this quality, and although it certainly is not the whole story, an audience that is sensually intrigued clearly is an audience already on its way to admiring and relishing a performance. Casting directors have never been oblivious to this, and you shouldn't be either.
- A person is relaxed in front of others—and when performing for others— and can be seen to *enjoy* performing. This enjoyment is often said to result from an exhibitionist instinct, and nothing in our experience contradicts this. Though actors may be as shy as anyone else (and not a few are painfully shy), some part of their personality relishes contact with others, even via the formal medium of theatre or film.
- A person can sing, dance, juggle, tell jokes, walk tightropes, and/or do striptease, backflips, handsprings, or t'ai chi ch'uan on short notice and with apparent ease and skill—and even enjoyment. Most talented people can do some of these, and many more *think* they are talented because they can do one or two of them. A person who is genuinely talented need not always be able to sing on key, but can probably "sell" a song if called upon to do so. Indeed, *musical* talent (singing and dancing) can be a tremendous asset to any actor, certainly in live theatre today. When this book first came out in 1986, musicals comprised only

a tenth of the stage productions on Broadway; by 2017, they account for roughly two-thirds of them, and are also the longest-running shows in town. The Broadway audience has almost doubled as well, so the more you can sing and dance the longer you may be gainfully employed. And singing and dancing are also now displayed often in many otherwise straight plays, feature films, and television shows; obviously, the more such skills a person has, the more employable he or she can be.

All of these are aspects of "talent," and the word is often used to denote one or more of them. There are no firm prerequisites for "making it" in show business, but the necessity for great talent—hard as it may be to define or acquire—comes as close as any.

Personality

Personality is the second most important characteristic of the successful actor, a ranking that often draws shrieks of dismay. "What does my personality have to do with it? Use me for my talent and ability! My personality is my own business!" Sorry, but no. As the great American actor William Gillette wrote in his *The Illusion of the First Time in Acting* in 1915:

> Among those elements of Life and Vitality, but greatly surpassing all others in importance, is the human characteristic or essential quality which passes under the execrated name of Personality. The very word must send an unpleasant shudder through this highly sensitive Assembly; for it is supposed to be quite the proper and highly cultured thing to sneer at Personality as an altogether cheap affair and not worthy to be associated for a moment with what is highest in Dramatic Art. Nevertheless, cheap or otherwise, inartistic or otherwise, and whatever it really is or not, it is the most singularly important factor for infusing the Life-Illusion into modern stage creations that is known to man.

A century's passage has not changed the import of Mr. Gillette's well-capitalized observations. If anything, it has emphasized them further. American theatre performances have been dominated, at least since the Second World War, by the Konstantin Stanislavsky/Lee Strasberg "Method" school of acting, which emphasizes the actor's personal (or "real-life") truthfulness—and therefore the actor's own personality—within the fiction of the role. The revolution toward *cinéma vérité*, or "truthful filmmaking," has brought the Method—or something like it—to twentieth- and twenty-first-century moviemaking as well, and has made the personality of movie actors central to whatever characters they play. Actors who can, in Stan-islavsky's famous expression, "live the life of their character on stage" are now most likely to live it in the casting office and the audition room as well. Which means they can live it in daily life. Which means it *is* their life—their day-to-day personality.

This is particularly true of film and television acting (not to mention real-ity television), where the snappy production schedule virtually requires instant characterization and immediate performance. There is precious lit-tle rehearsal in commercial films or television: "More often than not, you arrive and you're expected to start acting immediately," says John Lithgow, the Broadway, film, and TV actor. "The director hardly has a word to say to you. You'd be amazed. You arrive, the camera rolls, and you start acting." Natascha McElhone, who played Picasso's longtime mistress in *Surviving Picasso*, reports that she never had a chance to even discuss what her rela-tionship with Picasso (played by Anthony Hopkins) might be. "We just did it," she says. "We met, effectively, on day one, when we shot the scene where I'm running down the road.... We have a big row, and he's shaking me, and it ends up with his tongue down my throat. That was literally the first thing that the two of us had to do with one another."

If you are a day player on television—someone hired to do a small part with lines that can be filmed on a single day—you can be cast the day before, get your script that evening, arrive on the set at 8:00 the next morning with your lines learned, be shooting by 10:00, and be home by lunch. Your "per-sonality" is your character. It's as simple as that. There's no time for studying the character or "working your way into the role." The director yells "action" and suddenly you're Linda, the shrieking delivery woman, and no longer Jane, the actress. That's why your personality is crucial, because in your audition you shrieked the way they imagined Linda would shriek and you got the part. Don't be alarmed if the directors and producers don't know your real name—they wanted a Linda and they've got her. It's you, just the way you are.

Your personality enters the room with you at every audition. Indeed, cast-ing directors have often made up their minds about you the moment you walk in the door. The small talk that accompanies an audition can represent the largest part of any casting decision. Small talk is not just an icebreaker; it is the first way in which you express and reveal your acting personality.

Yet it is not sufficient merely to have a personality that is "right for the role." You must also have, or seem to have, a widely *appealing* or *exciting* personality. Likeability is the crucial factor in acting, and audience appeal (along with audience excitement) translates into fiscal success. In Holly-wood, a numerical personality rating system known as TVQ, created and operated by Marketing Evaluations Inc., creates a "Performer Q database" of 25,000 celebrities, which evaluates film and television actors (as well as newscasters and musical performers) on a "Q-scale," which they update twice a year—solely on the basis of their apparent personal attractiveness and "demographic appeal." In case you're interested, Robert Duvall had the highest Q Score (31) in 2015, while both Meryl Streep and Bradley Cooper landed at 27, Steve Carell at 24, and Reese Witherspoon and Benedict Cumberbatch at 22. You can find out more at TVQ's website, www.qscores.com—but not much more, because TVQ has, according to the *Los Angeles Times*, "maintained a lower profile than the average CIA mole."

What is a good acting personality? It is no one thing in particular, but it is *definable*: you are shy, you are fascinating, you are profound, you are dangerous, you are aggressive, you are hostile, you are nasty, you are fiery, you are sensual, you are youthful, you are hip, you are fussy, you are nerdy, you are idealistic, you are wacky, you are serene. These are all thumbnail descriptions, but they convey specificity. They separate you out from the mass of nice people. Think of your favorite movie star, and you can probably thumbnail him or her in a single word. That's how you'll hope casting directors will thumbnail *you*. It doesn't mean that's all you can do; it's just your flashcard that conveys (brilliantly, you hope) how you appear when people see you for the first time.

Of course, you must know that mere *nice* will get you nowhere. Nice isn't a personality. Thousands of aspiring actors have failed in interviews and auditions simply through excessive—and uniform—politeness. What's wrong with being nice? Well, nice is proper, but it's also dull, it's unexciting, and it doesn't bring people into theatres. Politeness is an essential lubricant for business dealings, of course, but it's a lousy interview and audition technique.

Yes, there *is* an "interview technique," and you will have to learn it (some tips appear in the following section). A hundred actors will grouse, "I didn't get the job because I don't play their games at the interview—I'm just not that kind of person." But it's not a game, and you *must become* that kind of person. Interview technique is nothing more than letting other people see just what kind of person you are—*when you're not in an interview*. The trick is that you have to show this *in* an interview. In fact, this may be the truest test of your acting ability!

In your interview, if your day-to-day personality is hidden behind a dozen "pleased-to-meet-you" smiles and a score of "thank-you-very-much" grins, you may never be looked at further. When you retreat into timid subservience at an interview, you not only fail to "play the interview game," but you also insist on playing another game: the "good little girl" or "good little boy" ploy that got you so far in the principal's office. Well, perhaps for the first time in your life, this is the wrong game to play.

Successful actors are not bland people. That does not mean they are wantonly brash or abrasive. Most actors of our acquaintance are people with depth, sensitivity, dedication, and artistry. They do not apply their personalities for the sake of calling attention to themselves. The surest way to lose your personality is to spin out a fake one.

Your real personality will accompany you in every role you play; it will become your trademark. In the classic days of Hollywood, such trademarks included Humphrey Bogart's smirky toughness; John Wayne's casual virility; Henry Fonda's sensitive passion; Marilyn Monroe's simpering sexuality; Marlon Brando's vulnerable egotism; W. C. Fields' cocky cynicism; Mae West's leering defiance; Grace Kelly's elegant poise; and Clark Gable's whimsically arched eyebrow. These personalities were not "put on" but, rather, were intrinsic to their owners and vital to their owners' successes. The stage and screen personalities of today's rising stars are no less subtle and are just as ingrained in their performances, even in varied characterizations.

You cannot create your personality—your stage personality—but you can liberate it. What are your personal characteristics? What do others see in you? Find out, and let those characteristics come out. Do not worry about "your good features versus your bad features." Just have features. Don't be afraid to be different. Don't settle for the ordinary, the timid, or the nice. Don't try to be what you think they want you to be. Don't worry about yourself. Be proud of yourself. *Like yourself.* If you don't, it's hard to see how somebody else will.

One other aspect of personality deserves some attention. It is so obvious that most young actors completely ignore it: Will the director *enjoy* working with you? There should be nothing surprising about this. Like everyone else on this planet, directors want to enjoy their work, and they would rather work with people they like. A common question at the casting table is simply "Who would give us a good time?" That person more than likely will get the job.

This does not mean that you must become a party animal—a "good time" should be fundamental to the artistic process, no matter how difficult the work. Filmmaker William Bayer advises directors that *rapport* is the most important quality to look for: "Are you going to be able to work with this actor on a basis of intimate friendship? When a film is shooting and the pressure is on, friendship and understanding may be the qualities that have most to do with failure or success." So, if you project a positive attitude, one that combines vivacity with sensitivity and sincerity with charm, then you might be seen as the kind of person a director would choose for company—and for *the* company.

Looks and physical "type"

Acting is one of the only professions (modeling is another) in which looks count *openly* and *legally*. Looks count in other professions as well, but nobody talks about it. In acting, everybody talks about it.

Of course, *good* looks, as everyone knows, have always been a marketing tool for actors. Elia Kazan admitted in his autobiography that he cast Kim Hunter as Stella in the Broadway premiere of *A Streetcar Named Desire* because "I was attracted to her, which is the best possible reaction when casting young women." This is hardly anything new. Back in 1750, John Hill wrote in his book *The Player*, "Tell people that there is a new actress to appear upon the stage such a night, the first question they ask is, Is she handsome? And 'tis ten to one, but they forget to enquire at all whether she has any merit in the profession."

Whatever your physical "type"—beautiful or ugly, tall or short, lean and hungry, or rotund and ebullient—it will always play a role in the role you play. The role may be according to type, or it may be against type. Janet McTeer, over six feet tall, won the Tony best actress award for playing Nora ("my little lark," her husband playfully calls her) in Henrik Ibsen's *A Doll's House* on Broadway in 1997. McTeer put herself up for the role knowing she could bring something very special to it. "If you are extreme, you can do a lot," she reports. "Being six foot tall is very extreme. I've been very gawky. I've been ridiculously elegant. I've toyed around with my looks because it's very interesting." And Peter Dinklage, star and heartthrob of HBO's *Game of Thrones* in the role of Tyrion Lannister, is 4' 5" tall, which hasn't prevented him from receiving both the Emmy and Golden Globe Awards for Outstanding Supporting Actor. "Everyone's different," he says.

Of course, you can get *rejected* on those same grounds, for example, if you are too old, too young, too fat, too short, too "ethnic"—or not ethnic enough—in the eyes of the producer or director. Or, in those same eyes, if you are a member of the wrong sex or the wrong race or are differently abled than other folks who happen to be available. Or even if you are considered "too pretty," as was Oscar nominee Keira Knightley when she started auditioning for serious film roles.

Indeed, the acting business is just about the world's last remaining *unequal* opportunity employer—and this is all perfectly legal. Casting inequalities are simply endemic to acting. This is not a matter of prejudice or mean-spiritedness: an actor is hired not just to perform a role, but to depict a specific character, whose race, sex, and general appearance may be deemed—by the author, director, producer, and/or even you— absolutely necessary to the play's or film's meaning and impact (not to mention its box office appeal). It is certainly understandable, to give an extreme example, that Martin Scorsese cast Robert DeNiro rather than, say, Billy Crystal as Jake LaMotta in *Raging Bull*; it was hardly an insult to Crystal's acting abilities that he was not asked to play this great American boxing champion—indeed, DeNiro himself felt he had to gain 50 pounds in order to play it.

Your type, of course, is not fixed for all eternity. Actor Christian Bale went from playing an emaciated machine worker (in *The Machinist*) to a hunky superhero (*Batman Begins*) in a matter of months, and Jared Leto went from a sexy teen idol to a chunky would-be assassin (John Hinckley, Jr.) in the same period, and went on to win an Oscar playing a transgender woman in *The Dallas Buyer's Club*. But, of course, these were both well-established actors when they were cast; newcomers to the profession won't have this option.

Your *gender* is, of course, a major aspect of your look and type, and women should understand that their casting potential—at least statistically—is daunting, as men clearly get the lion's share of the action in virtually all acting media. In the most recent statistical analysis of film and TV casting (by the Center for the Study of Women in Television and Film at San Diego State University in 2014), women garnered only 12% of the protagonists, 29% of the major roles, and only 30% of all speaking characters—with the majority of all of them younger than 40. As English stage star Imogen Stubbs reports, "sadly, actresses spend about 50% of their working lives crying, and much of the rest of the time taking their clothes off."

But there is also reason for optimism in this sector: the percentages of women cast in both leading and supporting roles are more than half again as high as they were when the first edition of this book was written 40 years ago. With the emergence of women as major film producers—Megan Ellison of *Zero Dark Thirty* and *American Hustle*, Darla Anderson of *Toy Star 3* and *Monsters Inc.*, Nina Jacobson of *Hunger Games*, and Kathleen Kennedy of *Jurassic Park*, *Schindler's List*, and *Star Wars: The Force Awakens* —as well as becoming the president of Lucasfilm—women have now become 25% of Hollywood's producers. Also, stage directors such as Julie Taymor, Susan Stroman, Diane Paulus, Kathleen Marshall, Tina Landau, Leigh Silverman, Anna Shapiro, and Twyla Tharp are now highly prominent, while numbers of female playwrights are rapidly increasing around our country and abroad, and female actors are increasingly playing male characters (e.g., Hamlet, Malvolio, King Lear, and Kings Richard II and III) that were previously played almost entirely by men.

Your *ethnicity* may be a factor as well, though less so than many people realize. Indeed, the casting of ethnic minorities has steadily increased in all acting media in recent decades, particularly in American TV, where in 2015 no fewer than 15 new TV shows (*Blindspot, Minority Report, The Player* and *Quantico* among them) were created with black actors playing major roles. Latino/Latina actors were playing such roles in at least 25 shows the previous year (including *Jane the Virgin, Bad Judge, Gracepoint,* and *The Flash*), and the percentage of minority actors in American films and television has increased by a staggering *three thousand percent* since this book's first edition. In the 2016 pilot season, in fact, several agents were discovering how increasingly difficult it was to get their non-ethnic actors audition appointments.

Nor are minority actors, despite what many think, typed mainly into criminal roles; today's black actors play barely 8% of the crooks on prime-time TV, while white ones commit crimes against blacks twice as often in that medium as the other way around. And today, black actors are more likely to appear as lawyers, doctors, or business professionals in TV than as blue-collar workers or as unemployed. In film, however, minority actors only performed 16.7% of the leading film roles in 2013, according to the *Hollywood Diversity Report*, which is less than half the percentage of minorities in the U.S. population. In 2016, film admirers were outraged to discover that no minority actors had received Tony nominations in that year or the previous one, and efforts are currently being made in Hollywood to turn that percentage around by 2020.

On Broadway, black actors, while accounting only for 7.1% of Equity members, often represent an even higher percentage of performers during a given season, at times accounting for up to 25% of the performers on what is still sometimes called (for different reasons) New York's "Great White Way." And as of 2015, no fewer than 53 Tony-winning actors and actresses have been African American, including, since 2010, Denzel Washington, Viola Davis, Nikki James, Audra McDonald (twice), Billy Porter, Patina Miller, Cicely Tyson, Courtney Vance, James Iglehart, and Sophie Okonedo.

But most ethnic groups other than African Americans remain seriously underrepresented in the nation's professional casting. While Latinos/Hispanics account for 17% of Americans, they constitute only 4.9% of the speaking parts of the top-grossing movies, according to a study by the University of Southern California. Still, this is roughly double what it was ten years ago. Asians and Pacific Islanders, representing 13% of the U.S. population, receive 3.4% of the country's acting roles, although their numbers have gone up by a third in the same period. North American Indians, seeing only 0.2% of the acting action, remain severely underrepresented.

If you are concerned about improving ethnic equity in the acting profession, get in touch with the Alliance for Inclusion in the Arts, at www.inclusioninthearts.com, which was founded within the Actors Equity Association and is now fully supported by that union as well as SAG-AFTRA. The motto of this remarkable and dedicated nonprofit organization is "Promoting full diversity in theatre, film and television," so if this could excite *you*, then you should give them your attention!

Your *age* is also, obviously, a factor in your looks and type. Particularly in Hollywood, where youth-oriented demographics face TV advertisers and movie theatre exhibitors, statistics are not encouraging if you plan to grow older—and they get much worse if you're female. For men, only 40% of roles go to actors over 40; for women, only 26%. Despite the occasional turns by Betty White (playing Dr. Beth Mayer in TV's *Bones* at the age of 93), Angela Lansbury (starring in *Driving Miss Daisy* at 90), or Ed Asner (in TV's *The Good Wife* and 21 other film and TV roles at 85), "the outlook for senior actors in Hollywood remains surprisingly glum," as *Backstage* reports. And "at forty, women seem to drop off the face of the earth," says a SAG-AFTRA spokesperson.

Of course, your physical type is not a matter of gender and race alone. Whether you have standard or nonstandard abilities—whether or not you are differently abled—is also a factor in casting. Indeed, to be differently abled may be a factor in your favor. Websites where you post your résumé (see Chapter 4) allow you to list specific disability categories into which you might fall, including having a visual, hearing, or walking impairment; being an amputee; or being developmentally disabled—and casting directors seeking such actors can filter their search on these sites to locate just such individuals. There are increasing numbers of theatres that favor differently abled actors, including the Theater Breaking Through Barriers in New York (formerly Theater by the Blind), the Deaf West Theatre in California, and many others elsewhere in the country. This takes personal initiative, however. Howie Seago, a born-deaf actor who has starred in live stagings by Peter Sellars and Robert Wilson, in TV shows including *Star Trek: The Next Generation*, and in major roles as a company member at the Oregon Shakespeare Festival, writes: "I have made the work myself by my own perseverance."

Some physical characteristics, however, are more variable than sex, race, and physical handicap. Your weight, dress, health, posture, hairstyle, teeth, complexion, and grooming all allow you great latitude. How can an actor use these variables? As with personality, there is no classic norm;

the premium is, rather, for a specific and *definable* "look"—which is sometimes called a "character type." Of course, in real life people are not types, and they don't like being typed—but you should face the fact that when casting people are looking to fill roles, they are certainly not going to be looking at all the 200,000 or so actors who are out there, but will be trying to narrow down their pool of potential candidates. So, when you post yourself and your résumé on a casting website today (see Chapter 4), you will be specifically asked to define your "character type." Here's your list of options on one very popular site in this area (nowcasting.com): "athlete, blue collar, character, ingénue, leading man, leading woman, model, precision driver, stunt person, triplet, twin, white collar." The same site will also ask you to characterize your "physique" as (choose one only) "athletic/fit, average, large, muscular, petite, thin" and invite you to list any of 21 distinct "disabilities."

Types may not exist in life, but they exist in casting, and whichever "character type" and "physique" box you check on a casting website determines whether your photo and résumé will show up on a casting director's search of that site when he or she filters it with any of those designations. Some descriptions, of course, you have no control over (such as "triplet"), but others you do, both in how you plan to appear (which you can control by diet, exercise, and grooming) and in how you describe yourself. The latter is tricky: do you want to be seen as "blue collar" or "leading man"? "Both," you could say—but you can't always check "both" on the list. How do you know which to check? How (in other words) do you know who you "are"— in casting terms?

> ASIDE FROM ROBERT: I once recommended a New York actor I had often worked with to the casting director of a play I was directing in Utah. When the CD came to New York, she called him in to read, but I was astonished when I later found out that he had decided to read for the role of the young lover instead of the older guardian (the lead role) for which I was considering him. Naturally, he did not advance to call-backs; his idea of his "type" was clearly different from mine and the casting director's!

Some of the character types—such as "leading man" or "ingénue"—are more than a century old. Such historic designations aren't as commonly heard as they once were, but they still often apply, and you should know what, in general, they imply:

> "Children" designates actors 12 years old and younger. "Preteens" are those from 13 to 15, and "teens" range from 16 to 19. Ordinarily these character types are not involved in romantic affairs—on stage, anyway.

"Ingénues" (girls) and "young leading men" (at one time—but rarely to-day—called "juveniles") are in the "first love" category. Usually they are in the early to mid-twenties and send off vibrations of youth, innocence, and charm.

"Leading men" and "leading women" are, in contrast, wiser, more experienced lovers; they are glamorous, romantic, mature, sophisticated, in their mid-twenties to mid-forties and beyond.

"Character men," "character women," "comedians," and "comediennes" are not romantic in a conventional sense. They are usually older, and their appearance is likely to be distinctive rather than attractive.

Notice that these types are defined not solely by age, but also by a position on some sort of romantic/sexual scale. This is simply an accurate reading of the typing that is done in theatre and film casting. No one assumes that an unattractive character cannot be portrayed in a romantic role (as in Stephen Sondheim's *Passion* and Terrence McNally's *Frankie and Johnny*). It is just that to do so is to cast deliberately against type, and such casting is done rarely except when a specific play or film calls for it. Since the time of Aristophanes, audiences have expected ingénues to be young and innocent, lovers to be beautiful and sensitive, and comics to be old and pudgy. Few casting directors wish to disappoint an audience.

It is important to find your type, if only to know which box to check on a casting submission site. More than that, your type will categorize you in the producer's mind. It provides you with a convenient label—a basis for comparison with other actors. You protest: you are an individual, not a type! Well, if you are Meryl Streep, you don't need a label. If you aren't, though, you will have to start somewhere. Even "male" or "female" is a label, and you can at least be a little more specific than that.

If you are hoping to get romantic leads, particularly in film or television, it is helpful to be attractive—indeed, *extraordinarily* attractive. This may be a bit unsettling, but it's simply a fact: casting calls openly call for "gorgeous" or "beautiful" women, sometimes even stipulating, quite shamelessly, "staggeringly beautiful." And the quest for male "hunks," whose very entrances will send the (largely female) daytime audiences into a rapturous fantasy, animates most television casting directors.

Please don't underestimate the lengths to which TV and film casting directors will go to hunt down stunningly *beautiful* people. They are not just looking for cute. They're seeking knockout sex appeal, the kind that will make viewers leave, if not their spouse or significant other, at least one soap opera for its rival. When the feature film *Flashdance* was being cast, Michael Eisner, then head of Paramount, assembled a room full of male

truck drivers and stagehands and showed them the screen tests of the finalists for the female lead, then asked them which one they most wanted to
bed down. Jennifer Beals won the vote—and was cast in the role. Realize
that a single percentile change in the ratings can mean several million dollars for the producers—and if a sexier smile or a bouncier bosom will generate that percentile bump, that's where the casting will go. This explains
why you'll find all those ads in the trade papers for tooth capping, porcelain
laminate veneers, nose jobs, face-lifts, chin tucks, and both breast implants
and breast reductions. "Everyone on television over the age of 25 has had
something," said the late Joan Rivers, who, having felt since childhood that
her face was "an albatross around my neck," admitted to many trips under
the knife throughout her long career.

And even some under 25, like former teen stars Ashley Tisdale (*High
School Musical*) and Dianna Agron from *Glee* fame, have admitted to having "work done." Of course, the nips and tucks are more an L.A. than an N.Y.
thing, as facial complexion reads far more vividly on the tube or screen than
from the middle of a Broadway house. For as a Los Angeles surgeon notes,
"You can imagine what a face wrinkle or a baggy eye looks like multiplied
100 times and shown on a movie screen 60 feet high."

Plastic surgery can go too far, however. One plastic surgeon to the stars
asks you to think of Jennifer Grey. "She did *Dirty Dancing*, had her nose
done, and never had a hit after that. She became just like everybody else.
Sometimes the thing you're trying to get rid of is actually the thing that
makes you unique and stand out above other people." Many actresses
who've had breast implants, finding that they're being called only to bimbo
auditions, return for a downsizing. Most actors today don't want to look
like they have had a "procedure"; they just want to look good. More, therefore, are turning to newer, non- or minimally invasive procedures, such as
laser treatments, dermal fillers, and Botox injections. As Dr. Joseph Eviatar
of Chelsea Eye and Cosmetic Surgery, who specializes in such treatments,
explains, "For my patients in the performing arts, it is important they look
natural. They want to be 'refreshed,' so people think they look great without
knowing they had anything done. The trend of wearing facelifts like badges
of honor seems to be history."

It is beyond the scope of this book to make surgical suggestions, but know
that if you are planning to be up for on-camera romantic roles, you should *at
the very least* consider your teeth, your hair, your cosmetic makeup (for women,
anyway), and anything that might detract from your marketable allure.

What about your weight? Unless you're bound and determined to be a
corpulent character actor (think of TV Golden Globe winners John Goodman in *Roseanne* and comedienne Melissa McCarthy in *Spy*), get your belly

down, and work your physical condition up to par—and even better than par, since, as one casting director bluntly explains, "There is a direct correlation between unemployment and being overweight." So, go to a gym or run on a track. For the fact is that most Americans are a bit overweight and a bit unfit, but most performers aren't. Few roles are written for chubby, flaccid actors, and this is no accident; characters in plays and films serve as role models to the public, and role models these days tend toward the lissom, lithe, strong, supple, and sexually desirable. The physical demands of performing also reward those who are physically capable of meeting them, so you need to exercise, diet, and get in *great* shape. This is particularly true if you plan to act in film and television, where the camera adds 10 or 15 pounds to you. It was only after an agent told Jennifer Aniston that she had better lose some weight that the young actress shed 30 pounds and won the role of "Rachel" on *Friends*.

And consider having Lasik eye surgery, which is high on actors' wish-lists these days. Wearing contacts can cause your eyes to redden on camera, and worry that a lens might pop out in performance, while wearing glasses may make you less confident when reading for glamorous roles. If you are a student reading this, hey, don't delay—do it now! Don't wait until you hit the big city casting offices. Get in shape, lose the weight, gain the muscle; just *do* it! Then you can hit the ground running, not plodding. We have visited many training programs around the country only to witness overweight, out-of-shape, unfit actors who say they're training to work. But they're not preparing themselves to get that work, and will face a rude awakening when they leave the comforts of the campus setting—and its surrounding fast-food emporia.

If, on the other hand, you think you have a crack at becoming a character actor, throw this advice out the window. Character actors since Roman times have invariably been old and fat, or old *and* fat, or old and fat and ugly. If these words could be used to describe you, there are roles that will fit you, so don't try to hide such features, *cultivate* them. Make them work for you. Become the star of some future *Modern Family* or *Law and Order*. Use what you have to create a *distinctive* appearance—the only "bad" appearance is a bland, characterless, type-less one.

What *should* you look like? That's your choice, to the extent that you can choose. Classic good looks, out of fashion for a while, are back in. Keira Knightley and Daniel Radcliffe could have made it in the 1950s as easily as the 2010s. All these "looks" can be cultivated, and in fact they *have* been cultivated by most, if not all, of the actors who exhibit them.

The specifics of personal physical appearance are not individually critical. What is important is the effect that your person and your "image" create—and the power of that effect, which should be enormous. When, at the end of a year-long casting search, Brazilian opera singer Paolo Szot, a virtual unknown in the American theatre, was called back for the lead male role of Emile in Lincoln Center's 2008 revival of *South Pacific*, he was asked to sing "Some Enchanted Evening" to all four women who were finalists for the role of Nellie. He reduced all four to tears with his rendition and got the role hands down—receiving the Tony Award three months later. If you are to be a leading man, this is exactly the romantic power you must possess.

Above all, cultivate a *distinctive* appearance. Separate yourself from the rest of your friends. Find an exciting hairstyle for yourself, a natural one perhaps, but one that looks better on you than on anybody else and is not seen around too much. Dress distinctively. If you are a woman and you like going around in pinpoint shirts and slim leather coats, then get some that fit absolutely perfectly—along with some great accessories—and look terrific. And the impeccable jacket or sweater or slacks can make a nondescript male very descriptive indeed. But if you wear jeans and a t-shirt better than anyone else—well, then do it! People have to remember you *somehow* when you leave the room—and for that they have to remember at least some of your individual qualities. Extravagance and propriety are not worth a dram in this business, but distinction *in your own terms* is. Find yourself, and find in yourself a unique appearance that will intrigue others.

How will you *use* your appearance? It precedes you in every interview and every audition. No actor can begin to look for work without a set of photographs. They are your letters of introduction. (You may want to turn now to the section on photographs in Chapter 4.) Your photographs must show just what your appearance must show: originality, vitality, and, above all, distinctiveness. If you look like something out of a high school yearbook, the chances are that you will never be heard of again.

Training and experience

Every actor must have training and experience. No matter how naturally talented, attractive, sexy, and individual you are, you will flop in the audition if you don't know what to do. In the old days, actors without formal training were the rule. As English actress Hermione Gingold once said, "I got all the schooling any actress needs. That is, I learned to write well enough to sign contracts." John Wayne bragged that he just learned his lines and went out and said them. Gingold broke into stardom in the 1920s, though, and Wayne in the 1940s; nowadays, this slackness is the exception. Henry Winkler says, "Training is the foundation to your career. Every single thing that I ever learned, whether I thought it was important or not, or understood it at that moment or not, I have used over the years in my career." "Training, training, training, training!" are the four most important things you need for a career, according to Bonnie Gillespie, who headed the casting at Twentieth Century Fox and NBC before becoming vice president of Talent Development and Casting for Big Ticket Television. Training is virtually a necessity for a sustained successful career. If you *are* hired at first without it, as child actors or retired athletes may be for TV shows, you will almost certainly need it before going further.

Indeed, your training will likely continue even if you become a famous performer. When rap star and hip hop tycoon Sean Combs (aka Puff Daddy) wanted to be a part of the 2004 Broadway *Raisin in the Sun* revival, he worked with an acting coach for months before coming in to read for the part—just to convince the casting director (one of the co-authors of this book) that he was up to the task. As actor-manager Seth Greenky reminds us, "The top concert pianists in the world continue to take lessons. Alex Rodriguez and Derek Jeter have a batting coach. That coach may not be able to do what they do but can spot flaws and ways to improve." No one should think they are too good to train.

What sort of training should you have? A virtual explosion in the area of arts education over the past two decades has spawned an extraordinary proliferation of drama schools and actor-training institutes, and the aspiring actor has many options. But know that you should have a comprehensive—not just a sporadic—acting education. Jane Jenkins, a casting director of 184 films and TV shows since 1980, puts it this way: "A lot of young American actors are limited because they go to an acting class here and there and they learn about being realistic and true to themselves, but when it comes to dressing in a costume and creating a character larger than their own life, they don't always have the technique to do that." For that reason, Jenkins often prefers actors from England over the "majority of young American actors, with the exception of those who go to proper schools." And because of that, you might well look for a "proper school" if you plan to acquire a truly versatile and long-lasting career.

University or college training

A general college education, perhaps with a drama or theatre major, which can be at the BA or BFA (Bachelor of Fine Arts) level, followed by a Master of Fine Arts (MFA) degree from a qualified institution, has clearly become the most desirable training base for professional *stage* actors, many of whom go on to become film/TV actors as well.

Stage acting—which remains based to a certain extent on the performer's sensitivity to literary values, acquaintance with political and social history, understanding of philosophical dichotomies, and general appreciation of art and culture—is favorably developed in an environment where classical as well as modern works are regularly analyzed, criticized, and performed. And with nearly 200 university drama departments now offering graduate acting degrees, the opportunity to receive *advanced* training, usually from instructors who have professional backgrounds and continuing professional contacts themselves, is available throughout the country.

While it remains true, in the classic expression of the late Joseph Papp, that "a Ph.D. won't get you through the turnstile of the IRT [then a branch of the New York subway system]," a college drama or theatre degree followed by advanced university-based actor training (usually leading to an MFA) can give you that important entrée to regional and New York theatre stage work and help you move from there to other media. Most MFA programs showcase their graduates before agents and casting directors in New York and/or Hollywood to help them jump-start their professional careers. "We are hard pressed even to *look* at someone without either an Equity card or an MFA," says a former casting director for Southern California's Tony-winning South Coast Repertory Theatre, "and most of the other LORT [League of Resident Theatres] companies feel the same way." In New York, another CD reports that "many of us only want to see actors with MFAs at the bottom of their résumé—usually an MFA from one of a very select few programs. The MFA is, to us, something like the USDA-PRIME stamp on the best meat at the supermarket." And those who graduate successfully from MFA acting programs will undoubtedly be able to head toward their hoped-for profession with the support of fellow graduates (and former teachers) who can provide support, comradeship, and up-to-date advice as they whittle their way into this difficult field.

First-class Bachelor of Fine Arts (BFA) degree programs can also provide a firm training foundation for a professional acting career. The BFA should not be confused with the BA; it's sort of an MFA at the undergraduate level. All you need to get into a BFA program —besides loads of talent—is a high school diploma. The best BFA programs can be every bit as focused, demanding, and intense as their masterly equivalents, and some of them produce New York and/or Los Angeles showcases for their graduates as well. They also have the benefit of getting you out in the field two or three years earlier than an MFA program: in film and TV particularly, those years can be crucial in a youth-oriented business. Of course, you won't be taking all those Medieval English and Physics-for-Non-majors courses as a BFA student (BFA programs generally require only a few general education classes, in addition to the theatre curriculum), so you—and perhaps your parents— will have to decide whether this is a proper educational track for you. Your BFA program also means putting almost all your academic eggs in the acting basket, of course, which doesn't give you many fallback options if the theatre and film jobs don't come your way after graduation.

And how about a BA program in theatre or drama—or even in political science, for that matter? The fact is that *any* serious program of study in act- ing can be the basis of a fine professional career—if you take it seriously, and your instructors do as well. Much that must be learned in actor training can be learned on stage, and in university theatre rehearsals and performances. And when the dedication is intense, the artistic ambition high, the direc- tion inspiring, the craft level of your fellow artists elevated, and your efforts unstinting, you may have a very strong chance of getting your foot in the door.

The best college theatre departments provide not only preparation for stage acting but also opportunities to act for the camera as well. Even if they don't, university stage training has become increasingly important in the film and TV casting worlds. *Friends* and film star David Schwimmer, who graduated with a BA in Theatre and Speech from Northwestern University, writes this about how his college training segued into his career:

> It made me realize that acting is a craft. With training, you can play vari- ous roles from different periods and styles of theatre. Doing a Joe Orton black comedy is very different from doing a Neil Simon play, which is very different from doing Noel Coward. ... I think the actors that have the most longevity in their careers are those who can transform themselves into playing beyond just who they are. Northwestern arms you for that.

Casting directors almost always look for training credentials on an actor's résumé. "I love stage-trained actors; they are believable, they are funny, they know what to do," says Jeff Greenberg, casting director for TV fare such as *Modern Family, Cheers, Frasier*, and *Wings*. "Training is the first thing that I check out on the résumé of a new actor," concurs Judy Blye Wilson, award-winning casting director of *The Young and the Restless* and *All My Children*, who adds that "an MFA from a good school makes a huge dif- ference." Susan Bedsow, longtime executive producer of *One Life to Live*, explains that she and her casting colleagues prefer to cast college-trained actors, specifically *classically* trained actors, in soap operas because these actors are more readily able to create an "ongoing character in depth."

This is why academic theatre training has become the rule rather than the exception in all acting media. Actors who previously may have hidden their university credentials behind a rock now brag about their academic and classical credits in their "Who's Who in the Cast" program write-ups and magazine interviews. One reason for this is the great growth in nonprofit regional professional theatres outside of New York City—more than 460 such theatre companies today are listed in TCG (the Theatre Communications Group), of which 74 of the most accomplished ones are also members of LORT (the League of Resident Theatres), which bargains collectively for its members with their professional acting unions. Such companies, all nonprofits, often have academic roots. Many, if not most, were formed by the faculties or alumni of MFA or BFA programs, and the majority of their stage directors also have MFAs; naturally, these directors like to "go with those they know," and often prefer to work with actors with whom they have developed working relationships during their school years, as well as those who have trained with the same teachers who mentored them in their own studies.

This evolving relationship between the academic and the professional worlds has many ramifications. Many universities run their own professional theatres, some in the summertime and some during the school year, which provide "half-way" employment situations in which students work with professionals. Other colleges provide apprenticeships and internships with nearby regional theatres, offering students regular opportunities to act with, study with, and rub elbows with professional actors; some students obtain union membership credits in the process. Most major campuses employ working professional directors on their faculties, either full or part time, who may involve student performers in their off-campus professional activities. The annual Kennedy Center American College Theater Festival, founded in 1969, now brings approximately 18,000 students from more than 600 American colleges and universities to dramatic competitions in eight regions throughout the country, concluding with final dramatic competitions at the Kennedy Center in Washington, DC that lead to prizes, scholarships, and awards. All KCACTF's activities celebrate university training as a base for the emerging actor's career.

However, not all is wonderful in university drama and theatre departments, and there are several things you must watch out for.

Perhaps the most important caution is that the university environment, even under the best circumstances, is an amateur one—and sometimes it is amateur*ish* as well. Because universities have a disproportionate number of young people, university directors often cast young people in older roles. This can create a resigned attitude with regard to casting standards: the production may aspire to only a minimal level of competence and may settle on an artistic standard that is simply what can be achieved "under the circumstances." Audiences in the professional theatre, however, are not as indulgent regarding circumstances, and not as amused by the often-affected performances of adolescents playing aged kings, queens, and master builders. Performing such roles may not be all that good for *you* either.

In addition, many theatre departments project a back-patting coziness that can lull student actors into a false sense of security, preventing them from developing their craft in a disciplined manner and encouraging them to rest on ill-deserved laurels. Many students come to New York with MFAs and glowing reviews in their portfolios—but with only slender skills, laxly honed because of their bearers' too-easily acquired campus popularity.

And, to be frank, some academic acting instructors are simply not up to the task of training professionals, because either they are out of touch with the profession, or resentful of it, or they have become embittered because of what they view as their own failed careers. No theatre program is any better than its weakest teacher, who could end up being yours.

Choosing a BFA or MFA program

How should you pick a BFA or graduate theatre program? How do you avoid choosing an inadequate one? Ask around, of course, and seek recommendations from teachers, school counselors, and professional actors and directors. Many of these programs advertise in journals: get any copy of *American Theatre* or the annual *Backstage* College Guide (published as an insert in their mid-November issue), each of which features dozens of ads for university theatre programs. Look closely at the websites of theatre programs that look good to you. Forty of the country's leading MFA programs are members of the University/Resident Theatre Association (URTA), which holds collective auditions for admission, and you can check out any or all of these schools at www.urta.com. If you already have a BA or a BFA, and are interested in any URTA schools for your graduate training, you can ask to be nominated by your school—and if you successfully pass URTA's local screening, you can be seen by most of the programs in a single audition at any of the sites they annually arrange around the United States.

So, if you're interested in a drama or theatre school, at either undergraduate or graduate level, check the ads in *American Theatre* or *Backstage* or the listings in *URTA*, or any college that your friends and previous drama teachers can recommend, and then check out the websites of whatever schools interest you. Then you can write to them for brochures and other information, and, if you can, write and ask to *visit* the three or four departments that seem most suitable to your interests and finances. Ask to see both faculty-directed and student-directed productions if either can be arranged. Ask to visit an acting class. Hang around the call board—there is *always* a call board—and talk to the students you see there. Ask what the students do when they're not in school, such as during the summer. Do they work in summer theatres? In Shakespeare festivals? Try to get the inside picture. Wherever you decide to go, you'll be there for a long while, so be active in your search. Find out as much as you can before committing your time and money.

Here are some things to look for in choosing a theatre school:

- A faculty with *professional experience*. At least some of the faculty in acting should be professional actors or directors, preferably in a variety of acting media. It helps enormously if the faculty is supplemented with *guest artists* who are active—and innovative—professionals.
- A faculty *currently working* in professional theatre, or a program with active apprenticeships in professional theatre. You want to be taught up-to-date techniques, and you want to work with people who have professional contacts. Best of all, of course, is working with professionals themselves, who, after graduation, could hire you for one of their professional plays!
- Ideally, of course, you should consider a school that has a *direct connection with a professional theatre*, such as the Yale Drama School (tied to the Yale Repertory Theatre), Florida State University (with the Asolo Theatre), or Brown University (Trinity Repertory Theatre); such hybrid programs can provide you with, in addition to expert professional training, the 50 weeks of professional work that will qualify you for membership in Actors Equity Association. Schools with attached professional theatres, however, are few, and sometimes the relationship between school and theatre is frostier than you might expect, so check this out carefully before plunking down your tuition deposit.
- An *organized plan* for the training of actors. A fine acting program is not merely a collection of fine actors revealing the secrets of their craft. A good program has a working methodology, or pedagogy, with various courses directly feeding into each other so that you will graduate with integrated and comprehensive training, not just a mishmash of information and critiques.
- *Proximity* to ongoing professional theatre activity. This means your college is within commuting distance of New York or Los Angeles, or near a city (or cities) with one (or hopefully more) professional theatres. You should have the opportunity to view professional work frequently, and to see it in relation to your own work.
- *Facilities*, *staff*, and *budgets* sufficient to ensure quality work at all levels. This does not mean that the college or university must boast a battery of fancy stages and equipment (although most do). It *does* mean that works put on by the department are ambitious, exciting, professionally

executed, and not prefaced by bundles of apologies or disclaimers. It also means a hardworking and energetic staff willing to put in time with you.

- *Good student morale.* Drama students traditionally gripe to each other yet put on shining faces to outsiders. Both behaviors indicate healthy morale. Watch out for any program where the students are unwarrantedly complacent or openly bitter.
- Opportunities to study *dance* and *voice* (singing) as well as acting. Stage actors particularly should seek as much training in music theatre as possible, because more and more contemporary stage plays demand musical abilities. Versatility is important for every stage actor. You should find and take every opportunity to enlarge your performing repertoire. Check also for opportunities to learn stage combat, mime, period movement, and audition technique.
- Opportunities to study *classical* acting. You may not think Shakespeare is your métier, but you should study his plays anyhow: he is *by far* the most produced playwright in America today, and his works have been seen in 410 feature-length films or on TV so far, and excerpted in no fewer than 1,110 films. And while England—Shakespeare's home—only has one Shakespeare-named theatre (the Royal Shakespeare Company), America has well over 100 Shakespeare Festivals! And most accept, often whole-heartedly, college drama students for the bulk of their casts. Norbert Leo Butz, who is known for his Broadway stage roles (*Wicked, Big Fish, Rent, Dead Accounts*) and for his burgeoning film career (*The English Teacher, Dan in Real Life*), prepared himself with an MFA at the University of Alabama/Alabama Shakespeare Festival. "If you do Shakespeare, you'll learn everything you ever need to know," Butz insists.
- Opportunities to work *on camera.* Some universities have video studios where you can learn to work on camera and study how to hit your marks while playing a scene. You *can* learn this later, but a school that provides such opportunities gives you a jump on the competition.
- *A showcase performance* in either New York or Los Angeles—or both—that presents the graduates' work to professional agents and casting directors. At least 70 schools now provide such actor presentations.
- A strong *alumni placement* record. What are the program's recent graduates actually doing? What percentage of their last three classes are actually working actors or have agents or have become members of acting unions? Feel free to ask. Good programs should be able to discover and document the success of a reasonable percentage of their recent grads. You should be able to get real information about this—actual alumni names and their professional credits—not just vague statements.

- Also note *where* a program's successful alumni tend to work profession-ally. If New York City is your dream location and a large alumni net-work is there—all the better. And similarly for Los Angeles. Most drama departments that produce showcases in New York and/or Los Angeles for their final-year graduates also host alumni reunions in those cities at the same time, allowing their current graduates to meet previous ones who are now working in that city—and can give the newbies good advice when and after they move there!
- *Superior acting*. Above all, be sure that the acting level of your chosen school's productions is excellent. If you are able to visit the schools that interest and/or audition you, try to see one or more of their drama pro-ductions, and then hang around afterwards to talk with some of the student actors you admired in the shows. And if you *didn't* admire any of them, take the school off your list; don't ever go to a school simply because you think you'll have an easy chance to walk off with the star-ring roles when you get there. You want the *best* possible school, the *best* teachers, and the *best* fellow students. You might as well start getting used to high-level competition, because you'll face it from now on.

A final word about college: while you're there, don't waste your time. Study all the theatre you can, of course, but also learn to sing and dance— ballet, tap, and jazz. Learn to fence if you can. Study literature, history, psychology, politics, economics, and philosophy. These subjects will not only feed your art, but they will also feed you. Listen to what Emmy-nominated Lee Pace (*Pushing Daisies* and *Halt and Catch Fire*) has to say: "I get obsessed with the artist Henry Darger, then read a book on Mao, then I plan a trip to India while staying home and learn how to cook. So when it's time to go to work, I've got a whole plate of things to bring to the role I'm playing." Actors these days are smart and they are active. They branch into writing and directing, they engage in politics, and they teach. Train, but also *learn*: use, explore, and expand your mind.

Professional classes

Professional classes refer to a collection of schools and teachers, mainly in New York and Los Angeles, that teach acting (and often related theatre disciplines) for set fees. These institutions and individuals are not affiliated with universities and do not ordinarily offer subjects unrelated to theatre.

The number of professional acting schools and studios has increased tremendously in the past 30 years. *Backstage*'s annual article on "Acting Schools and Coaches" currently lists 596 such schools, mostly in New York and Los Angeles, but many others around the country. And they're easy to find: many advertise in the weekly trade papers on both coasts, and many more are described and sometimes even rated in various publications available in drama bookstores when you arrive in town.

Professional schools and teachers vary enormously, both in the nature of their offerings and in the quality of their instruction. Some are comprehensive theatre schools; others are devoted to a single teacher's acting system. Yet others are specialized academies for certain skills: camera acting, TV commercials, improvisation, voiceovers, stage speech, comedy, singing, dance, audition technique, and like subjects. Many schools offer a variety of classes, usually a basic acting sequence plus specialized workshops. Naturally, the comprehensive schools are geared to the student without prior dramatic training, while the independent teachers and class offerings are more suited to the MFA-bearing actor located in New York or Los Angeles. Specialized classes provide a source of continuing education for actors and are very much part of the actor's life, even after roles start coming in. Internationally known actors frequently show up in acting classes in New York and Hollywood to refresh their skills and learn new ones.

Finding a professional class is tricky, because, unlike universities and colleges, professional schools have no system of regular outside accreditation and go in and out of business—sometimes as often as the teachers move into and out of acting roles. Even the schools with the "legendary five" names attached—the Lee Strasberg Theatre & Film Institute on both coasts, the Stella Adler Studio of Acting in New York (and the Los Angeles Stella Adler Academy of Acting and Theatre in L.A.), the Sanford Meisner Center in North Hollywood, and the HB Studio (created and taught by Herbert Berghoff and his wife, Uta Hagen) in New York—are all staffed by their now-deceased founders' descendants, both professional and familial. At these, you will at best be studying with a student of (or, more likely, a student of a student of, or a student of a student of a daughter of) one of these great acting gurus.

Other professional schools are connected with professional theatres. The Circle in the Square's Theatre School, in midtown Manhattan, is connected with the Broadway theatre of that name, and provides a two-year training program in both acting and musical theatre; the Circle's graduates have included Idina Menzel, Kevin Bacon, Lady Gaga, and the late Philip Seymour Hoffman, among many other acting and singing stars. Also in Manhattan is the off-Broadway Atlantic Theatre Company, which operates a variety of programs, conservatories, and summer intensives, following the training programs of David Mamet and William H. Macy. Other schools around the country that offer such professional training include the Actors Theatre of Louisville, the Steppenwolf Theatre in Chicago, the Berkeley

Repertory Theatre in California, and the Shakespeare Theatre Company in Washington, DC.

There are hundreds of other private schools and private coaches, however, with instruction ranging from full multiyear curricula for beginners to broad menus of individual intensive courses for ongoing professionals. If you can't find a copy of *Backstage*'s "Acting Schools and Coaches," you can hunt up leads by typing "acting teachers" into your favorite search engine. You'll find hundreds. Then you can call and ask to audit a class, and talk to their current students—and even their former students if you can track them down.

Remember, however, that professional acting schools survive on the tuitions they take in, and that they therefore have a vested interest in making you think their classes are "the way and the light." Be cautious, and particularly wary of *any* acting program that implies that its classes will lead directly to professional employment. No one can promise you this. Watch out also for acting classes that require you to pay extra for photographs and "management services" or pay to appear in showcases to which "important casting directors" will be invited. Often, such casting directors will instead be sending their assistant—or their intern.

Above all, steer clear of "star search" agencies that seem to be posting auditions for paid acting jobs but are really seeking only paying students. Virtually all of these are scams. "The Search for New Stars Is Happening Now," trumpeted an ad in *Teen*, *Seventeen*, and *Cosmopolitan* magazines a few years back. The studio ad promised that "you'll be auditioned on camera and interviewed by some of the top acting and modeling 'career makers' who will be there to judge you. We're looking for girls who want to be the 'new stars' of the decade." What the ad was really offering was a $2,100 acting course with no guarantee of professional visibility. (You'll be happy to hear that the studio was fined $50,000 by the Los Angeles Attorney's Office's Consumer Protection Unit and put out of business.)

The best courses and teachers are frank in their advertising, fair in their prices, honest in their evaluation of your potential (and your chances), and aboveboard in their registration and tuition policies. Don't be afraid to ask questions, and don't be willing to accept less than complete answers.

Who *should* study at professional schools? Probably just about everybody. The main advantage of a professional school is that it is right in the midst of professional activity; it is run by professionals, with "real-world" values dominating every classroom exercise and discussion; and your fellow students will be like-minded professional aspirants—good people to hang out with—especially when you're new in town. Even veteran actors continue to study throughout their careers. As Hilary Swank explained, well into her career, "you have to just keep working really hard and keep studying your craft. I would do a job and then [go back to] working on acting, reading a play with a bunch of actors, reading books about acting, and watching actors. It's an ever-evolving craft, something you always need to work at." No wonder she is now a star.

When you get into a professional class, get right to work—and work hard. Commercial schools do not have grades or examinations. The only motivation for study is your own drive to learn. Hard work and energy, not money, are your main investment. You will get out of these classes precisely what you put into them—a cliché perhaps, but one that is never so true as in an acting class. Meet the other people in the class and get to know them, because they will be your first contacts in the professional world you wish to enter.

Remember: whatever your training, academic or professional, you'll learn as much or more from your fellow students as from your teachers, and you'll be in touch with them further down the road. Richard Dreyfuss (star of *Jaws* and *Madoff*) remarked that "the people you sit next to [in class] are more important than the guy sitting up front. Because it's them that you will work with, pal with, share with, have information from about life. And from them you meet other actors. [Training] is not about becoming someone's student, it's about being an actor among actors." This seems to us outstanding advice.

Apprenticeships

Apprenticeship programs are a third possible training ground for actors, and the best of these offer excellent opportunities for professional development—when you can get them.

Apprenticeships (or internships, as they are sometimes called) put you in direct daily contact with working professionals and usually have you working side by side with them. Some offer acting classes in addition, and some even offer credits toward union membership under Equity's Membership Candidate (EMC) program (see "Unions" in Chapter 4). Most offer stipends, though you will ordinarily pay for room and board, and perhaps a tuition fee as well, but in some cases these may be negotiated if the company wants you and your skills badly enough.

The best apprenticeships (though they may not be known by that name) are at those LORT theatres that offer seasonal and year-round programs. For the last 50 years, for example, the Milwaukee Repertory Theatre has engaged in a paid residency program for up to 10 to 15 Emerging Professional Residents (EPRs) who "join the company in order to gain valuable experience, learn from experts in their field, and enjoy an entry into professional theatre." The Actors Theatre of Louisville is another outstanding example, but there are other LORT theatres that have similar year-round programs, and though these may not lead you into playing speaking roles in their productions, they certainly offer you a step or two (or three) up the professional ladder. And they can also provide you with the 50 weeks of work necessary to qualify for an Equity card under the EMC plan (more about this under "Unions" in Chapter 4), as well as a sound education in professional theatre practice.

Summer apprentice programs at outstanding theatres such as the Williamstown and Berkshire festivals in Massachusetts, the Powerhouse Theatre at Vassar College, and the many Shakespeare Festivals around the country are also great training grounds for professional actors, as has been demonstrated over past decades. You can find information about apprenticeships through summer theatre publications (see Appendix), through the University/Resident Theatre Association, and by writing directly to professional theatre companies that you know have such programs or that you think might be interested in creating one.

> ASIDE FROM JAMES: An apprenticeship with a regional theatre was my first move after graduate school. Not only did it provide a great opportunity with working professionals but it also got me to New York. Or as close to New York as I could—New Jersey—without going broke. It allowed me to dip my toes in the water before I knew that the water was just fine.

Summer festivals

Theatre festivals in the summertime can also be terrific stepping stones into the professional acting world. The vast majority of these are America's hundred-plus Shakespeare Festivals, most of them hiring both Equity and non-Equity actors, of whom the latter are generally college actors close to—or recently following—their BA or MFA graduations. Their festival engagements ordinarily come with cash stipends, housing, and speaking roles—and their roles might be paired with those of professional actors, and staged by professional directors. Some of these festivals—such as the Oregon and Utah Shakespearean Festivals—have won Tony Awards, and having played roles at either of them will look awfully good on an actor's résumé!

> ASIDE FROM ROBERT: In 1961, when I graduated from UC Berkeley with a BA and was headed to the Yale Drama School for my DFA, I applied for and received an invitation to perform with the nonprofessional Colorado Shakespeare Festival. The fee was only $300, and I had to pay for my travel, meals and housing, but I gladly accepted. I played roles in all three of their shows, and learned more about acting that summer than I had in my entire high school and college theatre classes and experiences. And

because of it I was invited to act with the Oregon Shakespeare Festival—
also not yet professional—the following summer. And two years later I
was at the Williamstown Theatre Festival—this one professional

A word of caution

One final cautionary word about pre-professional training: it can be over-
done. College, acting classes, and the local community theatre can be very
comfortable places. A lovely security envelops you. You are known, liked,
respected, and well reviewed by the locals and by your teachers. But check
your goals. If you want to move on, you better go when you are ready rather
than hang around merely because it's safe. Recognize the point of stagna-
tion when the competition gets soft. Some actors become so devoted to a
favorite acting class teacher that they study for eight or ten years without
going to a single audition, on the grounds that they are "not yet ready."
Such a "professional student" is really psychologically aberrant. Recognize
this trait in yourself, if it exists, and fight it. When you are ready to take the
plunge, take it. Only you can decide on the proper time.

Contacts and networking

Here we are. Contacts are the nemesis of the young unknown actor, and networking is often viewed as simply a debased form of social intercourse. Well,
you can whine, gripe, yell, and complain about it, but developing contacts
and then networking among them are important—*vital*—in getting jobs in
the theatre. Rather than just giving up on this account, *think*: what does the
term "contacts" actually mean, and what does networking actually entail?

Contacts are simply the people you know and who know you. If they
know a lot of other people as well, particularly people who are movers and
shakers in the acting business, then they're "good" contacts—and there's
nothing wrong with getting to know them. Networking is simply taking
the initiative to meet such people and spend time with them, and then to
remember just who they are, what they want, and what they do.

Switch sides for a moment. If you were casting a play and knew that Jane
was "just right" for the role, wouldn't you call her and ask her to audition?
Would you really search through the drama classes at Amalgamated State
University to find out whether somebody else is as good? No. You would call
Jane and say, "Hey, I've got a part that's just right for you." Jane would come
over and read for the part, and if you were delighted with her reading you'd
cast her. It's not that you owe Jane a favor, but you like her, you envision her
doing the part, and you can settle the matter quickly and move on. It makes

sense, doesn't it? And it saves time. Like it or not, "being known" is the *sine qua non* ("without which, nothing!") of getting that casting call.

There is nothing mysterious about "contacts," and it is fruitless to play sour grapes and say "I can't get anywhere because I don't have any pull." Of course you don't, but hardly anyone else does either at your level. It is not as though all your competition went to school with Tom Cruise or swam in Scarlett Johansson's pool. Everybody, or almost everybody, starts off just as unknown and unwanted as you. If you don't have contacts, you have to develop some. It is as simple as that. So, stop complaining that success is measured "not by what you know but whom you know." It's measured by what you know *and* whom you know. You say you want to make it "on your own." How could you do that? By being discovered? Where? Singing in your shower? Good luck.

The fact is that *nobody* makes it on their "own." It always takes *somebody else*, and that somebody else is your contact. This is no time to play around with semantics. Getting jobs in theatre involves getting people to know you, to know your work, and to like working with you. People like working with people they know and like. So do you. So, get on board.

Now, who said you have no contacts? *Everybody you know* is a contact, potentially even a "good" one. A fellow student may land a part in a soap next week, another might start an experimental theatre, still another might soon be producing a film, and one of your instructors might write a TV show. These people can become the initial core of your network, and the people they know can become the ring around them. This is hardly fantasy. Probably half the regional theatres in the country were started by drama school chums looking for something to do after graduation (see the final chapter for some examples). The person sitting next to you in class, in other words, might easily become your first employer. Therefore, it's to your advantage to get to know *everyone you can* in this business and get them to know you. And get them to *like* you. That's all networking is. Don't wait for the phone to ring—make some calls yourself. Send an email. Send a postcard. Send a photo. In other words, stay in touch.

The "important contacts" you probably don't yet know, but you will soon. Every time you audition, you meet at least one. At every class, at every audition, at almost every party, you will meet secretaries, directors, agents, and other actors. These meetings can be forgotten in an instant, but if you are personable and reasonably intriguing, a contact is made. You don't have to be pushy. Phony friendliness and phony friends are the most loathsome aspect of show business, and it is easy to completely misplay your hand. Theatre people are the worst name-droppers in the world, and "Oh, he's a good friend of mine" becomes a line that is too frequently applied to a person met once five years ago. You can build your *real* network of contacts—the people who know you and know your work—by simply and modestly finding ways to keep your friends aware of you. Also keep yourself aware of *them* by expressing a genuine interest in their activities, logging their names into your actor's journal (more on that later), gathering email addresses, making "friends" with them through one or more social networks like Facebook, and finding a way to get together again to see their work and to develop a truly professional relationship.

Remember these fundamental principles about contacts:

- No *one* contact is going to make it for you, and the fact that somebody else knows somebody important is not going to make it for him or her, either. Everyone you know can help you by trading information, tips, advice, and, ultimately, offers of employment.
- People you have known for years and who have subsequently "made it" may not help you out at all. It is not that success has made them indifferent to their old pals. Many genuinely try to follow the suggestion of Edith Piaf, who said that when you reach the top you should throw the ladder back down for everybody else. It is simply that your newly arrived friends are not as secure as they seem. In fact, they are in a particularly vulnerable position. Even if they can help you, they may not want to risk suggesting you to their higher-ups, fearing that if you fail, they'll be blamed. Beyond this, they may question their earlier evaluation of you now that they have new surroundings and a new perspective. They would prefer that you make it on your own—then they could be *sure* of their assessment. This is small comfort, of course, but you will probably have to live with it.
- Contacts may not *look* like contacts. The mousy-looking man hanging around backstage might just be getting ready to film *Grandson of Batman* and be looking you over for a part. Being yourself and making friends can't hurt you.
- Contacts may not *act* like contacts. People who give out jobs in show business are so besieged that they frequently hide the fact behind a veil of feigned clumsiness and innocence. Play along.
- All kinds of people will *tell* you that they are contacts, of course. Quite likely they're not. Maybe they are simply nice and want to help, and maybe they are after you for other reasons (which we don't need to go into). Some just like to sound important. Treat everybody the same, and retain a bit of skepticism.

A word or two about sleeping with the director. If you are a talented, personable, charming, and sexy person, all sorts of people will be interested in casting you, and all sorts of people will be interested in going to bed with you. These will quite possibly not be the same people, however.

A cartoon that used to hang outside the Screen Gems casting office window shows a young girl dressing in a bedroom and calling to an older man, "Now, when are you going to make me a star?" The older man is in the next room, smiling and cutting out a paper star.

Let's not be overly prudish. It is illogical to assume that if the casting director is your intimate, he or she won't be working a little harder for you than for others who come in for an interview. It is equally obvious that if your bed partner is a studio executive, all things are not going to be equal when it comes to casting the next show. Writer/director Paul Sylbert admits in his biting Hollywood exposé *Final Cut* that he was pressured to cast the mistress of an AVCO/Embassy executive in his film *The Steagle*. The larger point, however, is that when the poor lady proved unequal to the (acting) challenge she was fired, to everybody's chagrin and the actress's mortification.

Nobody gets a real job or builds a career *simply* by going from one studio bed or casting couch to another, not anymore at least. Why not? New awareness—and legal implications—of sexual harassment has put a firm damper on sexual trade-offs. "You never, *never* interview a woman in anything other than a very open situation," says 50-year veteran casting director Mike Fenton, one of Hollywood's best and with 280 credits to date, who keeps a woman assistant at his side whenever he interviews a female client. The potential for scandal in the tabloids, sexually transmitted diseases, and the inevitable loss of self-esteem are also inhibiting factors.

Most important, however: the great passion of the entertainment industry is for success, not sex. No producer, director, or casting director would dare put his or her show or career at risk just for a little playtime—which is readily available elsewhere. People in the business work too hard and have too much at stake for that. "These days, sleeping one's way to oblivion is more likely than sleeping one's way upward. Marry them—or date out of town," says celebrated producer Lynda Obst (*The Fisher King, Contact, Sleepless in Seattle*) in her apt and penetrating documentary *Hello, He Lied*. Everybody's working too hard, anyway, Obst explains. "Men are exhausted and enervated, while women are doing hundreds of military push-ups in aerobics classes." The bottom line: forget it.

Work!

No one has said it better than the great theatre composer Irving Berlin. Advising immigrants how to survive in America, he told them, "Do not take a moment's rest. Run. Work and *work* and then *WORK*." This is how Mr. Berlin built his career in the entertainment industry, and it's also the way you're going to have to build yours.

Your power supply is your sense of commitment and your will to succeed. These will keep you going despite the thousand and one ego reversals you are bound to encounter. As a young, professional actor explains, the greatest danger you face is going "DEAF—Depressed, Envious, Aching, and Frustrated." Your commitment and sheer persistence will vanquish DEAF-ness if anything can. They will keep you going through poverty and loneliness when you watch your friends marrying and having kids and making money while you eat out of cans on the Lower East Side and wait for your ship to come in. You must continue to hang in there, to train yourself, to seek information, to develop contacts.

To do these things, you must have an overwhelming desire for success. "Tenacity is a huge thing," says veteran actor Christopher Walken, who over the past 63 years has performed in 129 films and TV shows. "No matter how much you get rejected, don't stop. Be relentless." It is often said that the people who make it in the theatre are simply those who want it badly enough.

It is not necessary to step on other people's toes, to do zany things that draw attention to yourself, or to alienate friends, relatives, and competitors in your quest for success—but quest for it you must. Getting started in theatre means *initiating* actions: getting on the telephone and out on the pavement, looking up people, calling on strangers, arriving at places at 6 am and waiting around for three hours—all sorts of indelicate and unappetizing tasks. It also means weeks, months, even years of frustration, failure, defeat, and simple boredom. It means sitting around waiting for the telephone to ring when it has not rung in months. All these things are at best unpleasant and at worst may lead you to the brink of suicidal depression. Only a massive will to succeed will overcome them. Your commitment must be strong, persistent, and all-encompassing. All sorts of personal sacrifices must be assumed. "The only secret," says comedian Jon Lovitz, "is to keep getting better and persisting." Lovitz spent seven years after college trying to get a "first break," working as a messenger while his friends were becoming doctors and lawyers. "I was getting shit from my father and wondering if I hadn't made a giant mistake," he remembers. His persistence and relentless self-improvement have paid off handsomely.

Nobody can tell you how long it will take to "make" you an actor. Morgan Freeman claims his success didn't come until he was 50. Mercedes Ruehl, thinking of when she arrived in New York, says, "I remember glibly announcing to a friend that I would be a star in two and a half years. And seven, eight, nine years later, still nobody knew me." Stephen Spinella had decided he "was tired of waiting on tables" and was about to apply to law school when the first workshop for *Angels in America* came along, leading to his first two Broadway Tony awards and a subsequent starring role in *Spring Awakening.*

However, it is probably best to set yourself some sort of time schedule. Most actors do. Five years is an average allotment, ten years a generous one. Years during which you say to yourself, "I am an actor and I'm available for work." Years during which you hit the big towns, the casting offices, the studios, the agencies, and the professional classes. Years when you know that whatever you are doing, you will drop it immediately if it means you'll be getting a professional acting job.

During those years, you are prepared to scrimp on money for gifts, for food, for furniture, for an apartment. You will spend that money instead on pictures, résumés, trade papers, phone services, website listings, acting classes, gym membership, and auditioning clothes. You will get the sleep and exercise and medication you need, because you're going to have to look terrific on an hour's notice any day of any week. You will direct your time, your money, and your energy to two things: improving your acting and booking (getting signed for) work. Whatever is left over will go to less important things, like your social life or your marriage—yes, these are less important. If you aren't 100% committed to your career, you will almost surely be surpassed by someone who is.

You must also overcome the thousands of rejections and discouragements along the way. Actress Edie Falco described, in her postgraduate life, "some horrible years. You go to college and you go off and do plays and when the dust clears, you are left alone in your crazy apartment at four in the afternoon with no job, no prospects and a waitressing shift to go to. And real heavy-duty darkness can set in." Smitten by anxiety attacks, Falco went home to her mother, who "talked me through it." Not long afterward she went on to star in *The Sopranos* and *Nurse Jackie* on television, and the Broadway revivals of *'night Mother* and *Frankie and Johnny in the Clair de Lune.*

Don't think you'll escape some horrible times on your road, either. Start figuring out now how you will be able to transcend them.

Know, too, that even if you succeed, you will probably *still* think you "haven't made it." As the late Emmy award winner Peter Boyle explains, "You meet giants of the movies, people who are famous, powerful, successful, and who always think their last job was indeed their last." The late Oscar, Emmy, and Golden Globe Award winner Ruth Gordon likewise told her young *Harold and Maude* costar Bud Cort, "Listen, my dear, you *never* make it. I'm on that phone twelve hours a day. I make it happen for myself!" And "You can't hang onto your laurels," says 64-year veteran James Earl Jones. "I'm a troubadour, going from castle to castle looking to sing for my supper. That's the way it is; it never changes."

This isn't necessarily grim. A committed attitude, such as that personified by Boyle, Gordon, and Jones, carries with it something more than just a pragmatic advantage in selling yourself on the job market. Exciting people are committed people, whether in art, in politics, or in life. And it's to your advantage to be exciting: relish your accomplishments, however small. "Making it" is a step-by-step process; it rarely happens all at once. Aim for the top—but be prepared to climb there on a ladder, not get thrown there by a catapult.

Stay dedicated. It will offend the weak but inspire others. A life of dedication to your art is fulfilling. It galvanizes your talents and directs your energies. It characterizes all great artists. As famed playwright George Bernard Shaw wrote, more than a hundred years ago:

> This is the true joy in life, the being used for a purpose recognized by yourself as a mighty one: the being thoroughly worn out before you are thrown on the scrap heap, the being a force of Nature instead of a feverish selfish little clod of ailments and grievances, complaining that the world will not devote itself to making you happy.

Live as if you mean it, and become an artist in the same way. This involves a little presumptuous egotism; flow with it. Shaw, Bernhardt, Olivier, Beethoven, Heifetz, Picasso, Pavarotti, Hepburn—*all* great artists have been persons of great dedication, persons who have sacrificed easygoing pleasantness to the drive for perfection that has welled up inside them. If you are determined to make it as an actor, you are living a life with high stakes anyway. You might as well go all the way with it.

Attitude, discipline, health, and capacity for psychological adjustment

One of the saddest—but most common—things we hear about actors after a show is "He has a bad attitude!" or "She's undisciplined." Such reports keep talented performers out of work and land them on informal, rumor-fed blacklists, which they may not truly deserve. The biggest problem is that they never know about it. But the slightest whisper, from one associate producer to another, that "we've got enough problems in this show without dealing with *hers*!" is frequently the last exchange before "Thanks very much, dear. We'll be in touch with you if anything comes up."

Being daffy may be desirable, but being genuinely crazy—or having casting people think you are—is death. Crazy people are unpredictable and hard to contact, don't show up on time, forget their lines and their blocking, annoy other actors, antagonize directors, defy wardrobers, and in general are far more trouble than they are worth. If you are crazy, hide it. If you aren't, please don't pretend to be.

Mental health, however, means more than merely being on the near side of psychosis. Being relatively stable, well balanced, gregarious, and sensitive to the plights of others is a valuable asset. Arrogance, rudeness, self-centeredness, and carelessness are *huge* turnoffs. People may have liked you for your devil-may-care behavior in graduate school, but they will do more than wrinkle their brow at it on the professional set. You can be a prima donna only when you *are* a prima donna, that is, when your presence alone can guarantee a full house or a multi-million dollar gross. If you're starting out, you must be positive, professional, and ever-alert.

Much subtler "bad attitudes" can work against you that you may not even be aware of. For example, beware of knocking the industry, particularly television, which is always ripe for criticism. Lisa Miller Katz, who cast *King of Queens* and *Don't Trust the Bitch in Apartment 23*, is astounded when actors come in and boast "I don't watch TV!" "Like TV's beneath them," Katz exclaims. "But TV is what I cast!" What does Katz look for instead? Just the opposite: "People who are talented and enthusiastic. Enthusiasm and a vibe that they're happy to be there. The number of people I can't hire is mind-boggling, so when someone comes in and it feels like they don't want to be there, I think, 'You must pick another career!' "

Please remember that the vast majority of TV producers, directors, and casting directors—despite the silliness of some of their products—are intelligent, sensitive people. Although they may sometimes wisecrack about their industry, the vast majority take pride in what they are doing. If they didn't, they'd probably fail at it. To mock their show mocks them, so don't be misled by their occasionally self-deprecating remarks. Every director would prefer to cast an actor who will love the role, love the show, and love its medium.

Another attitude that will block your way is career complacency. "I'm waiting to be discovered" is roughly equivalent to "I'm waiting for death." Indeed, it's really a cover for timidity, a statement made by actors afraid of trying, afraid of looking foolish, and (at the root of all this) afraid of failing. Declaring self-promotion callous, such people don't seek out agents, set up interviews, or discuss career plans or goals with anyone but intimate friends. Beware of this outlook, because it masks itself with noble forms. Basically, it is egotism: the belief that your talent is so obvious you don't need to show it. But you do. The fact is that it takes work to get work, and *you* must do the work because nobody else is going to do it for you.

A third attitude to avoid is carelessness, slovenliness, a lack of preparation. If you want to be a professional, then you must *be* professional. It was one thing to be late learning your lines for an acting scene in college—or to paraphrase your text, come late to rehearsal, or show up with a drink or two under your belt. In fact, you might have thought these things were pretty cool, given how terrific you were. Well, they are absolute deathblows in the professional world, particularly for actors just starting out. "Actors who are late are out of my book," says Mike Fenton, who could hardly be more unequivocal when he adds, "There is no excuse short of being dead. None. Period."

Got that? Professional actors get it. As the great stage star Maureen Stapleton put it (and you better remember it), "Actors are the only people, good or bad, hot or cold, who show up on time."

"Being prepared" is the universal demand made by casting directors, particularly these days (as you will see in Chapter 4). Preparedness means spending every possible minute working up the audition you're heading into. Longtime stage and film CD Eddie Foy III put it very bluntly before he retired: "You've got to study, you've got to sweat, you've got to learn what it is to be hungry. Be a professional! I see actors walk in and they're not clean, they haven't shaved, they haven't washed their clothes. That's *professional?*"

Strict discipline is simply a must. Indeed, it's perhaps the chief distinction between amateurs and pros. Thus, the best colleges, commercial schools, and community theatres insist on it. Discipline is not contradictory to creativity but, rather, essential to it. Discipline means that whenever you're on call you're concentrating on your acting tasks to the exclusion of everything else. It means not only that you are always on time (actually, there *before* the time), but also that you always show up ready to deliver, with all your acting instruments—voice, body, imagination, and intelligence—well tuned and at the disposal of the director from the first moment of your call.

Discipline does not end when you leave the rehearsal hall, either. Your *physical health* is crucial to your success as well, and that must be tended to 24/7 throughout your career. Hear James on this subject:

> ASIDE FROM JAMES: There's no bigger turn off than an actor who shows up sick. And nothing more boring in an audition than hearing an actor tell me about his cold or her sore throat. I don't like such surprises: I expect you to be 100% healthy when you walk into the room. So, take care of yourself and *don't get sick!* Do whatever's necessary: get a good night's sleep, eat nutritious meals, go easy with controlled substances, schedule medical visits when necessary, *take care of yourself.* And dress warmly: notice performers in Broadway musicals coming out of the stage doors in wintertime with their hats on and woolen scarves wrapped around their throats. These folks know what a valuable commodity they are protecting!

We'd like to say an extra word about the perils of *eating disorders*, which are particularly common among young actors (along with dancers and models, whose problems with bulimia and anorexia are more widely publicized). Most victims of these diseases, sadly, refuse to acknowledge they have problems—even to themselves. A too-severely slimmed-down Calista Flockhart, star of *Super Girl* and *Brothers and Sisters*, once told 20/20 reporter Connie Chung "I would never say [that I had an eating disease] in a million years," before finally admitting that she had seriously struggled with anorexia while filming the TV show *Ally McBeal*. "At the time," Flockhart explained, "I was seriously stressed. I was working 15-hour days on the set and was dealing with the end of the show, which was basically my life. I started under-eating, over-exercising, pushing myself too hard and brutalizing my immune system. I guess I just didn't find time to eat." Fortunately, she has since recovered. Eating disorders are nothing new, either: multiple Oscar-winning actress Jane Fonda has confessed that she was a "secret bulimic" from age 12; other performers, most notably singer Karen Carpenter, have even died of such diseases. If you feel you are stepping over this edge, or your friends wonder aloud if you are, seek medical attention— immediately! It may save your career—and your life!

> ASIDE FROM JAMES: Working actors today have certainly learned this lesson. America Ferrera, who played the title character on TV's *Ugly Betty*, had an enormously busy schedule, and so had her three daily meals—all well balanced and nutritious—delivered to her door before work each morning. You may not be able to afford this, but you certainly can—and should—plan out a healthy daily diet and routine.

It's not always easy to recognize discipline in a professional situation. If you have the chance to watch the taping of a television show, you may see the regulars lounging around, talking to each other, joking on the set, drinking coffee, dropping lines during takes, and generally seeming pretty nonchalant about the whole experience. Don't be deceived. What you'll also see is the immediate attention the director commands and how everybody will snap into total concentration in a matter of seconds. These are pros, conditioned like flight crews to an ever-ready professional alertness. Their seeming nonchalance is only a rest break in a very busy day. Until you are experienced enough to know *precisely* when to break and when to deliver, concentrate fully on what you are doing. If you don't, you might find yourself laughing by the coffeepot while everybody else has suddenly gone back to work and your name is being called—furiously.

Discipline certainly includes a willingness—even an eagerness—to take direction. No good director will become offended or irritated by genuine questions or discussion about blocking, emphasis, or motivation. But continual complaints such as "It doesn't feel right," particularly when they are obviously meant to cover insecurity, drive directors up the wall and may land you out of a job—sometimes right then and there.

In summary, be positive and infectious, not distant, whiny, or superior. You love the part, you love the play, you love the medium, you love the direction, and you'll work your tail off to give the producers everything they want. Nobody is ever really offended by an actor who is genuinely eager, unless that eagerness pushes everybody else off the set. Be a yes person. Do your homework—*now*. Do more than they ask, sooner than they ask it. Anticipate tasks and anticipate problems. Knock their socks off at the audition. And while you must never cross over the line by obsequiously flattering the producers, your enthusiasm for the project will work to your advantage (and probably guide you to a better performance to boot), while sage notes of ironic weariness or indifference will work powerfully (albeit silently) against you.

Freedom from entanglements and inhibitions

Freedom is complex and does not exist in the absolute. Everyone is bound by restraints: practical, financial, social, and mental. Success in the pursuit of an acting career requires minimizing, not utterly eliminating, these restraints. An actor simply must be free to audition for roles and to accept employment when and where it is offered. When the important job offer comes as you're about to leave for your honeymoon, turning it down could be a career-buster.

Face it: commitment to an acting career means at least some slacking-off on other commitments, including those to husbands, wives, partners, children, friends, parents, outside employers, and teachers. When you were a college actor, you might have been able to ask your director for an hour off to pick up your mother at the airport; if you're a professional actor, however, you better tell your Mom to catch a cab. Obviously, it is better—if not essential—that you arrange your priority of commitments in such a way that your career plans can proceed unhindered.

For the acting career is an exceptionally demanding one, and you are going to have to deal with its demands. You must come to grips with the nature of the business you are trying to enter and make certain that the people who depend on you are aware of it, too—and are sympathetic to your ambitions. They may not be so at first. As an actor, you will be subject to an ever-changing and unpredictable schedule; you will be on call for location work in New Delhi or New Haven while your domestic partner is taking care of the kids in Culver City; you will be facing the terrific frustration of looking for parts and breaks in an industry where unemployment is routine; you will be sacrificing much of your income for classes and workshops and photos of your lovely self; and, finally, when you do start to get work, you will be deeply involved in the emotional crises, love affairs, and strange psychologies of the characters you are to play—and of the good-looking actors you are to play with—and these may not be exactly the emotional feelings you wrestle with in your own life. Face it: 30 well-known American actors and their spouses (many of whom are actors as well) divorced or separated in 2015 alone. Face the fact that you're no prize, and face realistically the trials your relationship will inevitably endure.

Should an actor get married at all? It is far beyond the scope of this book to recommend one way or the other, and it is also doubtful that any recommendation offered here would be very seriously considered anyway. However, it is obvious that a fully committed domestic relationship *can* become a serious entanglement to a stage or film career if both people fail to understand what they are getting into. If you enter into such a relationship without a clear understanding of what it means, either you will completely frustrate your partner and your relationship will end up in ruins, or you will frustrate yourself and your career will tank. You are already aware that the acting profession has a ridiculously high divorce rate. For some actors, it is simply an either/or situation. As the late, double-Oscar-winning Shelley Winters explained after her 50-year career with four marriages, "Honey, you've got to really make a choice in life. It's either a good role or a good marriage." Winters made her choice accordingly: "I loved working more than being married, so I gave up this great guy for this great role." And so it goes. You *can't* have everything.

You face other entanglements besides a committed relationship, of course. Some are financial, some emotional. You may be unwilling or unable to move around, to work with certain kinds of people, or to play certain kinds of parts. You may object to undressing in front of an audience (or a camera) or to performing in a way you find undignified. You must draw a line for yourself here, but naturally the lower that line (that is, the fewer your inhibitions) the more available you are. Insofar as that line must now be drawn to include or exclude doing nude scenes, increasingly common in Broadway and off-Broadway plays as well as feature films (see "The job offer" in Chapter 5), you will have to be prepared to define your views on this issue if you plan to work across the full spectrum of performance possibilities.

One "inhibition," however, is known as "taste." Performing in the nude for a porn flick is not the same as for a legit play or feature film. An actor known for pornography may become unusable for anything *but* that in the future. As Georgina Spelvin, the undraped star of *The Devil in Miss Jones*, has made clear, "if you make the choice to go into explicit pictures, it's for life." Marilyn Chambers, star of the 1972 *Behind the Green Door*, is still in the biz (with a voiceover in the 2009 *Porndogs*), but admits, "I thought there would be a chance to cross over, Boy, was I wrong!"

Good information and advice

You will need the most current information and the most up-to-date advice if you are to pursue an acting career successfully. This book may be filled with information and advice, but, like any book, it was written at least a year before you're reading it. You need to know the day-by-day, and sometimes the hour-by-hour, developments in your prospective field.

Trade papers and sites

Both the theatre world and the film world have their traditional (and by now historic) trade papers—universally known as "the trades"—as well as the more contemporary theatre websites that report on what's happening.

For actors the indispensable trade paper is *Backstage*, which, since its 2008 incorporation of *Backstage West*, now covers both New York and Los Angeles—as well as many places in-between—and films, stage, and TV. A yearly subscription to its weekly print is $200 in 2017, and for online editions $140, but you can get daily online issues for free at backstage.com, with dozens of details and 24-hour access to more than a thousand acting and acting-related jobs around the country. *Backstage* is an absolute marvel for newcomers to the business, as every issue includes multiple pages of casting calls, reviews of current productions, news of the theatre, film, and TV businesses around the country, articles on the acting craft, and hugely informative interviews with actors, agents, casting directors, acting coaches, and others with advice to give to both veteran actors and those hoping to join the ranks. A back page actor-advice column answers reader questions with sage counsel, and special pull-out inserts each year focus on important topics, contact information on agents and agencies, drama schools, voiceovers, acting on shipboard, and the like—indeed, many of the quotations in this book have been excerpted from the advice on these pages. A subscription to either version is perhaps the best investment—indeed, an almost essential investment—a young actor about to hit either of the big cities can make.

For entertainment executives and producers, the weekly *Variety*, founded in 1905, began its career by covering variety shows on the New York stage; however it is now almost entirely focused on Hollywood's film and television productions, and is available only on the web, being far more directed toward the entertainment business, and to its corporations and producers, than to day-to-day reports on stage plays, acting, or casting. The equally venerable but daily *Hollywood Reporter* (which also covers theatre), is its parallel, but given their high subscription prices, you're probably better advised to read these producer-oriented trades on their websites (www. variety.com and www.hollywoodreporter.com), unless you are fascinated with box office figures, the comings and goings of foreign exhibitors, and who's selling their Maine or Malibu mansion for umpteen million dollars.

Another great published source for New York-bound stage actors, but more useful for directors and producers, though expensive ($19.95 per month on the web, or $250 per year with web plus print per month, and $425 per year for weekly web plus print issues), is the monthly *Theatrical Index*, which lists every Broadway, off-Broadway, and national touring show currently being produced in New York—plus upcoming productions and activities of America's top regional theatre companies, along with the producers and casting officers of each show. This, however, is a trade magazine aimed at the wealthy; if you're not that, you can find a current copy in the New York Public Library for the Performing Arts.

Of course, if you're just starting out, reading the trades can leave you more frustrated than informed. Some casting calls in *Backstage* are for auditions you can't yet get (those for which you must be submitted by an agent or for which union members have priority) or don't want ("erotic telegram services" and cattle calls for shows you already know are cast), or with dismaying language such as "there is deferred pay" or "there is the possibility of deferred pay" or, the most common (and truthful), "there is no pay." You will also see casting calls for plays that will never be performed, films that will never be shot, and variety shows that will never see the light of day—or the dark of night. That said, however, the casting pages of *Backstage* are well monitored by the magazine's editors and will give you a pretty clear picture of the casting opportunities on both coasts, as well as some suggestion of what's going on deeper in the country's heartland.

Beyond the interviews, casting calls, advertisements, and advice columns, reading the trades—*Variety* included—gives you the feeling that you're part of the general goings-on in the acting industries. As such, they help you surmount the natural feeling of alienation and aloneness every newcomer has when hitting New York or Hollywood for the first time. They are simply the news of show business, and a half hour with any one of them will give you a good vocabulary of names, places, and shows and an idea of what's in the heads of the agents, producers, and casting directors who are active at the moment. The trades give you, at the very least, a vicarious sense of participation, and even a vicarious participation is a good start in a business that considers itself a club. Indeed, reading the trades is part of paying your dues, whether you read them in a library, on the web, or over someone's shoulder in the subway.

Trade books

In addition to the trade papers, dozens of acting handbooks—some quickly published with simple staple bindings and updated monthly or seasonally, and others (including this one) paperbound and revised over every few years—sit on designated shelves in the two stunning theatre bookshops in America's acting capitals. In New York, this is the historic Drama Book Shop, founded in 1923 and now located in the heart of the theatre district at 250 W. 40th Street (and now recovered from a near water-pipe destruction in 2016); in Los Angeles, it is the Samuel French Bookshop, originally founded in London, which has been at 7623 Sunset Blvd. in Hollywood since 1951. (The theatre bookshops in Toronto and Studio City mentioned in our previous edition have since dissolved.) Both of these stores can, of course, be contacted via the internet (www.dramabookshop.com and www.samuelfrench.com), where purchases can be easily made, but for these acting handbooks a personal visit will enable you to thumb through the editions first and see which ones really meet your needs.

The internet

Certainly the best place to find the most up-to-date information these days is on the internet, however, where most important sites update their materials daily, if not hourly. In the volatile acting business (particularly in television), a day can be forever, and the internet has taken over as the prime source of "staying on top" of what's happening in your field.

Virtually all important theatre companies, film and TV studios, acting unions, theatre publications, and purveyors of theatre photographs and other services maintain regularly updated and highly useful sites on the web. Scholarly resources abound as well, offering the complete plays of major playwrights, hard-to-find TV scripts, and whole encyclopedias of research materials; most are accessible without charge. There are also membership sites (much more on these in Chapter 4) where you can market yourself, ask questions, and "chat" with other actors and actor-aspirants.

The web also has lots of stargazers and scam artists, however. Keep in mind that anyone with modest web skills and the right software can put up a site rife with flashy graphics and blazing opinions—but with information and advice that's unsupported, outdated, and downright wrong. Often such groups will offer you an audition, and then flatter you outrageously ("You're terrific!"), so that they can then sell you "professional" photographs of yourself, or new hairstyles, or inept acting classes taught by inept acting instructors, all for large bundles of money. Stay away from them!

What should you look for in a theatre website? Mainly, it should be regularly updated and accurate. It helps if the site is solidly funded (these things cost money), generally by the hosting institution. Official websites of professional theatres, acting organizations, and the major trade publishers generally meet these criteria. Other sites boast the longevity and accuracy that indicate careful maintenance. Here are the four most informational, longstanding, honest, and likely-to-still-be-there-when-you-read-this websites for actors to check out; all are free and require no membership or registration:

www.playbill.com. Playbill Online, updated daily, is the nation's premiere theatre site, listing plays being performed in almost every city in the United States and most major cities abroad, Broadway grosses week by week, daily theatre news from all over, and a ticket purchasing service for all Broadway and off-Broadway shows, many of them with discounted prices.

www.imdb.com. The Internet Movie Database, offering a searchable database listing the film and major TV credits of *all* American actors (and directors, designers, playwrights, etc.) since the 1890s.

www.ibdb.com. The Internet Broadway Database, which does the same for actors, et al., in Broadway shows since 1832.

www.iobdb.com. The Off-Broadway Database.

Many other actor-useful websites—some more fully interactive and some requiring membership registration and monthly fees—are given in sections of this book specifically pertaining to them.

Other sources of information

Where else can you get information? Talk to people. Actors love to talk about their business—in fact, some of them talk about almost nothing else. Acting schools are a good place to begin. Another is theatre restaurants and bars, particularly in New York: check out such current Broadway hotspots as Joe Allen's, Sardi's, the Edison Diner, the West Bank Café, and just about any restaurant on 46th Street between 7th and 9th Avenues. And you can always strike up conversations at the theatre bookshops in New York and Los Angeles mentioned above; their employees all know what's going on in those towns.

Or simply go to lots of shows, such as the off-off-Broadway workshops in New York or the Equity waiver shows in Los Angeles. Even if you don't know a soul in the production, hang around after the curtain call and wander backstage. If you particularly liked the performances of any actors, congratulate them (an always-effective calling card) and introduce yourself. At worst, you will engage in an agreeable little conversation. At best, you will strike up a true and valuable friendship (some of the very best friendships have begun in precisely this manner).

> ASIDE FROM ROBERT: In 1968 the Royal Shakespeare Company came to Los Angeles and I saw *Taming of the Shrew* at the Ahmanson Theatre. I enjoyed the show so much I wandered to the stage door and asked the doorman if I could visit the bald actor who had played Grumio, a role I had myself played in my college years. The doorman ushered me back to the dressing room and I met the actor, and we have been close friends ever since. His name was Patrick Stewart—now *Sir* Patrick Stewart. So, don't be shy; if you don't ask the doorman, you don't get in the door.

Friends, of course, are a very fine source of information, and perhaps the best there is. With friends in the trade, you can get a feeling for the intangibles that drive this emotional and frequently mystical business. You can ferret out the tips, the hunches, the possibilities, and the probabilities that determine so much of the day-to-day course of the trade's events. You can also get a surer sense of the *feelings*—the hopes and dreams and fears—of the people in charge. Beware of being overly influenced by any single person's likes, dislikes, neuroses, or phobias, however, and be prepared to take comments with several grains of salt. Gradually you will gain a working knowledge of what casting possibilities are hot, which agents are not, which producers are open to what kinds of suggestions, and, in general, what your competition is going to be. All of this you can eventually put to use.

Theatre schools and intensive workshops that specialize in teaching job-seeking skills—"How to Audition" and "How to Get That Job!"— are also useful sources of information, particularly if you can get good responses from friends who have studied there. Also useful are actors' online information services, actors' discussion groups, and actors' counseling services. These are mostly well intentioned, and the online ones are free. You can find them, as well as public lectures on the actor's life, in the trades.

Of course, there are always a lot of people willing to take your money in return for "inside" tips and suggestions. If you deal with such people, however, you begin to reach the point of diminishing returns. No matter how much you may read or hear about the subject of "making it" in acting, nothing begins to approach the knowledge you get by working toward success yourself. The best way to learn the business is simply to get started *somewhere*, to participate in *something*. The suggestions in this book are designed to help you do that. Once you get your start, you can leave this book behind. You will find that you have access to information much more specifically applicable to your needs.

Luck and breaks

Luck and breaks are placed last on this list simply because you can do nothing to get them. When they occur, however, the alert and the talented make the most of them.

Luck is sheer happenstance. Matt Dillon was discovered by legendary casting director and then manager, the late Vic Ramos. Spotted while ditching junior high school one day, Dillon went on to star in *Little Darlings* and *My Bodyguard*, and continues to have a thriving career 32 years later. Actress Gretchen Mol (*Boardwalk Empire, Life on Mars, Mozart in the Jungle*) was discovered by her agent when she was working as a coat check girl. David Boreanaz had worked such jobs as parking cars, painting houses, and selling gourmet food door-to-door; he got his lucky break while walking his dog: a manager saw him, signed him, and called casting director Marcia Schulman to arrange an audition for the role of Angel on the hit *Buffy the Vampire Slayer*, which led to playing Angel on *Angel* and then Seeley Booth on *Bones*. Women and girls around the world have been admiring him ever since.

Breaks are much more common. They're a kind of luck as well, but luck that follows years of training, planning, and hard labor. Jessica Alba (*Dear Eleanor, Entourage, Sin City*) had good fortune in her 1993 film debut in Hollywood Pictures' *Camp Nowhere*. Originally hired for two weeks, she got her break when an actress dropped out of a principal role. Jessica cheerfully admits it wasn't her prodigious talent or charm that inspired the director to tap her to take the part, but her hair, which matched the original performer's. The two weeks became two months, and Jessica received a very impressive first credit. Mindy Kaling, actress and producer on TV's wildly successful *The Office* and *The Mindy Project*, spent years developing and writing a piece titled *Matt and Ben* that played the New York Theater Fringe Festival: the two-character comedy was a surprise success, showcasing not only her acting skills but also her gifts as a writer, and led to her job as head writer/producer and star of two of TV's biggest hits.

The dream of "discovery"—the lucky break—lies deep in the heart of every aspiring performer. Sadly, it's not in the province of this book to tell you how to get it. What, then, can *you* do about getting luck? That's between you and your divinity. But when you get it, you should know what to do with it!

3 Your First Decisions

Let's assume you have all the qualifications for an acting career that we've mentioned so far—or you think you have them. You are ready to look for work, so what do you do now? First, you have to make some very important decisions.

Your goal

As with every course of action, you have to begin with a goal. That means two things: choosing a goal (that's the easy part) and *committing yourself* to achieving your goal.

In acting, your long-range career goal is simply to get cast—and cast *professionally*. A role in a play, a film, a television show, a repertory company, an industrial production, or a TV commercial will start off your career, get you into an acting union, and begin what you hope will be a long list of professional acting credits.

Who casts? In your high school, college, or community theatre, the director probably posted tryout notices on a bulletin board or announced them in the local newspaper. You went to the appointed place, read from the script, and were cast in the production. In the professional world, things are quite different. Professional casting is done by many different people, participating at different levels. At the bottom are all the want-to-be-actors, including yourself (at level 1). Then there's possibly your *agent* (level 2), your *manager* (level 3), one or more *casting directors* (CDs) (level 4), a *director*—or two if it's the Coen brothers—(level 5), one or more *producers* (level 6), a battery of TV network executives (e.g. NBC, at level 7), and another level of studio executives (e.g. Universal, at level 8). Sometimes there will also be levels 9, 10—or even more. And *all* of these levels have to come onto your side—or at least not onto somebody else's—for you to be cast! So, it's not so easy as it was in high school or college.

There's not always such an extensive hierarchy, of course. You may not actually need a manager, and you don't always need an agent—certainly not if you can get in to see the CDs yourself. Sometimes, as in smaller stage companies, there are no CDs and certainly no network executives, and the director may also be the producer. That's how it worked in college, and it works this way sometimes in the big leagues too—but not very often.

Here's how casting usually happens in the *big* big time (i.e., major New York shows, Hollywood films, and network TV).

First, you get an *agent* (no easy trick, and you'll be reading much more about this—and everything else in this paragraph—in the next chapter). The agent agrees to "represent" you, usually under contract, and looks through a list of *breakdowns*—descriptions of roles currently being cast—to match you with roles you might play.

Then, the agent submits your name to one or more CDs for that part in that show or theatre company. If you're lucky, a CD then interviews and/ or auditions you, together with other actors submitted by *their* agents, and recommends you (and a few other finalists) to be auditioned by the project's *director* and *producers*. After these auditions, and subsequent callbacks, the director submits his or her first choices to the producers and studio and network executives.

And finally, a single choice is agreed upon by the producers and executives, and the CD is authorized to negotiate your contract—normally with your agent representing you.

Producers exist at various levels. In professional regional theatre, the producer is generally the company's *artistic director*, who is primarily concerned with each actor's skills (speech, movement, naturalness), looks (appropriateness to the character, attractiveness), and compatibility with the creative team and staff and the other actors who will make up the season. In films and TV, producers are more often concerned with budget (your salary demands) and your commercial appeal (your Q score and the size of your fan club). These interests are not all in alignment, of course, and so you might make a hit with the CD and the director, but then get axed by an executive producer (EP) who, say, doesn't find you sexy enough. Or you may make it through the EP too, but then get turned down by a network and/or a studio executive based on a wide variety of potential factors, from your salary demands to your height or your hair color or even the way you laugh. In any event, a whole lot of people are part of the casting business, as are the dismaying variations of casting criteria. You certainly have your work cut out for you if you are to impress all of these people with all of their individual interests.

For regional and many New York theatres, it's pretty much the same process, but often without the top and the bottom: sometimes there is no agent, and of course there's no network executive.

Getting auditioned

Professional casting people do not post tryout notices on a bulletin board. They do not send out press releases advertising their auditions. They're not easy to see, and often they're not even easy to find. They don't keep office hours available to you, they don't often answer or even open their mail (not your mail, anyway). And they most certainly do not pick up their own telephones—at least not the telephones whose numbers you can obtain. Emails with addresses the CD has never seen before are simply—and immediately—deleted. Indeed, most casting announcements are accompanied by the boilerplate language, in all-caps and with exclamation points, "ABSOLUTELY NO PHONE CALLS!!! NO VISITS!!!"

So, how do you see these reclusive folks? More important, how do you get them to see you? This is your basic problem—and the reason why people buy books like this one. Creating access between you and the casting office is the soul of acting professionally, and of *Acting Professionally*. Getting known, getting seen, getting accepted, getting cast, and getting work—this is the process you must negotiate.

Who are you?

Who are you, anyway? We don't mean "How good are you?" or even "How dare you consider yourself an actor?" You possibly anticipated that tone of voice in the words of our question, but what we mean is simply: what kind of actor are you able to become? What kind of roles might casting people see you in—and then put you in?

This may be the entry-level actor's biggest task: defining who you are. The command is as old as the Oracle at Delphi: know thyself! When you emerge from your training in Shakespeare and Molière, Rodgers and Hammerstein, Neil Simon and Samuel Beckett, you might begin to wonder just how you're supposed to present yourself in the agent's office or the audition room. And so your first task is to discover who you are as an actor—and who you can be—so that you can bring that "you" into every interview and audition.

Remember that with the exception of a few Shakespeare festivals and repertory companies, you are *not* going to be auditioning as a general-purpose actor. No one is interested in the fact that you can play old people *and* young people, ballet dancers *and* sumo wrestlers, classical tragedy *and* television sitcom. They are looking for only one thing, and they want to see that and nothing else. They don't even want to *know* about anything else.

As James tells you from his casting office, "We don't want to see the gamut from A-Z or your range from Laura Wingfield to Medea just yet. We want to know what your 'thing' is. Who you are, what you're about, and what is your true essence." And as Ron Surma, CD of *Star Trek* and *Bruce Almighty,* adds, "Actors have to know who they are. Whatever that is, bring only that choice into the audition. Discover who you are in life, and bring that in."

But finding your "thing" is not merely an intellectual task. A demo reel company (more on this in Chapter 4) will ask you to find what *music* describes you. "You, your product, the image that you're trying to sell. Find a song that embodies this," the company urges, and the resulting music will then provide your underscore, your "personal theme."

But what image are you trying to sell: Beethoven's Fifth, folk rock, or 1950s cha-cha-cha? And which of these is *really you*, and not just what you would like to be you?

Not easy, is it? Don't despair. No one has yet fully fulfilled the Delphic Oracle's demand, and this may be the hardest discovery you'll ever have to make.

But remember you're just trying to create—and narrow—your starting point. It's like finding your "angle of entry" into the acting profession. When a spaceship returns to earth, it must approach the planet at a precise angle: too sharp, and the ship crashes to the ground; too shallow, it bounces back into space. It's the same thing with getting that first acting job: you have to come in at the angle that meets their needs. You need to be the perfect key for their very particular lock. You need to be *better*, in their minds, than the hundred thousand other actors, already holding union cards, who are also looking to fit that lock and the other hundred thousand beginners who want to join them.

You haven't had enough metaphors? Martha McFarland, longtime CD for South Coast Repertory, the Oregon Shakespeare Festival, and several independent films, calls it your "vein of gold." Know it, develop it, and follow it.

But how do you do this? We have four exercises to suggest.

1   First, take stock of what sort of person you are physically. Short, tall, skinny, fat (we could say overweight, but this is not the time for euphemisms); black, white, Asian, Latino; balding, pimply, gangly, muscular. This exercise is easy. And it's the real you.

2   Second, what sort of person are you *emotionally*? Easily spooked? Moody, but quick to fly off the handle? Sexually aggressive? Socially gregarious? Athletically competitive? Are you primarily focused intellectually or romantically?

Don't answer these questions with "it depends on the situation." *Everybody* thinks their personality depends on the situation, and that only *other* people have fixed personalities.

So, grit your teeth and answer. Coming to terms with these and similar questions may let you know whether you should be aiming for the role of Titus Andronicus or Tiny Tim. This exercise is less easy than describing yourself physically. But it's describing the real you just as much as, if not more than, the first one.

3   Third exercise: on the left side of a lined sheet of paper, rank the following ten acting genres in a column, from top to bottom, in the order in which you think you are *most likely* to be professionally cast during the next three years. Do *not* make up additional genres.

Classical stage (e.g., *Hamlet, Oedipus Rex*)
Standard American repertory stage (e.g., *The Glass Menagerie, The Odd Couple*)
Musical theatre (e.g., *South Pacific, Kinky Boots*)
Experimental/avant-garde theatre (e.g., *Waiting for Godot, Sleep No More*)
TV sitcom (e.g. *Modern Family, Big Bang Theory*)
Romantic film (e.g., *Titanic, Sleepless in Seattle*)
Dramatic film/TV (e.g., *No Country for Old Men, Gladiator*)
Horror film (e.g., *It Follows, What We Do in the Shadows*)
Action film (e.g., *Deadpool, Star Wars: The Force Awakens*)
Soap opera (*Days of our Lives, The Young and the Restless*)

Now, make a second column, directly to the right of the first, of the same ten genres in the order in which you would *most want* to be cast. How do the two lists match up? Remember, the list on the left is—for getting that all-important first job—more important! The list on the right is for when you become famous.

Next, make a list of your five strongest selling points—those things in your favor—as an actor. Finally, make a list of the five things you think might possibly hold you back as you pursue your career.

When you are finished, share your list with people who know you well (they might be making their own lists at the same time). Do they think your evaluation is reasonable? Do you, after soliciting their opinions?

Don't think for a moment that they're right and you're wrong, but don't jump to the opposite conclusion either. Try to be objective. Look at yourself in a mirror—not the mirror on the wall, but the mirror of the stage. Look at those roles—as they appear in professional productions in the theatre or movie house—in which you feel you have your best shot of being cast.

4   Fourth and final exercise: make a list of actors you've seen who "play your roles," meaning the roles you think you can do. (Unless you live in a major professional theatre town, these will probably be roles on film or TV.) Then make an honest assessment of whether you could compete for these same roles. Are you really good looking enough to compete with Leonardo DiCaprio or Scarlett Johansson? Or emotionally deep enough to battle with Sean Penn or Angelina Jolie? Or sexy enough to outdo Johnny Depp or Keira Knightley?

Be frank with yourself, but don't be shy. And don't be afraid to ask your friends and teachers—those, at least, you believe could give honest and objective responses. If you have been reviewed in the press, what did they say about you? How did unbiased critics *see* you? (This is not so much about whether they said you were good or bad, but on how they *described* you.) Is this a lead for you?

Realize that finding your "thing," your "vein of gold," is not a final decision on the direction of your career or the roles you will play. Not at all. It's just your best chance at your first shot. But that shot could send you soaring: look at the new and current (2016) Broadway stars Beth Malone taking the "Great White Way" by storm, creating the role of (the adult) Alison in *Fun Home* at the Circle in the Square (and getting a Tony nomination for it), or Cynthia Erivo burning up the Jacobs Theatre as Celie in *The Color Purple*, or Alan Mingo taking over the star role of *Lola* in *Kinky Boots* at the Hirschfield. If they can do it, so may you be able to—eventually!

The last two exercises (3 and 4) are a combination of the real you and the stage you (or the film you). They can turn your physical and emotional aspects (exercises 1 and 2) into a real acting career.

Working through these four exercises will help you get to the bottom of your "thing." You are not, by this process, making your career choice for all time. Nor are you forging a new identity; you're only discovering the identity you already have. But *narrowing* and *defining* that identity more closely will help you focus on your career track. It is basically a marketing issue, not an ontological riddle.

No decision based on such exercises is final, and you may change your mind often before your first job—and very often afterward. But *having a defined sense of where you can best make your entry approach is the biggest single factor in getting your professional career off the ground.* All other decisions and actions, as described in the sections that follow, will be based, at least in part, by the discoveries you've made in this self-examination of your vein of gold.

So: where are you going to place that vein of gold? Where do you start?

Your starting medium

The three main theatrical media are, of course, stage, film, and television. These are divided into subgroups. Professional stage work can include Broadway and off-Broadway shows, regional repertory and stock companies, summer theatres, dinner theatres, theatre festivals, industrial productions, cruise ship shows, and guest-artist stints at drama schools and universities. Film acting work consists largely of feature films, plus occasional short features and documentaries. Television can include filmed or videotaped episodic or sitcom TV, TV movies and specials, TV streaming series, TV pilots ("test" shows for potential series production), TV commercials, TV voiceovers, reality TV, live hosting and announcing positions, and more recently "webisodes" (online telecasts).

It is natural to want to work in all these media, and of course many actors, over the course of their careers, do. But you're going to get your first job in only one of them. Which medium should you head for first? Where you will live, and what you will do, will be defined (in part at least) by your answer to this question.

By all means, you should seek some advice from people who know you and know your work, but your own choice (and it *is* your choice) should take into account some of the realities described below.

Working on stage

Professional live theatre is, simply put, language intensive. The majority of plays performed by salaried actors are essentially verbal constructs, performed live and often before large audiences. The repertoire of most professional stage companies includes a mix of classical or classically inspired works, plays of brilliant intellectual argument, plays of stunning wordplay and/or elegant diction, plays that make audiences cry their eyes out and/or laugh their heads off, and, in general, works of supreme linguistic challenge intended for live audiences numbering in the hundreds or even thousands who, in most cases, expect to hear every single word clearly. Naturally, then, the demands made of virtually all professional stage performers include truly stunning articulation, phrasing, rhetorical force, comic timing, and linguistic wit, all culminating in vocal variety, expression, and projection.

A lack of any of these assets would prove a severe—and probably fatal—handicap to any would-be stage performer.

In addition, the demands of memorization in stage acting require each entire role to be perfectly memorized and delivered whole, in a near-continuous performance of somewhere between 90 minutes and three hours.

To be a successful professional stage actor, you must also have a face that projects emotion without mugging, a body that moves liquidly and without apparent effort, and a stage personality that, without pushing, carries across the footlights. A familiarity with the standard stage repertoire, both modern and classic, and the fundamentals of verse speaking, comic inflections, and rhetorical builds and climaxes is also essential for most actors in mainstream theatres, while at least minimal (and hopefully maximal) performing skills in singing, dance, and dialects are increasingly indispensable as well. (If you're hoping to act on Broadway, know that as of the time this edition was written, no fewer than 44 musicals are on or about to be on Broadway's stages, compared with only 17 dramatic plays and comedies. Singing lessons never hurt.)

Above all, the stage actor needs the great intangibles: talent, presence, and timing. You must be able to enunciate the subtlest nuances clearly to huge audiences without looking as if you are reading from a speech text, and you must convey the sense of a vibrant personality whether you are playing romantic lead, ghoulish villain, or village idiot. If these are your key assets—and if you crave excelling in the theatrical repertoire, past, present, and imagined future—you should consider heading for the stage.

There's one great benefit for actors on the live stage: when the elder author of this book was graduating from college, there were no more than five full-time professional theatres outside of New York City that staged their own plays and paid their actors. Today there are 514 such theatres, all members of the Theatre Communications Group (TCG), which, as the Group requires, "meet minimum requirements for professional leadership, orientation and standards." The graduating actor's range of hiring opportunities has grown more than 100-fold in that two-generation period.

But, of course, there's a significant downside to stage work too: the salaries paid by nonprofit theatres (or, for that matter, by for-profit ones, on and off Broadway) are, in general, a small fraction of what you can earn in feature films or television.

Working before the camera

Working on film or TV, in contrast to the stage, is more visually intensive. It involves fewer words, more face. Less vocal training is needed, because except in special cases there's no verse, rarely a speech of more than two sentences, and—except in TV sitcoms performed before a live audience—rarely a situation in which you have to deliver more than one or two minutes of memorized text at a time. You can also forget about projection: the microphone is inches from your mouth—or you can loop in (dub) your words later, or technicians may do so with another actor's voice if yours turns out to be inadequate. There's also considerably less (and sometimes almost no) rehearsal, and thus more spontaneity. There's also, almost always, higher pay—since there are many more potential viewers.

Because they are visually intensive, film and television reward acting in which the script's subtext radiates mainly from your facial expression: particularly from your eyes and what seems to lie behind them. Your mouth, your smile, your frown, your hair, your idle toss of the head, your grimace of pain—all of these, rather than your manipulations of iambic pentameter or escalating rhetorical phrases, will be your main selling points in camera-oriented media. In Hollywood, you can get cast for your teeth.

Facial appearance, therefore, obviously counts more in film and TV than on stage, primarily because on the stage your scale diminishes in proportion to your distance from the audience. From the second balcony of a Broadway house, your face appears little larger than this capital O, while on a movie screen it can be more than 20 feet tall. Simple makeup can do wonders on the stage, whereas in film "the camera doesn't lie" is a truly apt aphorism.

Watch a TV sitcom for a few minutes and notice how few words are spoken and how much of the drama is conveyed simply by facial expression and background music. That's camera acting. What you don't say is often more important than what you do say. That's why Robin Wright cuts half her lines out of the scripts of the television series *House of Cards* and Clint Eastwood would cut half of his lines out of the script before the shooting started; in film, the eyes have it.

Finally, the structure of a finished film or television show is only *originated* during its acted moments; it's completed (some would say re-created) long after the actors have left the scene. Muff a line? Timing off? Trip on your hem? All will be taken care of in the editing room, with a cut here, a fill there, and if these don't work, a "Let's do a reaction shot" decision. It's not suspenseful? Beef up the underscore! Not so funny? Add a laugh track! No real tears? Digitize them!

So, if your looks are extremely intriguing and provocative (and knock-out beauty rarely hurts), your talents can shine in your naturalistic close-up performing, and you may find yourself more inclined toward honest and spontaneous performance interactions than by your studiously rehearsed role creation. And if that's the case, you'd be wise to consider heading toward a film or television entry job.

But which one, film or TV? You don't have to make this choice quite yet. And more than likely the choice will not be yours, but will be made by CDs, producers, and directors. Both film and TV are camera oriented, of course, and in fact, most TV is shot on film these days. Both media are largely headquartered in the same city—Los Angeles—and most film actors have performed on TV. However, there is both a craft and a status distinction between the two. Film seeks out the *dangerously* beautiful and the *ferociously* awesome-looking. It then exploits those looks relentlessly, not only in the films themselves but also in giant billboards and full-page advertisements that fill the entertainment sections of the world's newspapers. The great film stars, revealingly known as *monstres sacrés* ("sacred monsters") in French, offer not just a sense of excitement. Rather, they present a scary presence: a catch-your-breath intensity and carnal provocation. If they seem larger than life, it's because they are—sometimes two or three times larger. TV characters, in contrast, tend to be quirkier, safer, and quite a bit more comfortable coming into your home.

But recent years have seen some movie greats break down the barrier against TV "slumming," particularly for women of a certain age, for whom there are fewer roles available on the big screen. Thus, TV shows have recently featured well-established film stars including Claire Danes, Matthew McConaughey, Maggie Gyllenhaal, Meryl Streep, Steve Muscemi, Kevin Costner, Laura Linney, Woody Harrelson, Robin White, Brian Cox, Michael Gambon, Glenn Close, and Holly Hunter. As Matthew McConaughey says, "What other medium do you get to have…all that character development that we love? You don't get that anywhere else…That's what television has given us as artists."

Remember above all else, though, that if you make it in one medium, you'll eventually have a shot at all the others. A journey of a thousand miles begins with a single step, Confucius said, and now it's time to take that step.

Choosing your home base

Up to this point we've been talking about what's in your head: what you need, who you are, the decisions you're going to have to make. From this point on we'll be talking about actually making those decisions, actually doing things—moving, for example. Where do you locate yourself to get that first job?

In America, you really have only three choices: New York, Los Angeles, and the regional theatre—which means just about everywhere else. These choices involve different kinds of theatrical activity as well as different life-styles and business procedures: New York as America's theatre capital, Los Angeles its film and TV centers, and the regional theatre providing the bulk (about 75%) of American actors' paid workweeks. And since regional theatre is where you most likely will start your career, you might as well look there first.

Regional theatre

Regional theatre is very likely where you will start out and perhaps *should* start out, particularly if you're already in the neighborhood. First, regional theatre probably exists fairly close to home and/or close to your college or university; after all, there were 1,773 regional theatres in America in 2013, and there are certainly more now that you are reading this. Indeed, you may have already attended several such theatres on a regular basis—you may even know and be known by people working there.

Second, it's a far more *accessible* professional environment than New York or Los Angeles, and one in which you can contact the artistic staff fairly directly. Regional theatre, unlike that in the super-cities, is relatively free from the machinations of agents, managers, associate producers, and other intermediaries. Not only is it a good place to start out, but some actors also find it an equally good place to end up.

Regional theatre is a general term and not entirely specific. It includes the broad spectrum of professional but not-for-profit theatre companies operating throughout the country, plus commercial dinner theatres and stock companies that often cast out of New York. How many stage actors live and work in these American regions? Figures in 2015 showed that among the more than 50,000 Actor's Equity Association members (which include stage managers), 15,935 were based in New York, 7,013 in greater Los Angeles, and 1,589 in Chicago, these being the cities hosting the Equity offices covering, respectively, America's eastern, western, and central states. Other cities hosting significant numbers of Equity actors are San Francisco (968), Washington/Baltimore (854), Philadelphia (852), Boston (845), Orlando (591), Minneapolis/St Paul (437), and Seattle (397).

TCG and LORT

The vast majority of America's regional theatres are nonprofit (or "not-for-profit"), and, while independent and run by individual or partnering artistic directors, they are nationally supervised by two organizations mentioned briefly in the previous chapter. These are the Theatre Communications Group (TCG), which oversees 460 nonprofit professional theatre companies around the country, and the League of Resident Theatres (LORT), whose 72 member nonprofit companies are the most prestigious and well-funded major-city theatres in the United States, including the Guthrie Theatre in Minneapolis, the Denver Theatre Center, the Oregon Shakespeare Festival, and the New York Public Theatre, all of which have annual budgets in the $30 million range and higher. TCG is mainly informational, publishing its annual *TCG Membership Directory*, which lists all its members, affiliates, and colleges and universities with drama departments. It also publishes its monthly *American Theatre*, which, along with many useful articles, lists its member companies' performance schedules, plus a weekly ARTSEARCH, which lists 3,000 theatre jobs annually and current theatre books in its TCG Bookstore, and hosts conferences and forums on the state of nonprofit theatres today. LORT administers the primary bargaining agreements between its nonprofit members and the Actors Equity Association (as well as the Stage Directors and Choreographer's Society and the United Scenic Artists), and oversees the minimum fees for the five professional theatre categories: A+, A, B+, C, and D, depending on the size of the potential audience—with theatres having multiple stages often having different contracts for each stage. Such nonprofit companies have sent one or more of their successful productions on to the Broadway or off-Broadway stage (where, of course, they become profit companies!) and, occasionally, their shows go on to subsequent national tours and PBS telecasts. Indeed, almost every Tony and Pulitzer Prize-winning American play of the past three decades was first mounted by a LORT company. An acting assignment at any of these theatres, therefore, will not only prove to be a great artistic challenge but will also be a valued professional credit—a door opener—anywhere in the country. And LORT minimum salaries are the highest outside of Broadway and Broadway's national tours, the minimum salaries for actors in LORT companies in 2016–17 ranging from $637 per week (category D) to $992 (category A+).

Developing theatres—SPT and LOA

LORT is supplemented by TCG's growing list of Developing Theatres, operating under Equity's Small Professional Theatre (SPT) and Letter of Agreement (LOA) actor contracts. SPT serves theatres of fewer than 350 seats outside of New York and Chicago; the minimum SPT salaries in 2016 were $309 for actors playing four times a week, $382 for playing five times,

$430 for six times, $604 for seven times, and $664 for the full eight times. In 2015, Equity abolished its 28-year-old "99 seat plan," mainly operating in Los Angeles, and replaced it with the SPT agreement. LOA contracts are used only "in developmental situations" and are "individually negotiated" by Equity. Developing Theatres of this sort are indeed developing—they now account for over 50,000 annual actor workweeks, half again more than a decade previously. Often operating in small towns, many have ambitious agendas and offer outstanding artistic opportunities—though you may have to explain who they are when New York CDs see their names on your résumé. (Probably not the SPT New Theatre of Coral Gables, Florida, though, whose commissioned production of Nilo Cruz's *Anna in the Tropics* won a Pulitzer Prize.)

Stock theatre—COST, CORST, and others

Stock theatres present consecutive productions of different plays, often in the summer (hence "summer stock") and largely on the East Coast. Their activity has diminished in recent years, and they therefore represent a smaller source of actor income than during their heydays in the past. Actors Equity provides a minimum weekly salary between $664 and $951 for actors on COST (Council of Stock Theatres) contracts, depending on the size of the theatre, and from $564 to $879 for CORST (Council of Resident Stock Theatres) actors, while Outdoor Theatre, Musical Stock and Unit Attractions, and Resident Musical Theatre agreements apply to these separately regulated stock theatre operations.

HATs, CATs, BATs, OATs, dinner theatres, and all the rest

Forty other contracts—in or out of the TCG circuit—also offer regular employment for actors, and sometimes even better break-in opportunities for acting aspirants. Equity's CAT (Chicago Area Theatres) contract covers Chicago theatres, including the superb Steppenwolf. HATs, BATs, OATs, NEATs, and NOLAs refer to independent theatres and producers operating, respectively, in the major performance centers of Hollywood, San Francisco's Bay area, Orlando, New England, and New Orleans. Still more professional theatres—those with academic ties—may operate under University/ Resident Theatre Association (URTA) contracts: these include theatres associated with Cornell University in New York, Allen Hancock College in California, and the Illinois and Nebraska Shakespeare Festivals, and Music Theater Wichita in the Midwest. Other contracts—Guest Artist, Theatre for Young Audiences (TYA), and Special Production—may apply to these and other forms of nonprofit groups.

Dinner theatres, which burst upon the American theatre scene in the early 1970s, have fallen back somewhat since then, but they have now stabilized in number (there are currently 24 in Pennsylvania, in the National Dinner Theatre Association) and at last count provide actors with a $690 minimum weekly wage. The theatrical fare at these houses is generally light comedies and musicals; the plays are combined not only with pre-theatre dinners, but also occasionally with post-theatre dancing and merriment, and comprise a fairly encompassing entertainment medium. Some dinner theatres are beginning to offer apprentice programs, and apprentices who also elect to serve as waiters and waitresses can earn up to $500 per week while training. Occasionally, dinner theatres offer year-round employment, which is a godsend to most actors. Conversely, the dinner theatre credit is not always a particularly helpful stepping-stone to "eatless" ventures.

Some non-Equity companies—occasionally employing Equity Guest Artists—operate in the regions too, forming a sort of fringe to the professional theatre. Shakespeare festivals, now almost always featuring more modern fare in addition to the namesake Bard, and outdoor drama festivals, featuring pageants of American history, are often major operations, offering a range from well-paying to low-paying to no-paying opportunities in many states around the country. There are well over a hundred Shakespeare festivals in the United States (as opposed to none in England), including Tony-Awarded ones in Oregon and Utah, and distinguished others in Colorado, Texas, New Jersey, Vermont, Connecticut, California, Alabama, New York, Illinois, and Idaho, among many others. Most have at least some professional actors in key roles, but virtually all audition nonprofessionals, at least for smaller parts. Summer theatre directories (see Appendix) list addresses and audition dates for most of them.

Benefits of regional theatre

Virtually all regional theatres are permitted to cast at least some of their season's roles with nonunion actors—and they do so regularly. Regional companies may also offer you a *direct* opportunity to break into the field, in that you can normally apply to audition directly to the theatre company, without being submitted by an agent. Once on board a regional theatre, you may be able to work your way up to a union (Equity) card—if the theatre participates in the union's Equity Membership Candidate (EMC) Program, as do most LORT and Equity stock and dinner companies, and several SPT, CAT, and LOA companies as well. Under the EMC program, 50 weeks of acting work (which do not need to be consecutive) in one or more participating

Equity companies can propel you into union membership. (Further information about this program appears in the "Unions" section of Chapter 4.)

Overall, regional theatre (both profit and nonprofit) has become America's primary break-in place for actors and (sometimes more significantly) for playwrights, and it remains a significant area of employment for American stage actors, even Broadway veterans. Films and television also draw from regional banks. CD Mike Fenton reports that regional theatre is the source of 60% of the "unknowns" in Hollywood, and the number of regional plays that make their way to New York—with the same casts—is growing rapidly. Such Steppenwolf regulars as John Malkovich, John Mahoney, Laurie Metcalf, Joan Allen, Brian Kerwin, Terry Kinney, Glenne Headly, and Gary Sinise developed wonderful national reputations from their work in Chicago-based plays.

Drawbacks of regional theatre

However, all is not rosy for actors in regional theatre. The pay is substantially lower than in the big towns, and it takes at least a half-year of continuous employment—going from one role to another for most of the season—simply to cross the poverty line (more on this under "How much will you make?" in Chapter 5). Also, while there are fewer actors around to compete with, there are far fewer professional acting opportunities and CDs in any state in America than there are in the individual cities of New York or Los Angeles.

Worse, actors moving to a second-tier city for easier break-in opportunities will be dismayed to discover that the major theatre companies in these towns often cast many, if not most, of their leading roles in New York, and the major TV and film casting—no matter where the show or movie is set—is almost always in New York or L.A.! Why? Because New York actors are considered the cream of the stage performer crop by most CDs—and also because Milwaukee, Atlanta, and even Los Angeles audiences like to see New York credits listed in the actor bios in the "Who's Who in the Cast" pages of their local theatre's programs. Plus, a major proportion of the film and TV casting offices are in the gigantic film studios of L.A. Thus, regional CDs head to New York and Los Angeles (and occasionally to Chicago) for many or most of their auditions, and Actors Equity actually *requires* that the major LORT companies—those classed A through C, plus some of the Ds—schedule a full day of stage auditions every year in one of those three cities.

It seems unfair to local actors in Sacramento, Montgomery, and Baltimore to find themselves competing for roles in their hometown theatres against actors auditioning in the Big Apple, the Big Orange, and the Windy

City, but there you are. A fine young actor we know headed to Seattle upon completing his training and was initially overjoyed to find himself called back five times to read for the lead male role opposite a series of several actresses for an upcoming play at that city's major playhouse, but his joy lessened considerably after the CD cast one of the actresses—but then went to New York to cast the male role that the young actor had been reading for over a period of two weeks.

Another drawback is that you cannot assume that much communication takes place among the regional theatres themselves: Seattle's CDs generally know little about the acting pools in Boston, Washington, Atlanta, or Denver, and vice versa. And while *Backstage* conscientiously attempts to cover opportunities throughout the country, there are no comparable trade papers actually devoted to the regions. To combat this problem, actors in many regional acting companies, on their own initiative (and with their own funds), fly in CDs from other regions to audition company members for future work. The Oregon Shakespeare Festival is a pioneer in this area; their very productive "Shares" program brings in about 15 casting directors each year, from theatres such as Chicago's Steppenwolf, the Milwaukee Rep and Arizona Rep, the Actors Theatre of Louisville, Berkeley Rep, the Utah, Santa Cruz and Chicago Shakespeare festivals, and some Hollywood agents and studios. The Utah Shakespearean Festival's "Reach" program copies this, and actors in many other companies have created similar programs.

The bottom line, however, is that regional theatre mostly remains in the regions, relatively isolated not only from New York and Hollywood but also from Chicago, Dallas, and Minneapolis. And while important regional credits can look good on a résumé, they're basically only words on paper. They rarely provoke visions of how you look or sound on stage and rarely reveal the brilliance of your performing skills, which remain unseen and unheard by the theatre world at large. Your regional performances are not automatically going to prove stepping-stones to Broadway or Hollywood—if that's where you hope to be heading.

Some actors, of course, have no wish to "go Hollywood" or to head for the Great White Way in the East. Hundreds of actors all over the country happily spend their entire careers in regional theatre, finding there a high degree of artistic fulfillment and social satisfaction, particularly when they gain employment at a theatre that maintains a resident company. The Costa Mesa, California, South Coast Repertory maintained its core five-actor professional acting company for nearly 40 years, and its actors Hal Landon and John-David Keller have been performing there regularly for the last *50* years.

Such careers can also be combined with stable married lives. When man and wife Chris Hutchison and Elizabeth Bunch tired of acting in New York in 2006, they traveled to Houston and joined the Alley Theater's resident company; they are now, 10 years later, playing some of the finest roles in stage literature there—and have a house and a back yard to boot! Resident regional companies, where actors are assumed to have permanent or at least semi-permanent jobs, are not as common these days as many would wish, but when they do exist, their work can be exceptional. The Steppenwolf Theatre in Chicago has maintained an acting ensemble for more than 30 years, and reached an apex in 2008 when its production of *August: Osage County* came to Broadway and garnered five Tony Awards—for Best Play, Best Direction, Best Leading and Best Featured Actress, and Best Scenic Design. The Oregon Shakespeare Festival has engaged rotating "families" of actors since 1935. All of these companies, plus 36 others, have won Tony Awards for Regional Theatre, proving that continuous *and distinguished* stage acting employment *does* still exist in the American theatre. Nor are members of such resident companies limited to working in their hometowns. Most, in fact, enjoy outside acting careers between resident assignments: many Steppenwolf actors (e.g., Joan Allen, John Malkovich, and its 1970s founding trio of Jeff Perry, Terry Kinney, and Gary Sinese) have starred on Broadway and/or have played leads on television series and in feature films between their Chicago engagements.

Yet many, if not most, actors become frustrated just hanging onto the regional circuit. Lila Stromer, founder of the Director/Playwright Alliance of Chicago, reported in 2008 that a lot of actors she and her actor-husband know "who gets their card in Chicago either head to NY or L.A. within a very short span of time. In Chicago it seems the same twelve Equity actors get all the work and everyone else is jobbed in from NY." Rene Auberjonois, a superb regional actor who went on to great television success (most recently playing in *Masters of Sex*, *Pound Puppies*, and Paul Lewiston in 71 episodes of *Boston Legal*), gave a more elaborate reason for leaving LORT: "Most actors in regional theatre are schizophrenics; they cannot reconcile the feeling that they should be fighting the fight of commercial theatre with the feeling that they are chosen members of some great and holy theatrical crusade. This dilemma gives rise to a working climate which could be compared to a monastery filled with self-consciously zealous monks suppressing the desire to ravage the neighboring village." It is evident that some of these disappointments and "schizophrenic" discords are felt, if not to the same degree, by many in the LORT and other-lettered circuits.

Getting into a regional theatre—general auditions

Getting an acting job at your local regional theatre is no easy task for a professional, much less a nonprofessional, but you probably have a better chance of getting your proverbial foot in the door—and even an audition— at a regional stage close to home than anywhere else in the acting business. "Local performers shall have preference for local auditions" says the Equity–LORT agreement, although this, of course (along with everything else in that agreement), legally applies only to Equity members.

While the leading LORT theatres cast many of their major roles from a pool of New York-based Equity (union) actors (with regional directors often traveling to New York to do so), and from their own resident company, if they have one, and the pool of professional actors already well known on the regional LORT circuit, virtually all such theatres also arrange to see new actors from time to time at their home base. Thus, *general auditions* are scheduled at most theatres on a periodic basis, ordinarily twice a year, and sometimes more often: the Center Theatre Group in Los Angeles, for example, hosts Equity general auditions on the first or second Monday of each month. And while Equity actors are given a priority for such "generals" (as they are usually called), many companies will occasionally make room for non-Equity actors as well. "On occasion," says CTG, "for select projects we hold open calls for actors—please check back periodically for notices."

So, how do you arrange a general audition at your hometown regional theatre? First, go to the theatre's website and look under anything that says "Employment" or "Opportunities" or "Casting." The Guthrie Theater in Minneapolis, for example, gives a detailed summary of its general audition policies and procedures and, at the time of writing, had added an announcement for a specific audition for young (8 to 13) non-pros:

> **Guthrie seeks Boys & Girls with multiracial backgrounds** Guthrie seeks nonunion boys & girls with multiracial backgrounds to play Emile de Becque's children in *South Pacific*. Commitment from May 17 – August 28, 2016. Cast members will be required to sing & dance. No need to prepare anything in advance. Bring photo (snapshot OK) & résumé. Be prepared to stay for a few hrs. Experienced performers preferred. Weekly compensation offered.

Opportunities like this, though paying only a "gratuity," are surely worth looking into if you meet the proper demands and are in town, available, and hoping to start a career (and meet the people who might help you do just that).

Remember, though: the opportunity to audition for a professional theatre is—for a nonunion actor—a privilege, not a right. This is not the way it was in college, where your tuition payment guaranteed you a chance to be seen and heard in campus auditions. But no professional theatre staff member is *required* to see or hear you; they just have to *want* to do so.

However, virtually all regional theatres will see local nonprofessional actors who apply, look promising, have some training and/or experience, know how to smile, and are willing to wait around for their shot at the big time. Theatre companies are normally happy to have access to good actors who live in the immediate area (it saves the company paying their travel stipends and housing costs) and who might be available on short notice (for emergency replacements). It is good for the theatre's bottom line, and it makes for good public relations as well. We're not talking about lead roles here, of course—or even necessarily speaking ones—but, rather, foot-in-the-door opportunities for beginning actors.

What should you prepare for a regional theatre audition? You will find much more information on this later in the book, but most regional theatres like to see one or two pieces, usually one classical and one contemporary, neither more than two minutes in length. They may also be willing to hear 32 bars of a song, performed *a cappella*, if they have any musicals coming up. Of course, if you know the theatre's current repertoire, its upcoming shows, its philosophy, and its personnel before you show up, you can try to select your material accordingly—and you obviously should. There's no sense auditioning with traditional Shakespeare in a theatre solely dedicated to the avant-garde, or vice versa, unless you are advised otherwise—which sometimes you will be; legendary CD Nancy Piccione, of the Manhattan Theater Club, actually *prefers* to see Shakespeare at auditions, despite the fact that the Bard is never listed on the company's season schedule. Piccione claims that if the actor can handle the language of Shakespeare, then surely he or she can handle anything!

You will probably audition on a rehearsal stage, or on an actual theatre stage, and will probably be seen by the company's CD and/or possibly another artistic staff member. You should bring a photo and résumé with you, even if you've sent one ahead. Be sure your email and phone number are correct.

What are your chances? Very small, of course, but not zero. You should understand the complexities involved. As one artistic director writes, anonymously but with great sensitivity,

> The best chance a nonunion performer has is to be, first of all, an outstanding actor, and secondly a local resident. Then we know he or she

will be easily available and won't need much money to live on. The odds against the auditioner are, of course, incredibly high. We see a good many fine actors. We have a very good selection to choose from: it's a buyer's market. What isn't widely known is that we often see fresh faces that we want very much to give jobs to. I can think of three actors right now that I would dearly love to work with. But you already have actors who are just as good and who are already hardworking members of your ensemble; you're certainly not going to bump them out of their jobs to make room for the new face. For us, auditioning is a process for discovering a few new actors for our company, not casting all our roles.

So, understand the picture, and try to fit yourself into it one way or another.

Out-of-town regional auditions

Of course, nonprofessionals can seek audition opportunities at a LORT or SPT theatre outside of their hometown as well. Just check the theatre's website for audition opportunities as you would with a theatre in your own town. Many actors head for those few regional cities— Chicago, Seattle, Boston, Washington, and the San Francisco Bay Area are prominent ones—with a major concentration of professional theatres and try to audition for as many as they can at the same time. If you do this, of course, you should arrange for some of them ahead of time and plan to stay for a while. If you get work, you may find you have a new home.

As noted earlier, all LORT theatres also provide Equity auditions—either general or production specific—annually at their home base, plus at least one Equity Principal Audition (EPA) annually in New York, Chicago, or Los Angeles, or at one of their 28 liaison cities (go to actorsequity.org and click "Area Liaisons"). These "open call" auditions are, of course, rigorously prioritized for Equity members, but occasionally—when there is time—CDs will admit nonunion performers before they close the doors. Are these serious auditions, though? It depends—but you should be aware that a single CD is permitted to represent up to three different theatres at their Equity auditions, so the only real answer to the question must be, "not always." The dates and places of a theatre's open calls can be found on the theatre's website, and normally in regular announcements, two to four weeks in advance, in *Backstage* (see Appendix).

Regional combined auditions—focusing on nonprofessionals

Wouldn't it be wonderful, as a beginning nonprofessional actor, to go to one single audition and be seen by hundreds of artistic directors from around

the country? This happens in many other countries. Following their graduation at the Finnish National Theatre School, acting students are invited to
audition for all the stage directors in Finland, and at the end of their audition virtually every one of them has secured a year-long (and sometimes
permanent) professional acting job in a Finnish theatre! (Sadly, though,
only one in a thousand applicants makes it into the School.) But the diver-
sification of theatre in America's 50 states and the proliferation of our hundreds of drama programs and schools have made such national auditions
impossible in the United States.

Several major groups continue to hold unified regional auditions,
though, and they are of varying use to the actor seeking employment. Several are for a collection of summer theatres, others for both summer and
year-round companies, and yet others for graduate assistantships toward
professional training. If you're interested, you may download applications
from any of the following groups' websites and submit one or more applications, for a usually modest administrative fee. Understand, however, that in
most cases audition spaces are limited, and you may need to go through a
screening process to make it into the actual audition. So, plan to apply early
and present your strongest possible submission. Here's a current listing of
the main groups: if any interest you, go to their websites and, if you plan to
apply, study their deadline requirements for the current year very carefully,
as what you read below may have changed!

Unified Professional Theatre Auditions (www.upta.org) welcomed 92 registered theatre companies from around the country in 2016 (all figures in
this section are from that year's audition announcements)—mainly from
the Eastern and Central United States, with auditions taking place in Memphis, Tennessee in early February. UPTA's policies require pre-profession-
als to be pre-screened by first submitting a high-quality 90-second audition
video by mid-September in order to register; they will then audition in
person for another 90 seconds on the first day of the Memphis audition.
Actors who qualify must be available for employment and must meet *one* of
several key criteria: have a postgraduate theatre degree, have a nomination
from a UPTA-participating or TCG-member theatre, be a member or membership candidate (more on that later) of Actors' Equity Association, or be
a past UPTA auditionee. At the time of writing, the UPTA fee was $40, and
anyone thinking about coming should study their current policy (at upta.
org) very closely before seeking registration.

The Southeastern Theatre Conference (www.setc.org) is headquartered
at the University of North Carolina in Greensboro and hosts professional
auditions in the spring and fall for non-Equity actors who are not currently
in school and who have had a minimum of two professional jobs in live

theatre. At the spring audition, approximately 90 theatre companies from around the country audition over 800 actors, who must be 18 or above, not currently enrolled in school, and have had at least two paid professional acting jobs in live theatre. Actors not meeting all these requirements may also register for the spring audition by screening video pre-auditions. The Conference (SETC) also provides smaller fall auditions for actors who need to meet slightly different requirements but are available for work within 60 days of the audition. Audition costs for student actors, in 2016, were $140, for adult actors $220, and for senior (over 65) actors, $155.

The New England Theatre Conference, at www.netconline.org and head-quartered at Northeastern University in Boston, auditions approximately 700 non-Equity actors for about 50 companies, including Equity and non-Equity summer stock, Shakespeare and Renaissance festivals, music theatres, and others. NETC requests a two-minute screening audition before the main one; applicants must be 18 or above, and college students or adults (not in high school). Student fees in 2016 were $50 and non-students $60. Among the many companies attending have been New Haven's Long Wharf Theatre, Philadelphia's Walnut Street Theatre, and the Dorset Theatre Festival.

StrawHat Auditions take place in Manhattan in March; 30 summer companies audition some 700 applicants, and the company asserts that 85% of auditioners receive call-backs. Music theatre is dominant here, though the auditioners include a wide spectrum of theatres around the country, recently including Connecticut Repertory Theatre, Millbrook Playhouse, Olney Theatre, Finger Lakes Music Theatre Festival, TheatreWorks USA, and the Woodstock Playhouse. Your completed application (to www.strawhat-auditions.com) must include photo-résumés, which will be reprinted and distributed to the producers and will also be placed on the StrawHat online database throughout the audition period. If you pass the screening, you will have 90 seconds to do two pieces, one of which can be a song. Producers wisely advise that, while two-thirds of the actors hired will need to sing, if you can't sing at a professional level "don't try to bluff" your way through a song; do two monologues instead.

The Institute of Outdoor Drama (www.outdoor-theatre.org) conducts auditions for approximately 15 historical pageants performed (obviously) outdoors. Based in East Carolina University, in 2016 it auditioned 200 students from 21 states and 63 colleges and universities.

Midwest Theatre Auditions, held in St Louis in February, involve approximately 60 companies, provide a 90-second one- or two-piece audition, and require headshots, résumés, and a $45 application fee. For current information, go to the MWTA website at www.webster.edu and click MWTA on the "Search" button.

URTA

The University/Resident Theatre Association (or URTA, accessible at www. urta.com) is the really big one for students looking not primarily for professional hirings, but rather to study acting in graduate schools. URTA auditions undergraduate college seniors in New York, Chicago, and San Francisco, primarily for fellowships and assistantships in professionally oriented university graduate theatre programs, but also (in what URTA admits are "rare" cases) for independent performing opportunities with university-related theatre companies. All URTA applicants must be nominated by faculty from their undergraduate theatre departments, and applicants auditioning in New York and Chicago must first pass a tough screening audition. But if you want to take an advance look at one of the URTA auditions while still in your sophomore or junior year, you might be able to do so by contacting URTA to see if you can be permitted to do so before you have become a senior: URTA began a "sneak peek" program in their three auditions in 2016, and currently plan to continue this in the near future.

Many other regions, states, and even metropolitan areas have theatre associations that conduct regional auditions, often at a different location every year: among them are the New Jersey Theatre Alliance (www.njtheatrealliance.com), the League of Washington Theatres (www.lowt.org), the North Carolina Theatre Conference (www.nctc.org), the Ohio Theatre Alliance (www.ohiotheatrealliance.org), the Illinois Theatre Association (www. illinoistheatre.org), the Twin Cities Theatre and Film (http://tcuta.climb. org/), the Portland Area Theatre Alliance (www.portlandtheatre.com), and Theatre Bay Area San Francisco (www.theatrebayarea.org).

The super-cities

Sooner or later, however, you're almost certainly going to think about heading off to New York or Los Angeles. These are the super-cities, as we've said (and as you no doubt already know), and there aren't too many people who go into this business who don't harbor at least some ambition to measure their powers in these most celebrated arenas. But which one?

How to choose?

Which town is easier to break into? Neither, of course, is remotely easy, and this question has no simple answer. There are hundreds of variable factors; most actors eventually try them both. Beware of those who say that "New York is finished" or "L.A. is impossible." Both of these cities are tough, certainly, but both will be employing hundreds of new actors next year and each year following. Each town is finished for some, and just opening up for others.

Of course, you should know something about the towns themselves. They are quite unalike, and both take some getting used to. New York, though quite a bit tamed in the current century, remains gruff, tough, fast-paced, and volatile; its rattling subways and bitter cold winters could harden an angel. Manhattan rents, like the buildings on Sixth Avenue, are sky-high, and even middling midtown restaurants charge twice what they do in Cleveland or Spokane. On the other hand—well, this is America's culture capital, with staggering art museums, opera houses, and theatres everywhere you look. It's also the world's financial center and the focal point for most American publishing, broadcasting, fashion, and advertising. For most of us, New York's occasional problems are dwarfed by its sheer magnificence, and even a marginal life in Manhattan will provide a heady climate and a thrilling intensity to any passionate and committed artist choosing to live and work there. Indeed, how can you avoid it? Just think about how many plays, films, and television shows are *set* within 20 blocks of Central Park, or in the pulsing excitement of SoHo (South of Houston Street). Not to know this town is to remain inevitably apart, to some extent, from the soul of the American stage.

Los Angeles, in contrast, is hardly a city at all but, rather, a vast desert basin, alternately broken up by semi-urban concentrations (Hollywood, Century City, Beverly Hills, Westwood, Brentwood, Santa Monica, Universal City) and a "downtown" that, by 10 pm, is virtually deserted. And L.A. is surrounded by increasingly independent suburbs—principally "the Valley," Disney's and NBC's Burbank, and "NoHo," the wannabe SoHo of North Hollywood. All of this is loosely connected by interlacing six-lane boulevards (Sunset, Hollywood, Wilshire, Santa Monica) and numbered freeways ("the 5," "the 10," "the 405"). While L.A. does indeed have public transportation, nobody in the theatre world seems to know about it; in L.A., the car is still king, and you are simply toast without wheels of your own and a ton or so of steel and glass surrounding you. Therefore, there's little of an L.A. "street scene," since the city is so spread out and the local inhabitants are among the most privacy-conscious people on earth. The real action of L.A. takes place within private homes, tony restaurants, and exclusive clubs, and behind impassable studio gates.

Geography, however, is not the crucial factor in this decision. The key question is: which performance *medium* do you plan to act in, or at least to begin your career in?

The obvious answer is that if your best talents lie in the areas of stage acting and/or musical theatre, you should probably head for New York, for that's where most professional stage shows and musicals are cast. Virtually all Broadway and off-Broadway shows, most stock and dinner theatres, and many LORT, SPT, and LOA companies (even those located in Los Angeles and surroundings) are cast in Manhattan audition rooms.

Conversely, actors whose primary focus is on film and television work—particularly actors whose on-camera looks and personalities and naturalistic acting abilities are more likely to be selling points than their stage training and experience—should head for Hollywood, the land of feature films and TV studios.

It's not all black and white, of course. There are certainly TV shows out of New York, such as *Blue Bloods*, *Madam Secretary*, *The Path*, *Girls*, *The Affair*, *Orange is the New Black*, and *The Blacklist*, and there is plenty of live theatre in the Los Angeles area, including the Tony Award–winning Mark Taper Forum and South Coast Repertory Theatre, plus the Geffen, the Ahmanson, the Kirk Douglas, the Pasadena Playhouse, and many dozens of smaller but professionally run theatres that operate under HAT or Equity waiver contracts.

Still, the general division remains intact: film and television production in L.A. dwarfs that of New York, and the immense stage activity in Hollywood and its surroundings is generated largely by actors hoping to be seen by film and television producers and executives in the Equity waiver showcases. If you're bigger than life, musical or rep oriented, and eminently stageworthy, take a bite of the Big Apple. If you're drop-dead gorgeous, personality-plus, intimate, young, and contemporary, it's time to juice the Big Orange.

Most actors, however, fall somewhere in-between. Wouldn't it be wonderful to live in London or Paris, where classical theatre, commercial theatre, films, and television are all headquartered in the same city? Where should American in-betweens go? On margin (and this is a difficult call), the authors of this book recommend New York: first, because it is easier to get seen there; second, because there's more you can do there without an agent or manager; third, because you won't need a car; fourth, because minor New York stage credits are more important in Hollywood than major Hollywood TV credits are in New York; and fifth, because New York is the central casting locus for the regional theatre circuit. New York is also the site of most commercial photography shoots, cruise ship bookings, and industrial shows (musical extravaganzas produced by corporations for their employees or stockholders—see the final chapter), and half of the country's soap operas, all of which provide good income and acting—or acting-related—show business experience.

Also, New York actors are often viewed nationwide as simply better—or at least more serious—actors. As Hollywood CD Jerry Franks says, "I prefer New York actors to L.A. actors because in New York actors learn their craft. They're always in classes, be it acting, dance, movement, voice, and they're always honing their gifts. Actors in L.A. don't seem to do that." It's not certain that's the whole truth, but it certainly is widely believed. And there's no question that New York theatre credits and theatre training convey something of a cachet, deserved or otherwise. Thus, most CDs in New York—and perhaps the rest of the country, rightly or wrongly— think New York-based actors are superior to those in Hollywood. As one of them says from his lower Manhattan office, "the looks are out there, but New York's got the talent." And most of the others think he's right.

Finally, New York is an easier environment in which to connect with other actors. In New York, if you're an actor and reasonably outgoing, it won't take you long to feel part of the acting family, even if you're unknown and unemployed. Theatre bars, theatre bookshops, theatre lobbies, inexpensive ethnic restaurants in and around the theatre districts, and the TKTS line in Duffy Square (the northern part of Times Square, where you can buy half-price tickets to Broadway and off-Broadway shows) all abound with New York actors. By contrast, L.A. has little in the way of a comparable acting community. In New York, you walk or take the subway everywhere, elbow to elbow with humanity—and with other actors. In Los Angeles, however, you're mostly in a car by yourself—connected with the rest of the actor world (who are also in cars by themselves) only by your cell phone. So, if you can't decide between the towns, we say try New York first.

How good is New York if you want to act in film? Well, some of the best film actors today began their careers on the New York stage or in regional theatre cast in New York. These include, in no particular order, Tom Hanks, Denzel Washington, Gwyneth Paltrow, Sigourney Weaver, Richard Dreyfuss, John Goodman, Annette Bening, Mercedes Ruehl, Warren Beatty, Kathy Bates, Scott Bakula, Billy Crudup, Paul Giamatti, Jason Alexander, Laura Linney, Bebe Neuwirth, Stacy Keach, Robert Duvall, Al Pacino, Frank Langella, Meryl Streep, Barbra Streisand, Jane Alexander, Robert DeNiro, Robert Redford, Dustin Hoffman, and of course the late Marlon Brando. Very few actors have made the transition in the other direction—other than for a token Broadway appearance. Stage to film—and New York to L.A.— is the classic route. As the late James Coco said, "Off-Broadway auditions for Broadway, which auditions for Hollywood." More than ever before, film and even television directors look for actors well versed in improvisation, in stage acting—and even in classical performance technique. So, if you're undecided between the two towns and aim to make your first career moves in stage acting (although it might not necessarily work out that way), New York should be your destination.

If, however, you are charismatic only on camera, are extraordinarily beautiful, or are determined to be a film or television performer, we'll say it again: go west, young person! And if your father runs a theatre in Dallas, stay in Dallas!

Whichever super-city you go to, find a place to stay that's convenient to the casting action, where you can get to an audition anywhere in town within an hour. You're not going to want to commute two hours every time you get a call to read for a show, and no agent is going to sign you without feeling that you'll be immediately available when the call comes. It's true that there are L.A. actors who live in the San Francisco Bay Area, but they maintain L.A. phone numbers (which they pretend are in their homes), and they have to be ready to hop on an airline shuttle at a moment's notice—just to get turned down for a part. If you're headed for a super-city, *be* there.

4 Establishing Yourself

You have moved, then, to your new city. The first thing you must do is *establish* yourself. Obviously you need a place to stay, and rents in both New York and L.A. are quite high—in New York extraordinarily so (not to mention the rental agency, or "fixture," commissions you will probably be hit up for). If possible, move in with a friend and give yourself a couple of weeks to look for a rent-stabilized apartment in a decent area. Sublets—furnished apartments privately rented from permanent renters who are leaving town for a few months—are often quietly advertised on theatre blogs and can provide you (as they have for both of your authors) with a short-term home during your "get-acquainted" period in a new town. Better yet, move with one or two friends and lease a place where you can share the digs—and the rent— among you. (Hint: for those headed to New York, rental rates are lower in the outer boroughs of Brooklyn and Queens, or above 125th Street in upper Manhattan, and the subway connections can make these spots almost as close as Manhattan.)

Bring enough money to pay two months' rent in advance plus a deposit, plus $6,000 in reserve. (Why $6,000? It's a round sum, and you'll need some breathing room. Much less, and you'll be in a state of constant fiscal panic before the end of the first week.) If you don't have that sort of cash, beg or borrow it: you'll be doing a lot of that in the coming years in any case. If it's out of the question—well, go anyway.

If you head for Los Angeles, you can expect to find a more reasonably priced place to stay. It will also be cleaner and nicer to come home to. The limitation of L.A. is that you absolutely must have a *car* in good running condition. This will eat up whatever you may save on rent. (Not only is a car unnecessary in New York, but the parking rates also make one a genuine liability, so leave your Toyota in Toledo.)

Once you are settled, you can get to work. You will need many things. There is no particular order in which you should get them, but you should get them, and some of them you will need right away. The list includes:

To get right away

- A dependable source of *income*
- A battery of *electronic communication devices*: at minimum a *cell phone*, and reliable 24-hour access to the internet
- *Photos* that you will use to market yourself to agents and casting directors
- A *résumé* of your training and experience for the same purpose

To start thinking about right away

- A *website* where you can post your photos, résumé, and demo reel (if you have one)
- Access to *breakdowns* where you can see what's being cast

To be preparing for eventually

- Getting into an acting union
- Getting talent representatives—an agent and/or a manager
- And most critical—getting a job!

Getting a job

It's known as the day job, though it doesn't necessarily take place in the daytime. But you need to have it if you don't have an extravagant bank account.

Obviously you need a source of income that you can count on. You can't pay your bills, eat, dress, or go out into the world without money. Moreover, you cannot afford to scrimp on professional expenses such as photographs and classes. Perhaps you have regular income from home, from your working (and indulgent) partner or spouse, or from a parent or friend. If so, you need not worry as long as your source continues to take care of you, though generally something is expected in return.

But if you aren't so lucky, you will have to get a job, preferably one that has flexible hours and pays well. In Hollywood, where most work and interviews take place in the daytime, an evening job is ideal. For this reason, most L.A.-area waiters are unemployed actors: table waiting is *the* job of choice for most Hollywood thespians. In New York the same is true until you start to perform or work at night in off-off-Broadway shows, when a morning or graveyard shift will become preferable. The back pages of *Backstage* and other trade magazines advertise openings for temporary secretaries, telemarketers, drivers, couriers, parking valets, word processors, nannies, administrative assistants, guy/gal Fridays, receptionists, bilinguals, clerks, and typists.

And if you have catering or computer skills, you can make a living in either town. A salable office skill is particularly valuable—you might land a job in a theatre-related area, and you will start to make contacts while you work. Many young men and women have started in the office and ended up on stage. If you can, do something you can be proud of, something you feel is professional. Being a professional at something is good training for being a professional at acting. But stay away from porn movies and any illicit activities that may beckon; they will make you feel bad about yourself, which won't help your acting one bit.

Your communications

You can't do anything in show business without basic communications. As you've already seen (with the StrawHat auditions, Chapter 3), this is an industry that sets up appointments at 90-second intervals. Moreover, you will need to be in touch 24/7, at home or on the set or in-between. The essential required package is a *cell phone* with dependable *voicemail*, plus an internet-linked *computer* (preferably wireless, so you can more easily receive messages outside of your home) loaded with a reliable *email program*. Here's what these things can do for you:

Your telephones are your basic contact with the casting world. They're how your agent or manager can reach you—or, if you have no representation, how a casting director (CD) can call you directly. Your cell phone provides you with instant access. It's always with you, always at the ready when you might be getting a call. Miss the call and they may not call back; they may just go to the next person on their list. Actors who can make instant connections, as one CD reports, "work more than those that don't, particularly as regards to the casting director hiring readers to help in auditions in the last moment, extras or under-fives [parts with less than five lines] simply because there isn't a lot of time to wait for people to call back. I have to cast the show for the next day!" Another CD notes, "when we need a reader for one of our casting sessions, we ask the first person we can get in touch with." So, your mobile phone is your invaluable key.

Your voicemail will take care of any messages you might miss when you just can't pick up (such as when you're auditioning for another show or taking a shower). You just have to make sure you check it regularly—and keep your battery charged. Here's one more word of advice: keep your outgoing voicemail message short, cheery, distinct, and above all *professional*. You don't want to sound the least moody, distracted, or in the midst of a drinking party, and you certainly don't want to try your caller's patience. Time is money—and long (or "super-cute") welcoming messages aren't welcoming to people (agents, say) who may have to call dozens of people every 15 minutes.

Ready access to a computer and printer is essential as well. Email is now the medium of choice for both one-to-one and one-to-many communications. It's instant, it's printable, it's send-able, it's reply-able, and it doesn't wake you up in the middle of the night.

And the web is now—by far—the greatest source of up-to-date show business information that you can get without leaving home. As you will see further on in this chapter, casting notices, union–management agreements, theatre schedules, old TV scripts, agent and CD contact information, and current theatre and film news and reviews—all these are available almost instantly on the world wide web. So are the sides (partial scripts) from which you'll be reading at any audition you might score. The web is also a place where you can list yourself and make your photo-résumé instantly available to anyone who wants it. So, reliable 24/7 computer access is essential if you are to make use of these opportunities.

Your friends

What do your friends have to do with this? Well, they—particularly those you have acted in plays and/or taken drama classes with—may provide you with some surprising ideas about how you might proceed in getting a job. Yes, you may feel that some of them may prefer to compete with you for such jobs, but the fact is that this will be quite rare—unless you are the same sex, the same age, and the same color, and they perform in exactly the same style as you do. But even when this is the case, a good friend can remain a good friend, because they know that their helping you can lead to your helping them.

So, come up with the names of actors and acting students you've enjoyed working and/or studying with in the past, then look them up in imdb.com (the International Movie Database) and/or ibdb.com (International Broadway Database) and/or iobdb.com (Internet Off-Broadway Database, also known as the Lortel Archives), and see if any of these have already begun a professional acting career—as these three websites include all the known names of professional actors, with listings of all the professionally produced films and plays they have performed in. And when you discover any of your old comrades who have begun a career, try to look them up and get together—either in person or by phone or email—with the hope of restarting your friendship and discovering some methods that have helped them win some parts and join the appropriate unions. Nine times out of ten they will be only too happy to do this, and you will be happy to have them do it—and you will have a continuing comrade with whom to trade new discoveries and ideas about how to break step-by-step into the business.

We've now talked about the hard basics: a home, a job, a telephone, a computer, and a reconnection with your previous actor pals. These are things you get and keep. The next items are the soft fuzzies—things you get and then give away. And then you get new ones.

Your photographs and résumés

Your picture and your résumé are your calling cards. No actor can be without eye-catching photos and clear indications of an impressive (even if amateur) acting background. Study these photos and résumés carefully, and then read our discussions about them.

Your photos represent more than your appearance. They communicate your personality, your energy, your appeal, and your vitality. You should find the best photographer you can afford, have the best photo session you can arrange, and choose the best shot from that session that you can select.

One giant change from this book's previous edition: your photos must be *in color*. Black and white photos, still viable in the casting industry when that revision went to press (2009), are now virtually obsolete. The main reason is that the onetime price gap between black and white and color photography has virtually vanished; since most actor photos are now created digitally and transmitted electronically—with no developing or printing costs—color images cost no more than black and white ones; even printing costs have equalized. And color communicates not only details of your features (such as your hair and skin tones) but also your personal vivacity. As CD Adrienne Berg says, we "now request color photos because everything is being done online. And if you're looking at 60 images at one time, the person whose picture is in color is the picture that pops at you."

There are two basic photos that will be your most important ones, and you will want to have a hundred copies of one or both always at hand:

- Headshots. These are 8" × 10" vertical or horizontal photos (8 by 10s) that show your head and shoulders. Usually sporting your name on the bottom, headshots are the most prevalent actor photographs in use today—on both coasts and around the country.
- Three-quarter body shots, or "3/4 shots." These are 8 × 10s that you might use as alternates. Sometimes also called hip shots, they show you from the hips upward, giving a sense of your body as well as your face. Body shots came into vogue in the late 1990s and are still in use, but now mainly for dancers and younger teen actors: many casting people like them, others loathe them. If your body is a strong selling point, you

might consider a 3/4 shot as an alternate photo or even as your main photo, but the straight headshot remains standard—particularly in New York.

A gallery of headshots

The four headshots in this gallery were selected by this book's co-author, James Calleri, as particularly effective in representing the young professional actors that the Calleri Casting office has called in for auditions in the past year. In brief captions, Calleri explains why these photos – shown here in black and white but available in full color and no charge at www. palgrave.com/theatre/cohen – have captured the attention of him and his co-author and casting colleagues.

Sohee Yun

Sohee Yun - Beautiful, accessible, feminine, very little makeup makes it a natural beauty.
Photo: Matthew Dunivan

Sohee Yun (AEA)

Height/Hair/Eyes: 5'5"/Black/Brown

THEATER (U.S.)

OTHELLO	*Ensemble*	Classic Stage Company	Tyne Rafaeli
EXPOSURE	*Ensemble*	Gene Frankel Theater	Devin Brain
OUR TOWN	*Mrs. Soames*	Columbia University	Tyne Rafaeli
THE SEAGULL	*Masha/Nina*	Columbia University	Andrei Serban
4:48 PSYCHOSIS	*Girl*	Columbia University	Andrei Serban
LULU	*Geschwitz*	Columbia University	Ulla Wolcz
LA RONDE	*Parlor Maid*	Columbia University	Ulla Wolcz
WOYZECK	*Karl*	Columbia University	Ulla Wolcz
THE SHADOW	*Annnuziata*	Columbia University	Niky Wolcz
CAFÉ LE MONDE	*Death/Woman*	Columbia University	Tatiana Pandiani
ORESTES	*Chorus*	Columbia University	Scott Ebersold

THEATER (Korea)

THE SEAGULL	*Masha*	Dream Play Theater	Yeon Min Kim
A DAY LIKE TODAY	*Grandmother*	Homo Ludens Theater	Geung Ho Nam
CARNIVAL	*Laura*	JuByunin Theater	Chung Sik Seo
KING LEAR	*Cordelia*	BaekSu-GwangBu Theater	Sung Yul Lee
THE MAIDS	*Claire*	Dream Theater	Jin Hong Ju
YOU DON'T UNDERSTAND	*Eui Yeon*	Yu Rang Seon Theater	Seon Ho Song
PIG AND A MORTORCYCLE	*Wife*	Dream Theater	Jin Hong Ju
MEDEA	*Medea*	Korean National Univ. of Arts	Jin Young Kim
4:48 PSYCHOSIS	*Girl*	Korean National Univ. of Arts	Phillip Zarrilli
PORTRAIT OF A LADY	*Lawyer*	Korean National Univ. of Arts	Han Nae Kim
THE FIGURE	*Actress*	Korean National Univ. of Arts	Geung Ho Nam

FILM

TO ALICE	*Nancy*	Columbia University	Frank Ju Ning Liu
MR. DOBSON	*Lily*	Columbia University	Ryan Wen
U. F. O	*Nurse*	Queenie Productions	Kwi Hyeon Kong
ALOHA HAWAII	*Sumin*	Queenie Productions	Kwi Hyeon Kong
EMPTY LIES	*Woman*	Korean National Univ. of Arts	Oh Jung Lim

EDUCATION

COLUMBIA UNIVERSITY | MFA in Acting, May 2016 *(Theatre Arts Dean's Fellowship, Theatre Arts Program Scholarship)*
  Instructors: Andrei Serban, Anne Bogart, Kristen Linklater, Andrea Haring, James Calleri,
  Gregory Mosher, Niky Wolcz, Ulla Wolcz, Mark Olsen, Michael Sexton, Reed Birney

KOREA NATIONAL UNIVERSITY OF ARTS | BFA in Acting, May 2011
(Full Academic Scholarship)

SPECIAL SKILLS

Ballet, Modern Dance, Korean Traditional Dance, Singing, Fluent Korean

Jarvis Dewayne Griggs

Jarvis Dewayne Griggs   Great pop of color, straightforward, confident, eyes zero in on you.
Photo: Matthew Dunivan

Jarvis Dewayne Griggs

New York Theatre:

Othello	Ensemble/Dance Captain	Classic Stage Company/Tyne Rafaeli
Three Hours (Ware Arts Festival)	Joey, K, R	HERE Arts Center/Sharone Halevy
Our Town	C. Warren/Joe Stoddard	Columbia University/Tyne Rafaeli
Blue Window	Norbert	Columbia University/Ken Rus Schmoll
Waiting for Godot	Didi	Columbia University/Ulla Wolcz
The Seagull	Dorn/Trigorin/Konstantin	Columbia University/Andrei Serban
Café Le monde	Vershinin/Ensemble	Columbia University/Tatiana Pandiani
Jaques or the Submission	Jaques	Columbia University/Niky Wolcz
Master and Margarita	Master	Columbia University/Niky Wolcz
Woyzeck	Drum Major	Columbia University/Ulla Wolcz
La Ronde	Young Gentleman	Columbia University/Ulla Wolcz
Orestes	Pylades	Columbia University/Scott Ebersold

Houston Theatre:

Jelly's Last Jam	Jelly	Prairie View A&M University
Fabulation	Hervé/Guard	Prairie View A&M University
Once on This Island	Armand/Ensemble	Prairie View A&M University

Training:
Columbia University School of the Arts-MFA 2016
Acting: Andrei Serban, Gregory Mosher, Niky Wolcz, Ulla Wolcz, Mark Olsen, Michael Sexton, Anne Bogart
Voice: Kristin Linklater, Andrea Haring
Movement: Niky Wolcz
View Points: Kelly Maurer
On-Camera Acting: Todd Thaler, James Calleri
Prairie View A&M University- BA 2013
Theatre: Dr. Cristal Truscott

Dance Training:
Tuscan Summer Dance Intensive (Italy) Summer 2015
Alvin Ailey Extension Dance
Classic Dance Ensemble Company Member (2011- 2013)
Modern/Contemporary: Maxine Steinman, Arianna Bracciali, Michael Leon Thomas
Ballet: Danyale Taylor-Williams, Nicole Ortega
Hip-Hop: Johnathan Lee
Jazz/West African: Michèle Moss, Danyale Taylor-Williams

Special Skills: SAFD Basic unarmed combat; Tuba (9 years), clown and mask, Directing, Stepping, Improv
Dance, Basic Tap

Sepideh Moafi

Sepideh Moafi - Easy appeal, direct, exotic, captivating, easy beauty.
PHOTO: Gene Mollica

ABRAMS ARTISTS AGENCY

SEPIDEH MOAFI

sanders | armstrong | caserta
MANAGEMENT

TELEVISION

Notorious	Series Regular (Megan Byrd)	ABC/Dir. *Michael Engler*
The Deuce	Major Recur (Loretta)	HBO/Dir. *Michelle MacLaren, Ernest Dickerson, others*
Red Zone (pilot)	Series Regular (Frida Moussaf)	CBS/Dir. *James Foley*
The Black Box	Major Recur (Dr. Mahmoud)	ABC/Dir. *Various**
Elementary	Guest Star (Sofia Tannen/Szofi)	CBS/Dir. *Aaron Lipstadt*
Nurse Jackie	Guest Star (Mrs. Harrison)	Showtime/Dir. *Adam Arkin*
The Blacklist	Guest Star (Mary Henning)	CBS/Dir. *Andrew McCarthy*
The Good Wife	Guest Star (Sylmar Knausgaard)	CBS/Dir. *James Whitmore*
Limitless	Guest Star (Dr. Pauline Wilson)	CBS/Dir. *Doug Aarniokoski*
Forever	Guest Star (Melanie Sparo)	ABC/Dir. *Robert Bailey*
Blue Bloods	Guest Star (Aaliya Zaki)	CBS/Dir. *David Solomon*
Unforgettable	Guest Star (Lisa Martinez)	CBS/Dir. *David Platt*
		* *John Krokidas, Andrew McCarthy, Josh Marston, Eric Stoltz, Tricia Brock*

FILM

Quest	Lead (Susan Hayes)	Quest the Movie/Dir. *Santiago Rizzo*
Best Man in the Dark	Lead (Tereza Lopez)	Midnight Treehouse/Dir. *Alfred Padilla*
Violet is Single	Lead (Violet)	Scary Cow Production/Dir. *Alexandra MacArthur*

NEW YORK

As You Like It	Rosalind	Chautauqua Theater Co./Dir. *Jackson Gay*
The Screens** (workshop)	Various Roles	The Public Theater/Dir. *Mark Wing-Davey*
The Band's Visit (reading)	Dina	Atlantic Theater Co./Dir. *Hal Prince*
The Urban Retreat (reading)	Narrator	LAByrinth Theater Co./Dir. *Adrienne Campbell-Holt*
Fifty Ways (reading)	Zoe	New Dramatists/*Kate Fodor*
Everything is Ours	Catalina/Cheryl/Flora	Chautauqua Theater Co./Dir. *Adrienne Cam.-Holt*
		** *New adaptation by Caryl Churchill*

THEATER (PARTIAL LIST)

The Three Musketeers	Constance Bonacieux	Shakespeare Santa Cruz/Dir. *Art Manke*
Henry IV, Part One	Lady Mortimer / Angel	Shakespeare Santa Cruz/Dir. *Scott Wentworth*
The Fantasticks	Luisa	SF Playhouse/Dir. *Bill English*
Romeo & Juliet	Juliet	Palo Alto Players/Dir. *Bill Olson*
After Troy	Hecuba	UC Irvine MFA Acting/Dir. *Mihai Maniutiu*
The Rose Tattoo	Serafina	UC Irvine MFA Acting/Dir. *Shannon Ferrante*
Importance of Being Earnest	Gwendolyn	UC Irvine MFA Acting/Dir. *Phil Thompson*
Twelfth Night	Viola	UC Irvine MFA Acting/Dir. *Ryanne Laratonda*
The Wild Party (Lippa)	Queenie	UC Irvine MFA Acting/Dir. *Myrona Delaney*
Hello, Again	The Actress	UC Irvine MFA Acting/Dir. *Roger Castellano*
9 Parts of Desire	One-Woman Show	UC Irvine MFA Acting/Dir. *Sepideh Moafi*

OPERA / CONCERT (PARTIAL LIST)

Le Nozze di Figaro	Susanna	Livermore Valley Opera/Dir. *Jose Maria Condemi*
Agrippina	Agrippina	Oakland Opera/Dir. *Tom Dean*
Concert of Arias		John F. Kennedy Center
Händel's Messiah		Davis Symphony Hall

TRAINING

UC Irvine – MFA Acting 2013 (full scholarship, fellowship)
SF Conservatory of Music – BM Vocal Performance (full scholarship, presser grant)
The Washington National Opera – Institute for Young Singers, AD. *Plácido Domingo*

SPECIAL SKILLS

Fluent in Farsi, Basic Italian & Spanish, IPA trained for all dialects, Soprano, Read Music, Tango, Various Dance, Contact Improv, Certified Instructor: Yoga Alliance & Pure Barre, Driver's License, League Champion Wrestler, Crazy Yoga Tricks

Dan Amboyer

Dan Amboyer - Charming, sexy, confident, classy shot. Puts you at ease.
Photo: Luke Fontana

DAN AMBOYER

danamboyer.com | @danamboyer

NY: Harden-Curtis Associates   Authentic MGMT   LA: Abrams Artists Agency

TV / FILM

"Younger"	Thad & Chad (3 seasons)	TV Land, ex p. Darren Star
William & Catherine: A Royal Romance	Prince William	Hallmark, dir. Linda Yellen
Batman v Superman: Dawn of Justice	Lt. Christie	Warner Bros., dir. Zack Snyder
Love the Coopers	Jake	Lionsgate, dir. Jessie Nelson
"Benders"	Christian	IFC, ex p. Denis Leary
"Untitled John Cusack" Pilot	Douglas	CBS, dir. Niels Arden Oplev
"Unforgettable"	Eric Oliver	CBS, dir. Matt Penn
"Person of Interest"	Don Juan	CBS, dir. Chris Fisher
"Inside Amy Schumer"	Ron	Comedy Cen., dir. Neal Brennan
"Body of Proof"	George White	ABC, dir. Matthew Gross
"Law & Order"	Todd Barton	NBC, dir. Sam Weisman
Lily in the Grinder	Bean	dir. Michael Morgenstern
"All My Children"	Guest Star	ABC
"Grand Theft Auto V"	Various	Rockstar Games, dir. Rod Edge
"Red Dead Redemption"	Various	Rockstar Games, dir. Rod Edge

OFF-BROADWAY & REGIONAL THEATRE

THE METROMANIACS by David Ives (premiere)	Dorante	Shakespeare Theatre, dir. M. Kahn
AS YOU LIKE IT	Orlando	Old Globe, dir. Adrian Noble
RICHARD III	Richmond – King Henry VII	Old Globe, dir. Lindsay Posner
INHERIT THE WIND	Bertram Cates	Old Globe, dir. Adrian Noble
AS YOU LIKE IT	Orlando	HERE, dir. Moritz von Stuelpnagel
REMEMBRANCE OF THINGS PAST	Robért Saint-Loup	92nd St. Y, dir. Di Trevis
THE BAKKEN FORMATIONS	Tom	Ars Nova, dir. Jade King Carroll
THE ECLECTIC SOCIETY	Tom Rockwell	Walnut Street, dir. Ed Herendeen
THESE SEVEN SICKNESSES	King Theseus	EPBB, dir. Ed Iskandar
RESTORATION COMEDY	Berinthia	EPBB, dir. Ed Iskandar
DIDO, QUEEN OF CARTHAGE	Aeneas	EPBB, dir. Ed Iskandar
HENRY IV P1	King Richard II, Sir Vernon	Utah Shakespeare Festival
DOCTOR FAUSTUS	Beelzebub	Utah Shakespeare Festival
BASH'd! a rap opera	Jack, Dillon	The Zipper Factory
THE GREAT UNKNOWN	Capt. Walter Powell	Theatre at St.Clements
ORANGE LEMON EGG CANARY	The Assistant	PS122, dir. Michael Sexton
LE GRAND MEAULNE S	Augustin Meaulnes	Quantum Theatre, dir. Di Trevis
THE PLAY ABOUT THE NAKED GUY	Kit	Emerging Artists Theatre

TRAINING

Carnegie Mellon University, School of Drama -- BFA Acting -- **Interlochen Arts Academy**, high school diploma
New York: Private Coaching w. Harold Guskin, On Camera w. Bob Krakower, Scene Study w. Caymichael Patten

SPECIAL SKILLS AND INTERESTS

Piano, Singer, Accents, Narrow IPA, Stage Combat, Horseback, Driver's License, Swim, Hockey, Animal Enthusiast

You may also want these photos:

- Postcard shots. These consist of your reduced headshot printed on a postcard stock that still leaves plenty of room for an address and a message. They can be printed at the same time as your regular photos, and you can use them for confirming dates, inviting people to showcases, and, in general, reminding casting folks who you are. When you're doing a show, for example, a photo-postcard is an effective quickie advertisement that can circulate your picture, name, and informal invitation: "Hey, come see me play Juliet at the L.A. Shakespeare Festival!" They're also good ways to confirm dates, thank people for their attention and consideration, and announce your current activities. And they have the advantage of being easily thumbtacked to a wall if anyone wants to look at you for a day or two while casting a project—and who knows but that someone might? Occasionally the right postcard comes across the desk of a CD at the exact time it is needed. To quote David Ives' famous play, it's "all in the timing."
- Business card photos. These are mainly special-use novelties: small enough to carry around in your purse or pocket and hand out to people that you may run into by chance, say in a theatre lobby, an acting class, or the "acting" section (or, even better, the "producer" section) of New York's Drama Bookshop or Hollywood's Samuel French Theatre and Film Bookshop.
- Composite photos. Occasionally popular in past decades (particularly in commercial casting situations), these combine headshots and bodyshots shot in a variety of expressions, makeups, and costumes on a single 8 × 10. They are no longer useful, however, for film, stage, or TV casting, and many in the industry regard them as a huge no-no.

You can, of course, acquire photos for all of these purposes at the same time. Find a photographer who specializes in actor photos and arrange a sitting. Virtually all photographers shoot digitally these days; they will provide you with hundreds of images (still called "proofs" or "contacts"), either at the time of shoot or by email or by a posting on the website. (A few photographers, mainly in New York, have stayed with the older film technology: they will provide you with fewer proofs, but otherwise the procedures are the same.)

When you get your proofs, pick your favorites (you can and should email some to friends and colleagues for their advice), and make your best three to five choices, asking for these to be blown up to 8 × 10s. Then pick the best single one of *them*, and have that one as your master shot that will be printed in bulk for subsequent distribution. Keep the rest for the day you change your mind. Or for the day the agent tells you to get new shots!

Finding a photographer

How do you find a photographer? That's the tricky part. You're going to want a specialist here: someone who knows the field and has the gift. As one Hollywood photographer, Kevyn Major Howard (who was an actor for 25 years first), puts it, "your 8 × 10 has approximately two seconds to gain the casting director's attention and confidence. It must impress. Nothing short of brilliance works." Expect to pay for this brilliance, although you can negotiate a reasonable fee if you do your homework and choose well.

The best way to survey actor-savvy photographers is on the web. Do your research. There is ample material online nowadays of almost every photographer's work. In New York, go to nycastings.com and click "Photographers"—where you will find about fifty headshot photographers and their own pictures, addresses, phone numbers, and explanations. You can also look at actual headshot samples in the office lobbies of Reproductions in New York at 70 W. 40th Street. In the rest of the country, go to actingbiz.com and click on the various suggestions such as "How to Get Great Headshots" and "Headshot & Photo Examples." Plus, *Backstage* routinely carries as many as 50 ads from actor photographers at both ends of the country in each issue. If anything, there are too many photographers to choose from.

How do you choose a photographer from all these options? The best way, if you can do it, is to ask actors who have used their services. Talk to working actors you can meet—look at the photos they've had taken, find out who took them, and for how much, what their experience had been like, and whether they would shoot with that photographer again. You will surely hear war stories: not every matchup is made in heaven in this very competitive field.

When you have identified one or more possible photographer candidates, call and request a meeting. Your personality and a good connection with your photographer are as important as good lighting in this circumstance. You want to feel good and be a good fit before and while setting up your session, so study their portfolios, look at their studio, and get a sense of the photographer and how he or she might work for you. Does the photographer match your expectations? Do you feel sufficiently relaxed in his or her company? Does he or she shoot only in the studio, or outside as well? And, most importantly, would you truly look forward to coming back for a four- or five-hour shoot with this person?

Once you've arranged a sitting, what should you wear when you come? You should discuss this in advance with the photographer and arrange to bring a selection of three or four different outfits. Natural, contemporary, relaxed clothing that you feel good in and that brings out the "inner you" will always be best. Avoid bold patterns such as stripes or plaids, anything that's uncomfortable, and anything that's super-trendy (among other things, it will quickly date). Actor/photographer Ike Eisenman suggests that clothing with a physical texture—such as "tweed jackets, sweaters, denims"—looks particularly good. Clothing—though casual—should be spotless, hair clean, jewelry and makeup discreet (if used at all), and eyes open and shining.

As to makeup, particularly for women, consider using a makeup artist. You may bring your own, of course, but most photographers will be happy to arrange for one to attend the shoot—for an additional fee, of course. Find out if they have a makeup artist and/or stylist they typically use. You want to look your absolute best, but you also want it to look like you. So, makeup and styling are important. Find out any extra costs the photographer may have as well before you agree.

When the camera lens finally focuses on you, your face should be relaxed, open and personable (this is why you want a photographer you feel totally at home with—and not one you are intimidated by!). Should you smile? The answer is a definite yes if you're going for commercials—at least if you have great teeth. That smile has to be genuine and infectious, however; nothing will kill your photo's impact as much as a pasted-on grin. But theatrical photos may be more serious and somber—though frowns and glowers are probably best avoided—if those are the kinds of roles you are seeking. In either case, a relaxed photo session will help your best qualities—either smiling or pensive—to come out. If music turns you on, ask if you can bring a portable CD player with you to the shoot, or ask if the photographer already plans—as most do—to employ musical accompaniment at the lensing session.

How much will all this cost? A bit less than in earlier editions of this book: in 2016, fees charged by the more experienced photographers in New York ran from $350 to $850; in L.A. they can be the same. But you get a lot for this: usually 600 to 1,000 digital images (or 72–108 if the photographer works on film), plus, depending on the photographer, online viewable options for four to six wardrobe changes, touch-ups on two or three of the final blow-ups, and other services—like free drinks from the fridge! The going rate for the photographer's recommended makeup artist at that same date was $125–$200 for the shoot.

The photographer will most likely agree to send you a secured link to your selections, which can then be easily reproduced. The lab will add your name (you can choose where, and in what typeface, from an extensive menu) and will print your 8 × 10s by the hundred. Ask for a matte rather than a glossy finish. This is important. The cost at a representative studio with offices on both coasts in 2016 was $105 for 100 copies and $265 for 500 (obviously quantity provides savings), including an initial set-up fee of $18. Reorders of the same master shot receive a reduction from those numbers. Postcard-sized reproductions cost less ($74/$233 for 100/500), and business card size less yet ($62/$260). You can get cheaper reproductions by a lithographic process, but most people (your authors included) think lithos lack punch.

Of course, there are also package deals and additional services (retouching, color correction, emailing, etc.) available. How can you find a reproduction service? Several advertise weekly in the trades. You might check out reproductions.com, a premium service, but there are dozens of others.

What *kind* of photo should you be seeking? Part of it comes down to knowing who you are—and who you want to be. Reread the section in Chapter 3 on this delicate and awesome subject. Remember: you are going to present only *one* photo, and for all (professional) intents and purposes this photo is YOU. Do you grin from ear to ear, or do you glower behind furrowed eyebrows? Either pose may be effective, but you obviously can't do both in your one photo. Does your hair cascade down your back or tie up in a bun at the back of your neck? Don't say "It depends on the role" or "It depends on how I feel," because you can show off only one of those hairstyles on your single headshot.

One of two things will happen when you show your headshot around. Either somebody will say "You need new pictures," or *everyone* will say, "You need new pictures." Don't be discouraged; just get used to it. *Everybody* in New York and L.A. (along with your Mom and Dad) considers himself or herself an expert on what your photos—and you—should look like, or wants to impress you with their expertise on such matters. Everybody also feels complete confidence in declaring that brushstroke borders are in, or cockeyed angles attract attention, or 3 × 3 square pictures floating in an 8 × 10 white space really set you apart from the crowd. But that's just their opinion; judging photos is a notoriously subjective subject, and this fact can prove especially painful when *you're* the subject. So, let us make a few remarks, gleaned from many interviews with CDs on both coasts, about the decisions you will be making both in choosing your photographer and in specifying what you want.

Rule number one is, of course, the photo has to look like you. Indeed, if you read CD interviews, that's the single most important thing your photo has to do: "I hate it when actors come in and don't look like their photo!" shouts virtually every CD interviewed in the press.

But you must also realize that while rule number one is true from the CD's point of view, it's not going to be your biggest problem, because if your photo isn't brilliant, you won't "come in," and there won't be anyone to care whether the photo looks like you or not! The most memorable headshot veteran agent Richard Fisher of Abrams Artists ever saw was of an actor posed next to a giraffe in a zoo. He still remembers the photo, but he has never called in the actor. "I'm not sure he was taking this career very seriously," he said, laughing.

Your biggest problem, then, is that your photo has to be brilliant! It must catch immediate attention from at least half the people who look at it. (Don't worry about grabbing *all* the people; nobody's picture does that. Half will be just fine.) It has to have *instant* eye appeal, equal measures of surprise and fascination: a specificity that says, Oh, he or she is *that* kind of person. Sex appeal, individuality, charisma, intrigue: all these are qualities that the brilliant photo conveys.

Also remember that your photo must have what is known as "thumbprint appeal." Thus, it needs to look good small as well as big. The majority of time your shot will be looked at is at a casting service or, if you are lucky, when your agent or manager sends over a tiny link. The thumbprint size is on what is called a "casting session sheet." Trust us: they are on there! It's how the creative and casting team remember you as they audition throughout their day.

Remember, you're going to be cast because you're terrific, not because you look like your photo. So, get a brilliant photo. And if your brilliant photo doesn't look like you, then make sure you look like it!

The second most important criterion that casting directors recite, almost in unanimity, is that your photos show honest life and warmth, particularly in the eyes. This advice you should follow to a T. We want "someone approachable, someone you wouldn't be afraid to speak to," says CD Sheila Manning, who looks at hundreds of photos ("200 in a minute and a half") every day as she casts both TV shows and commercials. Manning hates show-offy formats, forced smiles, shticky hands-on-face shots, composites ("this shows me but it's old and out of date"), and "anything that looks phony." Her views are industry standard. Another CD seeks "life behind the eyes—something going on that tells you about who the person is as opposed to a flat, pretty picture." Another likes photos that show "life going on in their faces, intelligence in their eyes, as opposed to a vapid look of 'Aren't I cute?'

or 'Aren't I pretty?' " Your expression should not be passive; you should not be seen as simply "posing." CDs certainly don't want to see, "Look at me having my photo taken!" Rather, your headshot should suggest a point of view—*your* point of view—about something reasonably important.

Naturalness, liveliness, and a sense of excitement are much more important than clever poses and splashy formats. The rapport you can develop with your photographer, then, is crucial, so that your mind and emotions can become fully engaged during your shoot, bringing out your natural liveliness. So, it's essential not only to see a photographer's work, but also to see—or have a sense of—the photographer working. You certainly don't want to be intimidated or brushed off by your photographer, no matter how celebrated she or he might be. The shooting location may play a key role: outdoor shots, with natural lighting, can convey warmth and genuineness—but they can also make you squint from the sunlight or get lost in the background. (One New York photographer shoots subjects on the same cobblestone street in the Manhattan meatpacking district, but his photos emphasize their gritty locale more than their actor-subjects.) Indoor studio shots give you more control—your hair won't blow around, for example—but they can look more, well, studious. If you shoot outdoors, be sure the photographer can blur out the background, which is easily done by setting the proper focal length. If you shoot in a studio, be sure you feel at home there. Your photographer may even propose the increasingly popular combination of a studio shot with natural lighting, which may give you the best of both worlds.

When you examine your proofs, look at each picture very carefully. Disregard photos in which your eyes are anything but brilliant or that have distracting backgrounds (or foregrounds) or that show smudges on your clothing or that present your face in less-than-perfect focus. Email your proofs to your friends and get their opinions—taking the proverbial grain of salt as you do so.

Also ask the photographer, who will undoubtedly offer advice in any event. If none of the shots please you, ask for a reshoot. It may be a sticky request, but they're your photos, and it's your career, and your money. On the other hand, if you have a good photographer, consider his or her advice carefully. The photographer wants your pictures to be successful too. Their success is essential to his or her business as well as yours.

Retouching?

Should you have your photos retouched? Retouching on film tends to be easily spotted, but digital retouching is much simpler, and mild retouching of, say, minor facial blemishes (that may even be gone when you show up for your interview) may be accomplished with photo-editing software by a professional retoucher. Chris Melkonian, who does this at Isgo Lepejian Custom Photo Labs in L.A., reports spending much of his time "clearing darkness [under the eyes], smoothing out the lines,... [and] whitening the teeth and eyes, making them pop more." Hollywood headshot photographer Mark Husmann uses retouching to remove "flyaways"—distracting stray hairs—and minor wardrobe malfunctions. But don't go too far in these directions, or you might violate rule number one: the photo must look like you do!

Taking your own photos?

Earlier editions of this book suggested that you and a friend might have a crack at taking each other's photographs. Unless you are both experienced photographers, however, we think the time for this advice has passed, unless you live where you simply can't find or afford a good pro. If that is the case, however, grab your digital camera (preferably with image stabilization) and head down to your local park with a friend willing to shoot you in a variety of locales and poses. This is just a temporary fix until you hit the big towns. But it is not recommended. You want to be a professional actor? Get professional photos.

Your résumé

When you're asked through the trade announcements to "submit" for a CD, you are ordinarily being asked to submit—usually by mail or email—your picture and résumé. They are really one item, as the résumé is going to be stapled to the back of your picture. But you don't create it at the same time or in the same way.

Your résumé is a one-page (and no more!) document that tells casting people why you should be hired as an actor. It lists, in a fairly set order from top to bottom, your contact information, union affiliation (if any), physical characteristics, acting experience, training, and, at the bottom, any special talents or abilities you might have.

You can have résumés made by professionals, but here's something you can make up yourself, if you have decent composition skills and a computer. And this is something you should do, if possible, because you will want to experiment with all sorts of layouts, formats, fonts, and styles.

While the layout of actor résumés may appear relatively fixed at first glance, some very important, if subtle, variations (in typeface, choice of information presented, spatial arrangement of those choices) can make your résumé show *your* credits to maximum advantage. Let's take a look at résumé construction from the top down.

At the top go your name, your union affiliation (if you have any), your contact information, and your height, weight (though less often and rarely for women), and hair and eye color. Your singing range (e.g., "tenor") goes here too, if it's a true specialty. Union affiliation is so important for the entry-level actor that your union—the magic letters being AEA, SAG, and AFTRA (or SAG-AFTRA)—should go right under your name. (When you amass significant *professional* credits, you may leave off your union affiliation, as by then it will be presumed.) Your contact information consists of, at minimum (and possibly at maximum), your cell-phone number and email address. When you have an agent, the agent's contact info (and probably the agent's logo) will likely replace them, though entry-level actors are wise to leave their personal cell number and email address as well, as most casting directors appreciate the freedom of being able to connect with you directly if they so choose. The name and logo of your manager, if you have one, may be added as well. But *never* put a home address on a résumé unless you want to have household visits from unwanted guests.

Be honest in listing your physical characteristics: give your real—not ideal—height and weight. Casting people will be mad when you turn out fatter or shorter than you led them to expect, and they won't be happy with your lame excuse of too much dessert last week. Keep the description of your hair color up to date. If you list "tenor," be sure you can deliver the notes when asked. You *never* list your age on a résumé, and you don't even need to list an age range—this will limit rather than expand your cast-worthiness, and your photo, if it's contemporary, should show your age range sufficiently. Exception: if you are under 18, *do give your birth date.* There are legal restrictions on your hiring that the casting people will need to know about beforehand. After age 18, create a new résumé without that info.

The middle section is the key portion of the résumé: it details your acting experience. Here's where the format may prove crucial, for, as opposed to your height and hair color, your on-stage or in-film/TV experience is unique, and you need to show it in a clear and impressive fashion. Expect to spend considerable trial-and-error time finding the format that best shows off your credits. Generally, you will divide this portion into two to four horizontal blocks, with each devoted to those media in which you've worked. These could be titled "film," "TV," and "stage"—or "Broadway," "Off-Broadway," "Television," and "Regional Theatre." Then you will divide each of these sections vertically into two, three, or four columns detailing, from left to right, what role you played, where, and with whom. Unlike the horizontal blocks, the columns do not need to be titled; their function will be obvious from the information you put in them. How you present this information is up to you, but to make it truly impressive you must provide the information not as it may be important to you, but as it will appear important to *them*—to your readership of casting people. Some tips follow.

If you have professional experiences, they are *by far* the most important ones for casting people and therefore must be given prominence. If you are looking for film/TV work and have some professional experience in the media (even if nonunion), then make your film/TV experience your first horizontal block; if you are looking for stage opportunities, lead off with your stage experience. Oftentimes in New York you simply lead off with the theatre credits, since that is a theatre town. Vice versa in L.A. If you have acted with any union company, these credits should be listed above your amateur ones, even if the work was artistically inconsequential. If, for example, you have been a day player on a TV pilot, put it above the Hamlet or Hedda you performed in college. But do include theatre credits, if you have them, somewhere on your résumé, even if you are interested primarily in working in film or TV. Although he mainly casts TV sitcoms, veteran CD Jeff Greenberg explains that "if actors don't have stage credits on their résumé, I'm very reluctant to bring them in." According to Greenberg, an actor's ability to "re-create with consistency," which is generally stage-learned, is crucial in his projects.

Always remember that few casting people will read your entire résumé. If the first third of it doesn't grab them, they will only pretend to read the rest. So, lead off with the most important (and most important-sounding!) credits you have, regardless of where they stand chronologically.

If you have acted with known stars, known directors, known actors, or known theatre companies, be sure to choose a format that highlights this information. A column for "other" information can be useful here: for one show it can say "Susan Stroman, dir." and for the next "with Nicole Kidman." (Don't you wish?)

Don't list lots of names unknown in the profession. If your credits are all from your university, that's fine: just use one horizontal block, untitled, listing your top ten school credits by role, show, and the university group that produced it. But don't list the names of all your student or even faculty directors, no matter how much you admired them. Not only will it not further your chances, but it may also simply emphasize your distance from the profession. It is far better to list:

Barbara rather than	*Major Barbara*	Kansas State University
Barbara	*Major Barbara*	Harry Schmerd, director

Also, the CD may have *gone* to Kansas State University (before Harry Schmerd taught there) and you'll at least have lots to talk about.

For the same reason, don't try to disguise (as many do) a college credit by listing it under the name of the theatre building in which it was performed; you don't want to irritate the casting person, who then has to figure out where the credits were obtained. Believe it or not, it's much better to say "Pomona College" than "Garrison Theatre," because everyone knows of Pomona College but no one outside of Pomona has heard of its Garrison Theatre. There's nothing wrong with showing your college theatre credits if that's all you have: everybody starts somewhere, and casting people know that. Trying to puff up your college experience by pretending it's in some unknown building doesn't increase its prestige, it reduces it.

Don't ever lie about your experience! Aside from moral reasons, you'll probably get caught. It's really a small world out there, and people do check. If you say you've acted for George C. Wolfe, the director who's interested in you might very well *call* Mr. Wolfe to check you out, and if Wolfe's never heard of you, you're in deep muck. Indeed, the guy in the back of the room might even *be* Mr. Wolfe. You never can tell.

Do you need another reason not to lie? Here it is: *you'll be worrying the whole time that you'll be found out, and it will spoil your audition.* Furtiveness and anxiety are disastrous for actors taking part in an interview, and you only set yourself up for a sour stomach if you present forged credentials.

What else? A few don'ts: don't list high school or community theatre credits if you have college or professional ones. Don't ever list extra work in movies. Don't list chorus or ensemble roles as such if you can avoid it; list them instead by a name if you can (most producers now name all the roles, even if the name doesn't appear in the script) or by something like "street gangster" or "high-society lady and other roles." Never list roles with numbers, such as "second court lord."

At the very bottom of your résumé, you should list these add-on items:

- Special abilities that you do *superbly*: performance sports, such as high diving or gymnastics; circus acts, singing and dance experience, fencing skill, nightclub work and stand-up comedy, and so on. And be sure you can do them superbly if asked to do so at an audition!

- Any languages you speak fluently, and dialects at which you are already expert.
- Your training, with the names of any instructors that would probably be recognized in the professional world.

> ASIDE FROM JAMES: But be careful here! I see résumés where the actor's training credits take up more room than actual work they've done. Nothing is less sexy than a shopping list of voice teachers, styles classes, and master classes. I want my actors studied and trained, but that shouldn't be the meat of your résumé. Yes, your training by all means should be your badge of honor, particularly if you've studied with strong people, but it mustn't be the highlight of your résumé.

Keep this "bottom" material to less than 10% of the résumé.

You should *not* include, however, the following kinds of information on your résumé:

- Your interest or experience in directing or stage managing (it can be a turnoff).
- Your membership in Phi Beta Kappa (ditto). "It doesn't do to be too smart. Actors who insist that they're brilliant—that puts you out of the running for half the roles you want to play," said the late Edward Herrmann.
- Your high school or college grades (nobody cares).
- Your academic awards or scholarships, even prestigious ones such as the Irene Ryan Acting Prize (sorry!).
- Your hobbies (they're not hiring you for these).
- Your reasons for wanting a job (they know).
- Your dedication to acting (they know that too).
- Your willingness to do anything and everything (they'll find that out soon enough).
- Your psychological history (ditto).
- Your marital situation (it may change).

How cute should you be?

Watch it. It's best to be simple, honest, effective, and businesslike and show your experience at a glance. If you want to include a couple of humanizing details (such as your ownership of cocker spaniels), you might raise some coincidental interest among those sharing your interests, but you might also come off simply as an amateur. However, if your résumé shows a very special or unique skill, this might well spark a conversation—so be ready for it!

ASIDE FROM JAMES: There was an actress that came in for me. She was lovely and her audition was fine, but the one thing I really remember is that after her reading the director asked for her "Bjork interpretation" that she had listed as a special skill, and what she then showed us was remarkable and memorable. She didn't get the part, but I have never forgotten her and could well call her again.

Like your photo, your résumé is not a passive presentation; it is not simply an application form to be faithfully filled out. It is a creative statement, an advertisement of your skills. Approach it not as a duty but as art—and occasion to inspire. If your experience is limited solely to college or school shows, list them proudly, and make them seem as if they were the most important shows done in the three-state area where you lived.

Your résumé must, above all, be cleanly composed, professionally attractive, and quick and easy to read. No colored papers! No fancy fonts! While no actor ever got hired because of an expensive printing job, and while super-opulence can be an actual turnoff, *neatness* and *clarity* are very important. They indicate your professionalism.

Proofread carefully, and check all proper names against reliable web entries, such as on Wikipedia or imdb.com. We are always amazed at how many actor résumés include misspellings—of play and film titles, directors' names, theatre companies, and the like. While no one will hire you for your spelling skills, misspelling important trade information like this connotes a lack of professional authenticity on your part—implicitly suggesting that you're not really familiar with the work you say you did or the professionals you say you worked with.

Leave lots of white space. Don't pad your résumé by squeezing everything you can think of into it. A résumé is about quality, not quantity: actors who cram 35 amateur roles onto one sheet of paper only make it clear that they have been wasting away in the boondocks longer than has been good for them. Having a dozen interesting credits will look better than five dozen repetitious ones. If you are a young actor, the casting people do not expect you to have a lot of credits. Indeed, having too many is a red flag; you aren't that old! Your résumé can look as young as you are.

Once your résumé has been completed, proofread, and duplicated, it should be printed, and copies of it should be stapled to the backs of your photographs. The resulting hybrid document is your photo-résumé. Some photo labs can actually print your résumé on the back of your photo, but that's not such a good idea, as you'll be regularly updating your résumé (you hope!), and won't want to have new photos printed each time you do so.

You should also store a copy of your printed résumé on your computer for emailing and uploading onto websites—and it's best to store it as a .pdf or .jpg file, as these read identically on PC and Mac formats for those who may later download it for themselves. CDs will often call up a young actor and say "Email me your pic and résumé stat!" You best be ready to do so at the touch of a button.

Reels

It's now increasingly common—one might even say necessary—for an actor seeking TV and film work, particularly in the Los Angeles market, to have a *reel* (also known as a *demo reel* or a *show reel* or a *speed reel* or a *performance video*—each with slightly different meanings, which we'll discuss shortly).

Your reel shows you in performance, and has become a virtual necessity in the film/TV casting world. Casting calls in trade papers (like *Backstage*) or websites (like *nowcasting.com* and *actorsaccess.com*) that five years ago asked for "pix and résumés" now commonly ask for "pix, résumés, and reels."

But what is a reel, exactly? And how do you get one? And how do you submit one? Read on.

First, a "reel" is no longer a real reel, at least not a reel of tape or film wound around a spool. These days, a reel is a link to an online digital file.

Whatever it's called (and we'll simply call it a "reel" from here on in), it's a video presentation of you in action: of you acting.

And it's short! How short? In the previous edition we reported six minutes as the going maximum; by the time of writing (2016), the standard has dropped to *two or three* minutes—and in many cases the reel will also be shortened to an online *performance video* or *speed reel* of just *one* minute!

Don't be too surprised—or angry—at how short this is. Casting people are not simply looking at *your* reel—they're more likely shuffling through files of them, often with their phones ringing off the hook at the same time. And most of the time they find out everything they need to know (or think they need to know) in *the first ten seconds*.

If you think one or two minutes—not to mention the first ten seconds—is too short a time to get across how good you are, hear what actress/author (of *Acting Is Everything*) Judy Kerr has to say: "Watch awards shows. Notice how a clip that's 20 seconds long maximum can still give you the full essence of a character? That's what you'll want to strive for in your reel." She's right.

So, your challenge isn't to complain that one minute isn't enough; it's to make that first minute—even the first ten seconds—*absolutely terrific.* Your reel should be an enthralling, fascinating *glimpse* of your potential. It's not a documentary film on your career. It should grab—not bore—the viewer. And that's why reel-making is a tricky business.

Creating a reel

There are three basic ways of making a reel, and the differences between them are quite significant.

By far the best reels are compilations of clips from your previous *professional* film and TV appearances, and we'll discuss these first. But since entry-level actors, by definition, don't have previous professional film or TV appearances, this option won't be possible for them. For those without pro credits, you have four alternatives: (1) engaging a professional service to produce such a reel, (2) making your own reel on your home or school video equipment, getting together with friends to serve as supporting cast and technical crews, (3) compiling some work from your best scenes in a good on-camera class, or (4) finding the best film school and hoping you can acquire some great useable footage. Film and stage veteran Catherine Curtain, a star in *Orange is the New Black*, lives by this code: "You have to create your own work in this field. Every year or two, I try to do an NYU film or a Columbia grad film. I love them. I try to always meet new young filmmakers and to live by a code of 'Yes.'"

We'll discuss these alternatives after the preferred—and industry standard—pro clip-compilation reel, but you should look at the compilation reel first.

A compilation of professional clips

The best reels of this sort will show you performing in award-winning films or TV shows along with Robert DeNiro and Sarah Jessica Parker. Of course, if you have these sorts of clips hanging around, you're probably not reading this book—at least, not for the first time. But *any* part in a professionally produced film or TV show—if you have some face time on camera and a line or two—can provide you with a great 60-second spot that can prove both winsome and fascinating—and can indicate your potential.

So, as soon as you begin to land professional roles, no matter how small, you should start acquiring broadcast-quality clips of them. The easiest way to do this is when you are on the set. Make friends with the show's production coordinator (or second assistant director, or casting director) and ask—

at an appropriate moment, of course—how you can acquire a copy of the final show.

Once you have clips of the show, you (or someone you hire) can break it down to the most useful *clips* (very short sequences, measured in seconds) that show you at your most winsome—or ferocious, or glamorous, or funny, depending on how you want to be seen in it—which will later be edited into your reel, and on some occasions used by yourselves.

Failing to get footage of the show during its shoot, you can wait for it to air or stream and then lift it to your computer or, even more reliably, engage any number of video services to record it for you. Such a service (called "Aircheck"—available at actorsaccess.com/forms/aircheck/) will then provide you with a DVD of any TV show for a reasonable fee ($30 at the time of writing), and will actually upload individual *clips* (very short sequences of the show, measured in seconds) to your site, if you have one (see next section), for an additional per-minute fee. Some such services even maintain backlog digital files or tapes of your previously aired TV shows, and so can provide you with copies. Almost everything on television is available nowadays on demand or on streaming services of some sort. You can log onto the network website (e.g. nbc.com) and see if it's still on their site, or an alternative like Hulu, if it can be downloaded or inexpensively acquired through iTunes. CDs are always checking out past shows: while this book was in press, the creative team for the video streaming service Hulu's *The Path* cast an actor directly after seeing him in a reel from Showtime's *The Affair*.

When you've accumulated one or more suitable clips, you can then find any number of editing and duplication sites that will edit and produce your reel to your specifications. At the moment, actorsaccess.com, workingactors.com, and backstage.com list a number of such services in Los Angeles and New York. Such services will, under your supervision, convert your clips to the appropriate format, and then edit them as you direct (either with straight cuts or with fancier wipes, dissolves, freeze-frames, and so on). During the editing, they can put in titles, add your headshot, underscore the tape with music, and, when finished, label and package into a finished DVD, printing as many copies (dubs) as you want to pay for.

How much will all this cost? At the date of writing, $60 per hour is a common editing fee (with three to five hours a common standard), plus added fees for added creative services. Once you have such a reel, you can send it to any industry member that might want it. Or you can let CDs or directors watch it from a computer when and if they choose, after which you can email it to anyone who requests it. (Don't *ever* send one out unsolicited, however!)

And—which is increasingly common—your reel, or clips from it, may be *posted* as a performance video on one or more *websites* that you (or a service you contract) create and maintain.

The benefit of such posting is extraordinary: it allows your reel to be instantly transmitted to any agent or CD in the world—and it can be searched online by anyone who's looking for actors who meet your description. See the following section on "Your website" to investigate this crucial method of actor self-marketing, which has only come into its present dominance in the past few years.

Making your own reel

If you haven't yet landed any professional work, or what you have managed to do has never been recorded or has ended up on the cutting room floor, you can still make a reel by hiring a professional service company and having them produce it. You would be responsible for selecting and rehearsing the material yourself (with a partner, ordinarily), which would then be staged and taped in the service's studio or an available outdoor space. The service would provide the directing, camerawork, lighting, sound, and editing, all subject to your approval. But we must alert you at the outset that such privately prepared reels rarely attract the same interest—or have the same impact—as do the compilations of professional clips described in the above paragraphs. The fact is that the technical production work in even the least-admired professional TV shows is hard to match (and expensive to hire), and if the focus is fuzzy, the camera wobbly, the sound uneven, and the editing spotty, *even for one or two seconds*, the professional CDs watching it will, almost unconsciously, see your work as amateur. That this is *not your fault* and has nothing to do with your acting is, sadly, not going to change things. Thus, longtime CD Mike Fenton admits, "I will look at a reel only as long as it has professional work on it. That work can be student films, commercials, soap opera, documentaries, television, motion picture tests, but not taped stage work, and not something you paid somebody to film."

So, while we cannot particularly recommend this route—and certainly cannot recommend any specific professional companies that are engaged in producing such reels—you might give it a try if you have a good deal of money, skill, and determination to pursue it. In which case, *try to find the best video production company you can*! Search online for "video production companies" in Los Angeles and New York (and elsewhere if need be) that specialize in such reels, and ask your actor friends for suggestions. When you identify a likely studio, ask to see some of their existing reels: this will tell you far more than any fancy brochure, website, or sales talk.

If their reels look good (and if they don't show you any reels, head for the door), you can then ask your comprehensive questions about their service: where do they shoot? How long is the session? How large is the crew? How do they handle their audio? (Audio may be the most important consideration in choosing a studio—more demo reels are ruined by bad sound than by bad video.) And what quality of equipment—camera, audio, editing—do they have?

And, of course, how much will it cost? At the time of writing, the fees at top agencies such as Indigo Productions (in New York, L.A., and Chicago) begin at about $3,000 for a single (and simple) one- or two-minute scene, shot outdoors (i.e., in natural light and without a lighting designer or operator), and edited with straight cuts and a single title card. And this fee may grow exponentially with each addition: added pages, characters, or minutes; a musical underscore, or any sophisticated digital ("toaster") editing effects, such as wipes and dissolves, flips and tumbles, or multiple title cards. Such additions can easily escalate the cost well into multiple thousands of dollars. But local production companies can charge as little as $90 per hour or $650 per day.

If you have neither pro credits nor money, can you put something together with some friends at your school video lab or your home iMac? Well, yes, you can. There are plenty of first-rate, on-camera acting studios in New York and Los Angeles. If you can acquire some good work from a classroom project that shows you off well, it can sometimes prove useful in a pinch. Just be smart about what's good, what's professional, and what is going to be useful in showing you off to your fullest potential.

But let's be frank here: this is almost never a good idea. These amateur reels will be looked at if they were professional ones, not home movies of classroom scenes. It's not even clear that such home-made products are "better than nothing," for they may keep viewers from ever looking at you again (if they remember your name). But if you are fantastically good looking, or a rare and astonishing type that can be glimpsed in a few seconds, it may be worth a try.

So, realize that the best reels by far—as we said at the outset—will be those you aren't going to be able to make until you've begun to appear in professionally produced work. Or, at the very least, a fantastic student film by a graduate filmmaker. But then, you can go to town. And until then, you can get started.

Here's some final demo reel advice from the pros:

> Keep it short—discipline yourself! Individual clips should be 30 to 40 seconds at most; the total reel certainly shouldn't be more than two

minutes if it does not contain professional work, or three minutes if it is all professional work. (If they want more, they can always ask.)

Try to get a camera that New York CD Maribeth Fox suggests "is capable of creating compressed videos on a computer so CDs don't need to spend a long time downloading footage—if a self-tape takes me 10 minutes to download, you're out!"

Keep your titles and video effects simple and classy; you, not the editor, must be the star. "Don't let your website outshine you," says one classy and successful New York actor. So, while we've talked about dissolves and wipes, we don't necessarily recommend them.

Start and end with your full name on a blank title card. The most important aspect of a reel is that they remember whose it is.

Music can be important, but make sure it adds—not detracts—from the content and your acting.

Keep your character relatively consistent: Vary the moods and tempos, but not your basic image; don't try to be a one-person repertory company. Remember, this is not your grad school audition.

Look for shots "where you're laughing, crying, fighting, looking damn good, or turning away from or to the camera," not just where you're talking. (This good advice is from the website of Hollywood's Planet Video, one of the services that edit such reels.)

Don't get naked! "Sex sells, but it can sell you short," says a very attractive actress who knows what she's talking about.

If your reel is for a CD, just try to give him or her exactly what he or she wants. Agents and managers might want to see a full reel, but casting is more specific to the existing show. Give CDs exactly what they might be needing—whether it's comedy or drama. Split each scene into a separate clip on your reel and post only what is needed, ideally a specific scene that shows you off well in the light, with its own title and length indicated. This is known as a "scene clip"—the abbreviated form of a reel and the latest trend in 2016.

Finally, if any of your outtake video clips include a time code at the bottom (which is the running digital clock used in editing the final version), leave it *on*. It subliminally validates the clip's (and your) professionalism.

Slates

There's one reel we can mention that doesn't take a great deal of money or technical expertise: this is the *actor slate*, a very brief (generally seven seconds) clip of you speaking directly into the camera, and is usually put at the beginning of a demo reel. Since you use a fixed camera for this, there is no significant movement, the lighting and sound are relatively simple, and the production cost is minimal, you should make this a must. Contact actorsaccess.com (for which you must register, but can do so for free) and click onto "All about SlateShots," where you can see free samples of various slates, and also find out how to film your own or have them professionally done through their "SlateShot Affiliates" in New York, Chicago, Toronto, and L.A. The utility of such electronic slates (the term comes, of course, from the striped film clapper that introduces each take) is probably minimal, but it will get your face and voice on a globally transmittable video clip for a very reasonable cost.

Your website

You may create your *own* website, and/or your own, independently accessed webpage (URL) on an actor's website!

With such sites, or pages, you can *email* all your marketing materials—photos, résumés, and performance video/demo reels—with a few simple clicks of a mouse. And with some, you can search casting opportunities and *electronically submit yourself*—and your materials—to the CD mere minutes after the casting notice is posted. Indeed, your materials may be among those viewed by CDs you've not even contacted but who are "just fishing" for actors who may match your credentials. These reasons are why the actor's website/webpage has become one of the strongest self-marketing tools in the actor's portfolio in just the past few years.

There are three basic categories of such sites:

- independent ones that you create on your own (yourname.com)
- host-dependent "posting" sites where you post your materials on a service-provided webpage alongside those of other actors (such sites currently include actorsaccess.com, nowcasting.com, backstage.com, imdb.com, lacasting.com, nycasting.com, castingfrontier.com, and others, some of which require registration)
- general or social sites like YouTube or Facebook

Each of these categories—and each service—has its advantages and disadvantages, but you don't have to choose among them—you can maintain *any number of such sites or pages*, depending on your energy, patience, and pocketbook.

The *independent* site gives you the most flexibility—indeed, it gives you total flexibility. You can have it designed any way you like, and can use it to display your photos, résumé, demo reels, press clippings, biography, personal philosophy, anything you like. It can also reflect who you are as a person, which many actors think is important. (A suggestion: if you do make a broad personal website for casting purposes, keep your family and vacation pictures on pages wholly separate from your acting materials. Or better, create a separate site for personal—as opposed to professional—viewing.)

Creating an independent site can certainly be costly if you engage a professional designer, but most people we know think this is worth the investment in the long run, particularly if you have a busy career and lots to show. If you have one made, it should be attention-grabbing but not overly busy, and it should come up right away when your URL is entered; beware of sites that take 45 seconds to load, because that's longer than most casting directors will allocate to looking at them.

You'll also have to find a hosting service (such as GoDaddy.com) that can get you on the web with the unique domain name that this requires. (Clicking onto yourname.com would also work, but not if your name has already been taken.)

> ASIDE FROM ROBERT: Mine is a common name—and the robertcohen.com domain had already been picked up by a British cellist when I created my site. So, My website can be found at robertcohendrama.com, and this has worked out just fine.

The huge downside of the independent site is that no CD is simply going to stumble upon it; you've instead got to find ways to bring it to the attention of those you want to see it.

By itself, your independent site is only useful to include as a link on information you send out with your emails, postcards, photo-résumés, and the like. So, put the link on your résumé, on your personal letterhead, and above all in the "who's who in the cast" of theatre programs of shows you're in. (Don't be shy: Broadway actors increasingly put their website addresses in their *Playbill* bios.) Your independent site is useless for casting purposes unless you find a way to direct casting people to it.

Much more common are *host-dependent* sites—which are individual pages of managed, actor-oriented websites onto which, after paying a fee, you can post your résumé, photos, contact information, and reel.

Some of these are *inclusive* sites, meaning that anyone paying the fee may join: you do not need an agent, a manager, a union card, or any professional credits to sign on. Some of the best inclusive sites at present are actorsaccess.com and nowcasting.com.

Other host-dependent sites are *exclusive*, meaning that you must be a member of SAG, AFTRA, or Actors Equity; you can sign onto imdb.com (for which you must have a professional film or TV credit already on their site), nowcasting.com (where you must click onto "Actor Free Registration"), or playersdirectory.com if you are already registered on nowcasting.

There are other sites, both up-and-coming but also down-and-dirty, and among the latter are downright scams. CastingYou.com got an F rating from the Better Business Bureau, and InstantCast.com's website became inoperative after sending out mass emails teasing recipients with the lead-in "Richard Gere needs co-stars for his new drama! They're looking to cast talented actors like you!" We hope readers of this book receiving such tempting emails wouldn't think that Mr. Gere was hiding in the back of their college theatres to scout their performance of Juliet or Mercutio, but everyone should check such suspicious claims with ripoffreport.com, which has already filed over two million illegal reports and saved consumers more than 15 *trillion* dollars.

The main disadvantage of host-dependent sites is that you are restricted to the design and format of the host—no family photos here, please. But the advantages are big-time, and the major one is that since these sites are in various ways connected to casting calls and *breakdowns* (lists and descriptions of roles currently being cast, for stage plays as well as the more common film and TV openings—see next section), you can *electronically submit yourself* for consideration for any part you think you could fill. Thus, if you had been a member of Actors Access and on March 9, 2016 had seen this breakdown for the SAG feature film

> Female—18–65—Beautiful, Sexy, alluring as acting vulnerable to overpower her victims, deadly vampire.
> or
> Male—18–65—Sadistic, loves violence and uses it for his kill, deadly vampire.

you could, with a few clicks of your mouse, have put your photos, résumé, contact info, and one-minute performance video into the CD's computer in a matter of seconds, and been interviewing for a role in *Villainous* the following day!

A second advantage of the hosted site is that it will regularly be accessed by CDs and others in the occasional fishing expeditions that your individual site won't be in the stream for. This is particularly if you list specific attributes and skills (height, weight, hair color, ethnicity, sports played, accents performed, union affiliation) that can pass through sufficient filters to put you in consideration for certain roles matching those features. Putting "dreadlocks" onto your profile means you'll be among the relatively few actors—even without credits or SAG cards—who will be brought to the CD's attention for a part requiring them!

Finally, hosted sites are considerably less expensive than building your own, and on some sites (currently actorsaccess.com, nowcasting.com, and castingnetworks.com) you can begin your basic membership for free, paying only as you add or change photos and reels. Beyond the service charges that will eventually accrue, you don't have to engage a web designer or a hosting service, or, indeed, any other professional web expert.

To post your materials on any of these hosted sites, just log on and follow their directions. Since all such sites are changing very rapidly, some on a near-daily basis, there is no way we can predict which service will be best for you when you read this, but in 2017 Actors Access (actorsaccess.com), which has already been mentioned several times in these pages, has some distinct advantages for entry-level actors: first, it is inclusive and anyone can sign onto it, and second—more to the point—it is a subsidiary of Breakdown Services, which has since 1971 been the major collector and distributor (now through its adjunct, Breakdown Express) of the official cast breakdowns for virtually all professional films and TV shows being produced by U.S. companies. Actors Access is also directly linked to Showfax.com, the industry's major distributor of actor "sides" (script pages) that are used in professional auditions, so that the service's registrants are able to make instant submissions to projects being cast, and to instantly acquire the script sides they will need if selected to audition. (And signing onto Actors Access lets you sign on to Showfax.)

Other sites are hot on Actors Access's heels, however, and some have benefits that their rival doesn't. Now Casting (nowcasting.com) is currently its chief competitor, and has some technological advantages and a large and somewhat different pool of casting opportunities that Actors Access doesn't; it also now owns playersdirectory.com, which, in the print era, was the "bible" of actor-listing sources and is still the only place where you can literally "thumb through" the photos of thousands of "Leading Ladies," "Character Men," and the like. You can sign up for Now Casting's or Actors Access's free registrations for nothing, and then move upwards to their relatively inexpensive monthly fees ($21 in 2017 for Now Casting). And the Players Directory eBook allows CDs to bookmark pages, add notes, and save an actor's profile to an electronic file cabinet. And these Players Directories are given to CDs complimentary of Now Casting. So, it might be worth a shot at listing yourself. You can also post on backstage.com, the free online version of the major acting trade paper of that name, which, in addition to its film/ TV listings, remains the leading source of live theatre casting opportunities around the country, as well as the best source of actor-related articles and advice columns taken from its print edition. Castingfrontier.com is now a major site for actors in TV commercials, and will give you a barcode that you can have scanned into an auditioner's computer to instantly access your materials. And L.A. Casting and New York Casting (lacasting.com and nycasting.com) are also valuable sites for finding current opportunities, particularly in commercials.

All these sites have distinct advantages of their own—such as the capacity to put demo clips straight onto your résumé—as well as different categories of membership. So, check them all out closely when you're ready to make your move into the profession—and check on any that may have come online since this book was written. You might indeed want to register for—and maintain a presence on—two or three of these sites; most actors do, and the costs for the paid levels are not really exorbitant considering the exposure and information they provide.

Regardless of what site you create, make sure it is mobile friendly and can be viewed on any smartphone.

Social media

Finally, there are the *social networking sites*—Facebook, Twitter, Instagram—where you can begin to build your presence online and in addition optimize your "brand," build industry relationships and followers, and promote, essentially *for free*, your work, your photos, your résumés, and a lot else—along with more generic sites such as YouTube, where you can post your entire demo reel. Two nice bonuses of YouTube are that you can upload both your reel and also individual clips, directing interested parties (i.e., agents and CDs) to whichever URL you want them to look at, and you can check out how many people are viewing these materials whenever you wish. And, if your clip makes YouTube's "most viewed" or "most popular" lists, it could land your face on several thousand home—and casting office—computers and make you a cyber-celebrity.

Such social sites are often "cruised" by CDs. You only have to look at Darren Criss's original YouTube videos, which he sang in his apartment, to understand why he went on to star on television's *Glee* and then become the star of the National Tour of *Hedwig and The Angry Inch*. These videos are not linked to other acting-related services, such as electronic submissions. But a good Google search might send the right person to your name and link if you set it up properly. Facebook and YouTube will more properly serve as your adjunct posting spot rather than your primary one (currently Instagram), but they can become vital search tools for your visibility in a very crowded field.

Online video

Online video has also now become a popular way for stage actors to be seen. Bernard Telsey, one of New York's most famous CDs, launched what he named the YouTube Project in 2012, which allowed him to reach actors on a national and global scale. "It's almost like a continuous open call," he explained, since if actors don't have the financial means or the personal connections to get into an agency, they can send a tape to his company and somebody will watch it. New video technology has opened the door to undiscovered talent.

Facebook fanpages and Instagram

Unlike a personal Facebook page, a Facebook fanpage can be very useful for the young actor. A fanpage is a place where you can safely promote your work without sharing the latest picture of you hanging out with your drinking buddies, or personal photos of your family's pets. The fanpage can hold your headshot, résumé, press photos and reviews, and even a demo reel with which you can update your fans and followers on your most recent projects. This is hugely popular with actors on national tours, and even most Broadway shows have their own hashtags so that internet fans can locate their recent, current, and upcoming works. These can also be connected to your Instagram account (owned by Facebook), and are a common way to keep in touch and build your fan base. Indeed, budding young actors can watch their followers increase by the thousands with a single job, since Broadway groupies are rapidly (and rabidly!) following their favorite chorus boy or music theatre starlet.

Twitter

Got things to tweet? Then Twitter is your site of choice. Twitter is an online social networking service that enables users to send and read short 140-character messages called "tweets." Registered users can read and post tweets. Actors love to tweet and share their point of view on just about anything. This is particularly common with comedians, who have funny and astute things to say.

Breakdowns

Breakdowns—full character descriptions of roles currently being cast—are the next thing you need, but as an actor (and particularly as a would-be actor) you can't get them directly, at least not all of them.

When a major film, TV, or theatre show goes into production, the casting director prepares a "breakdown" of its roles, describing each, and distributing the resulting "breakdowns" to agents, managers, and, in some cases, the acting community at large. That intermediary, in the United States and Canada, is Breakdown Services, Ltd., which has had a virtual monopoly on these media since its 1971 founding. From its offices in New York, Los Angeles, and Vancouver, Breakdown Services distributes approximately 30 film and TV scripts a day, including TV episodics, pilots, feature films, movies for television, commercials, print projects, student films, industrials, reality TV, and both union and nonunion theatre productions, along with other types of projects, to talent representatives—agents and selected managers (those in the Talent Managers Association, or those who submit three written references from authorized SAG agencies)—around the country, after which the talent representatives, based on the breakdowns, submit their clients to the CDs via their BreakdownExpress subsidiary.

Unless you're a talent representative, or registered on ActorsAccess or Showfax, you can't get the film/TV breakdowns directly; however, CDs may authorize Breakdown Services to release some or all of their shows' roles online to actors they're hoping to assist—which certainly suggests that the $16 fee per half-year is a reasonable price to get them directly. Here are three examples of small or highly specialized roles or projects that represent the kinds of roles beginning-level actors are, by far, most likely to get.

> ARMY WIVES, Episode 403. Lt. Brenda Foster. Female, any ethnicity, mid 20's. Lost arm and shoulder from IED. From Chicago, with Midwestern values and attitude. Attractive. Strong personality but also overwhelmed by what has happened to her. No accent. Co-star. NOTE: seeking (arm) amputee actresses.

> FUERZA BRUTA, Off Broadway. Non-jurisdictional production. Seeking union and nonunion, men and women, early 20's–late 30's. All ethnicities. Should be charismatic, dynamic and in excellent physical shape for this physically demanding show; must be comfortable in a bathing suit. Preferred performers with experience in one or more of the following: tumbling, dance, acrobatics, gymnastics, and/or aerial acrobatics.

ON CAMERA TEASER PRESENTATION. Seeking strong young actors with great improvisational skills to play suburban teens circa the 1970s. Actors must be comfortable with strong sexual content and look convincingly of the time period. Must have the ability to portray the range of adolescent emotions in the midst of an outbreak of a mysterious STD that only affects teenagers.

Not all breakdowns are submitted through the websites mentioned in the above paragraphs, of course, and many others—particularly for stage work but also for major roles in films and TV—are not posted on websites at all. Some, however, are occasionally mentioned in the pages of *Backstage*, the country's major trade paper for stage actors on both coasts and in-between. In fact, Actor's Equity absolutely requires advance mentions for professional stage roles!

Can *you* acquire the breakdowns for those major roles in plays, films, and TV shows currently being cast? The answer, now, is yes—and we have told you how. But remember to keep your wits about you. It can be a healthy way to motivate yourself and find out what's going on in the business so you can get yourself into it. But some actors have found it an unhealthy habit that spirals into a rabbit hole of self-doubt and insecurity. Viewing all the things you might not have access to can be tricky. Cinderella knowing about the ball but not being invited to it can lead to frustration. It can be super-challenging having information about things you can't or don't have access to. So, put knowledge to good use and focus on how it can lead to success.

Unions

Money and industriousness will get you everything mentioned up to this point in this chapter. From this point on, however, the bar is going to be raised a bit. From here on in, apart from a few exceptions, you will need to prove yourself as well as simply pay the bill. Which is to say, you will have to get into one or more of the acting unions.

Your union affiliation, as we have said, goes at the top of your résumé. That may strike a note of terror in your mind—for how do you get into the union? You are probably already aware of the great "cycle of impossibility" that defines union membership: you can't get work until you are a member of the union, and you can't be a member of the union until you get work. Well, that's not exactly true anymore. (It never was true, of course; it only *seemed* true.) You can get into the unions now somewhat more easily than in previous years, but union membership may not mean quite as much as it did then.

You have to understand at the outset that it's the *job* of unions to keep you out. That's one of the main reasons why there *are* unions: to keep you out of the picture (literally and figuratively). Unions protect their existing members, to whom you represent a threat—and, to be brutally frank, a cheap threat.

You will come to be pleased that there are unions. They will protect *you* if you become an actor. If there were no actors' unions, actors wouldn't get minimum salaries, wouldn't receive health benefits, wouldn't have fair working conditions, and wouldn't have pensions when they retire. Just try one of the dozen non-Equity tours on the road right now. It is not without reason that some of Broadway's biggest and most recent hits then find great success on the road in non-Equity productions. *Bullets Over Broadway* and *Once* were both out on tour at this time of writing—and very cheaply; the salaries and working conditions are well below Equity's Broadway standards. But for the young actor, these road tours are often a fertile training ground to hone their skills and garner experience.

And do you really think theatre owners would come up with retirement programs for actors on their own initiative? No. Theatre owners have their hands full planning next year's season, and the unions take care of the actors' long-range welfare. So, the unions aren't the enemy, even though they may seem lined up against you at the beginning.

There are now two principal actors' unions, already referred to often in these pages.

Actors' Equity Association (or simply "Equity," at actorsequity.org), is the union for all professional stage actors and stage managers; in 2016 it had more than 50,000 members in good standing. Founded in 1913, it's the oldest performers' union in America, and has its main headquarters in New York, along with branches in Los Angeles, Chicago, Orlando, and San Francisco.

Actors working professionally in film, TV, and radio are unionized by SAG-AFTRA (sagaftra.org), which since 2012 combines the previously separated SAG (the Screen Actors Guild) and AFTRA (the American Federation of Television and Radio Artists). In 2016, the now-joined union represented roughly 160,000 actors, announcers, broadcasters, and other media professionals, which included about 35,000 Equity members who worked on both stage and screen. The SAG portion of the combined SAG-AFTRA oversees all film and filmed television, including filmed commercials, while the AFTRA half covers professional performers in videotaped television (including most soap operas), radio, sound recordings, non-broadcast/industrial programming, and new technologies such as interactive programming and CD-ROMs, as well as sportscasters, game show hosts, political commentators, and program announcers. SAG is a national union, with its headquarters in Los Angeles, where more than half its members are based (roughly a quarter are in New York, and the rest are in 18 other jurisdictions in the country). AFTRA, despite its national name, is actually a federation of local unions.

These actors' unions are joined by the American Guild of Musical Artists (AGMA), which covers dancers and opera performers, and the American Guild of Variety Artists (AGVA), which, though pretty moribund these days, in theory covers Las Vegas and other variety and amusement park performers. All of these unions constitute a loose association known as the quaintly named Associated Actors and Artistes of America (the Four "A's"). All also operate under American Federation of Labor–Congress of Industrial Organizations (AFL–CIO) charters. SAG-AFTRA, particularly, emphasizes its AFL–CIO constituent status to achieve greater political clout than it could achieve on its own.

Joining a union

How can *you* join a union?

Method one, the cleanest and most effective way by far if you can swing it, is simply to be offered a "principal or speaking role" (i.e., not an extra) by a union producer—that is, a producer willing to sign you to a union contract. In that happy event, the union will be obligated to let you in, subject only to your submitting an application and paying a hefty initiation fee ($1,100 for Equity, $3,000—with two-year loans available—for SAG-AFTRA in 2016), plus a first installment on your semi-annual dues (which are dependent on your salary, but a minimum of $59 semi-annually for Equity, and a bit more for SAG-AFTRA at the time of writing).

Do you *have* to join the union just because you have a union job? Not immediately. A provision of the 1947 Labor–Management Relations Act (universally known as "Taft–Hartley" after its principal authors) permits you to work in a single union production for up to 30 days without joining a union—but on the 31st day you have to sign up or you're out of the show. You have to be a good actor—hardworking and lucky—for this to happen. And they have to want you above anyone else.

You can also be hired for two shorter film or television shootings without joining, but on the third assignment you've got to sign up—this is known as the "three strikes and you're in" clause! The Taft–Hartley provisions—which are closely monitored by the casting offices and unions—may prove helpful for entry-level actors who might not be able to manage to cover the initiation fee until they have a couple of paid engagements under their belts.

Method two is working as an extra in a SAG-AFTRA film or TV production. This can earn you a "background voucher" each day that you work; earn three of them and you can apply for an "open" membership. If you're lucky, you can also join a union if, while working in a non-speaking background job, you are given a line of dialogue that upgrades your role to that of a "principal." Believe us, this actually happens!

Method three is to "sister into" one union by being a working member of another. Under the "sister" provision, anyone who has been a member of SAG for a year or more can join Equity, and anyone in Equity for a year can join SAG. But AFTRA members have no such privileges unless they have been an AFTRA member for a full year *and have actually worked and been paid under an AFTRA contract.* Since you needn't have worked professionally to join AFTRA, neither SAG nor Equity recognizes it as a true "sister" for membership purposes.

Method four is what is unofficially called the SAG "voucher system," whereby "background actors" [i.e. extras] can join the union "upon proof of employment as a SAG-covered background player at full SAG rates and conditions for a minimum of three work days" (if you're interested, check www.sag.org for current info).

The problem in taking advantage of the voucher provision is that the majority of background actors are nonunion extras, who are hired at much lower than the full SAG rate, and if you're nonunion, this will include you. But here's the catch: the SAG contract with L.A.-based producers requires that, in films, the first 50 background players must be paid SAG rates. If on a given day fewer than 50 SAG members show up, enough non-SAG performers must be bumped up to SAG rates to reach the minimum 50 (presuming the producer wants 50 or more extras that day). Members so bumped up not only get the extra pay, but also receive a "voucher" indicating they have worked at SAG rates. Get three of these "SAG vouchers" and you can join the union! (The same procedure works in TV shoots, except that the minimum number of SAG extras required there is 19.)

How do you become the actor who gets the voucher? Work often as an extra, arrive early, and get to know the assistant directors (ADs) every chance you get. Let them see how dedicated, uncomplaining, and hardworking you are. It's the AD who usually does the picking, and they'll most likely give their available vouchers to actors they like, and like to see on their sets. (We should enter a caveat here: although this voucher system has been in operation for well over a decade, it is easily corruptible, and "SAG vouchers" have recently been surreptitiously sold for cash for up to $350 on Craigslist. So, this system is under constant scrutiny by the SAG and the producers, and may be revised or eliminated by the time you read this.)

Method five, for live theatre only, is Equity's *Membership Candidate Program,* which is a more logical stepping-stone into the profession. This program permits you to become eligible for Equity membership by working as a nonunion actor or understudy for 50 weeks at any Equity-approved participating theatre operating under Equity's LORT, stock, or dinner theatre contracts. You needn't be paid any set salary for this qualifying work (indeed, you must pay a $100 registration fee to the union), and you don't receive any Equity benefits: during this time, you're an Equity Membership Candidate (EMC), but not an Equity member. (And if you are a SAG-AFTRA member, you can work as an EMC for 25 weeks without joining Equity, if that were important to you.)

If you can secure such employment, you simply need to register with the union as an EMC; your $100 fee will be credited toward your eventual initiation. When you complete your 50 weeks, which need not be consecutive and may be accumulated over any period of time, you can join the union at any time over the next five years by simply paying the balance of your initiation fee and your first installment dues. Equity recommends that your Membership Candidate application be filed as soon as you start your work. Your application is an affidavit of nonprofessional status and certifies that you "are interested in obtaining training for the theatre and/or intend to make a career in the professional theatre." You can then list "Equity Membership Candidate" in the space on your résumé where union affiliation goes; it isn't union membership, but it's something. See actorsequity.org/membership/emc.asp for full (and updated) details, and a list of participating Equity theatres.

Note also that your "open" AFTRA membership, obtained by method two, may actually *prevent* you from becoming an EMC! Equity looks dimly on AFTRA members who have signed into AFTRA simply by being an extra, and requires such AFTRA (or even former AFTRA) members to make a "special request" for permission to join the Membership Candidate Program. "This request must contain a copy of your résumé and a detailed description of your professional work history," Equity states. Only after such a review will Equity waive your "method two" AFTRA card and permit you to come aboard through its Membership Candidate Program.

Method six is enrolling in a graduate program that provides you with your Equity card upon graduation. These programs (The Old Globe theatre in San Diego or Columbia University in New York City, for example) are typically connected with professional Equity houses that can assist in this. The Old Globe, for example, employs its rising graduates with an Equity contract in its summer Shakespeare season. Columbia's School of the Arts partners itself with the Classic Stage Company in New York City to provide educational workshops and performances all over the city and beyond. These are just two examples of graduate training assisting with the guarantee of the golden ticket of an Equity card upon graduation.

Finally, method seven, which is not really a method at all but is the way most people make it, is to keep battering at the doors every way you can. You can be seen, you can be auditioned, and you can be cast professionally without being in a union. It's harder, but it's obviously possible. It happens every day, and the pages that follow contain a lot of advice on how to do it. There are doors that are closed, but there are always keyholes to peek through. Talent rises. And remember, if they find you and decide they want you, they'll hire you—they'll even pay a fine to hire you. No actor's lack of union affiliation ever stopped a producer from trying to make a better movie or a better play or—let's face it—a bigger gross.

And there may be new ways to join a union by the time you read this. A few years back, 1,600 persons were able to join SAG by volunteering 80 hours on the SAG picket line during a strike or by turning down—walking away from—a principal role in a scab (union-defying) commercial in which they had been cast. So, check the union websites, listed above, for any recent updates.

Should you join the union?

Should you join a union? Yes, but …

It would be odd *not* to join the union if you had the chance, but there are some things to think about.

First, you have to understand that being a member of the union means that you *cannot* accept nonunion work. Indeed, this is the famous "Rule Number One" of SAG-AFTRA (which, since it now extends to worldwide production, has been renamed "Global Rule One"). Indeed, the SAG-AFTRA site takes it "very seriously; violating it can result in disciplinary action ranging from reprimands to fines to expulsion." Completing your 50 weeks in an EMC Program means the same thing. Thus, being in Equity, or having completed your weeks, means you can't join, for example, the non-Equity acting company of a Shakespeare festival. So, you're left home by the telephone while your friends are braving the Bard in Utah or Oregon. Another recent actor out of school got a call to join the non-Equity company of Shakespeare in the Park, but had already been given the opportunity to join Equity through a theatre's educational teaching program. This situation, for the young actor, can be both a blessing and a curse. Many a non-Equity opportunity can arise for the young actor. As a union member, your hands are a bit tied unless you can find your way around (or beneath) your union's bylaws, which is decidedly *not* recommended.

And second, more and more touring of current (2016) New York productions, such as *The Color Purple, Fiddler on the Roof, Legally Blonde, Grease,* and *Spring Awakening,* is going the way of modern economics and moving to non-Equity contracts in 2016–17. So, weigh your options depending upon your skill set! This can be a dilemma especially for the music theatre performer, as there are so many opportunities for the young actor starting out. Make sure you weigh your options before moving too quickly on any decision.

And finally, you will have to front the initiation fees and dues. But hey, let's get serious here. Obviously, if you are going to be a professional, you're going to have to pay professional dues. We don't have to tell you that, do we? And if you don't have the money yet at hand, the union will provide you with a reasonable payment plan so that you can "pay your dues" over an extended period, perhaps by finding flexible work as a dog walker or baby sitter or doing similar free-time but cash-producing duties.

So, unless you are absolutely aching to accept that non-Equity summer acting position in Colorado or Cape Cod (in which case you need only defer your membership application and sign up afterwards), you will want to join Equity at the very first opportunity, simply because your new union membership will give you an implicit priority within your field—and an *explicit* priority in the open casting auditions ("cattle calls") for virtually all Broadway, off-Broadway, regional theatre, and national touring productions. Of course, you'll have to line up at six in the morning to sign up for (and then wait around for) your all-important audition slot—knowing that the Equity rulebook only requires that slot to be one minute long! But that minute can be the golden entrée to your budding career. And make no mistake, casting—even of unknowns—takes place in such calls. Your Equity card is also the single best way to get your foot in the door of New York casting offices and expose you to creative teams you would rarely encounter without such access.

Union membership also supports the efforts that will make your professional life easier: efforts to negotiate minimum wages and maximum working conditions, for example. And you're going to want to have easy access to the information sources that unions provide, including their own membership section on their websites, plus their magazines, lobbies, bulletin boards, housing notices, hotline telephone numbers, seminars, meetings, and informal networking services.

But the main factors concerning union membership might be psychological. An Equity or SAG card makes you *feel* better about yourself and your career, and if you feel better you'll probably act better. Remember that "talent" is largely self-confidence, and card-carrying unionism, in this field, breeds professional pride. Rightly or wrongly, you'll walk a bit taller—and probably look a bit larger in other people's eyes as well. The fact is that most folks in show business simply assume, probably at an unconscious level, that only union membership conveys "big league" status and that nonunion actors are somewhere in the "minors." That's hardly the truth—or hardly the entire truth—but why fight it when you have so many other battles yet to win?

And if the Utah Shakespearean Festival wants you and then finds out you're not a member of Equity, they may just give you an Equity contract. You never know until you ask.

And if you're still not in the union? Don't despair. As your co-author James says, "Young actors constantly ask me if I care about their lack of union affiliation. I tell them I never pay attention to that stuff. It is the last thing I think about when casting for a TV show or play; if I want to hire you, I will find a way to do it!" So, be of good cheer.

Talent representatives

Even when you're in the union, there can be a huge gulf between you and the actual casting people. The major roles—both on stage and certainly in films and TV—are rarely cast through open call announcements in the trades. Most such roles are cast through auditions for which you don't submit your materials but *are submitted* by somebody else. That somebody is your *talent representative*, or more simply, your *representation*.

Your representation comes in two very different forms: *agents* and *managers*. The professional activities—and hence value to you—of each group are changing even as you read this. You should, therefore, read this section quite carefully.

Basically, *agents* are responsible for finding you work and negotiating your contract for such work, while *managers* are responsible for planning and guiding your career. These differentiated responsibilities are not only a matter of custom, but are also regulated by law. There are huge areas of overlap, however. Each advises you on your career, each seeks to help you develop contacts with useful people, and each takes a commission (a percentage of your acting income) for services rendered.

But they do these things in different ways that are sometimes complementary and sometimes not. Should you have both an agent and a manager? Neither? One or the other? And if so, which one? To the extent that such decisions are in your hands, your criteria will be both personal and professional. Let's look closely at the differences.

Agents are licensed by the state in which they work. In California, licensing is by the California Labor Commission, operating under the Talent Agencies Act (you can see if any California agency is CLC licensed at dir.ca.gov); in New York, it's by the New York City Department of Consumer Affairs. And most agents are also certified by their official organization, ATA—the Association of Talent Agents (agentsassociation.com)—which maintains negotiated franchise agreements with Actors Equity and SAG-AFTRA. (ATA's longstanding franchise agreement with SAG expired in 2002, and while that agreement has not been renewed, its main tenets are still adhered to by both parties.) For each of their certifications, agencies must pass rigid qualification tests, be bonded, adhere to stiff guidelines, and pay fees. Having acquired their license and franchise, agents are then legally authorized to submit actors to CDs and negotiate their clients' resulting contracts, for which they receive a commission of 10% of the client's salary or fee for that role.

Managers play quite a different role—in principle, at least—since they are legally prohibited both from actually submitting clients to casting offices and from negotiating contracts. Rather, their role is to advise the actor and shape his or her career. In answer to the question "What is a Talent Manager?" the Talent Managers Association (TMA—at talentmanagers.org) says that he or she "is a professional engaged in advising and counseling talent ... in every facet of their career." For doing this, your manager will receive a negotiated commission of 10% to 15% for all the work you book—regardless of whether they were directly involved in landing you the job! most managers work on a sliding scale depending upon how well you do, which means 15% of your earnings up to $50,000 during a one-year period, but allowing their commission to drop to 10% for what you make beyond that. And don't forget they will take commission from *all* of your actor earnings, including theatrical, commercial, voiceovers, and such, whether they helped book you in them or not.

When you sign with an agent, you are generally offered a one-year to three-year contract with the option of terminating it after 91 days if you have not received any work from the relationship. When you sign with a manager, you are generally offered a three-year contract, since they are committing themselves to you on a more long-term basis.

The basic idea of having two representatives—if you do—is that while your agent handles the practical aspects of your day-to-day casting opportunities (reading the daily breakdowns of new scripts, submitting you for selected roles in them, and negotiating your contract if you are cast), your manager, with far fewer clients to serve, helps you shape your long-term career: advising you on putting together your package of photos, résumés, and reels, helping you select the right roles to advance your presence in the profession, and shaping a stronger visibility for you among the CDs, directors, and producers that he or she presumably is regularly meeting at both professional and social events.

But the dividing line between agents and managers is not as clearly drawn in reality as this description implies, and is, in fact, getting fuzzier every year. Since our previous edition, most managers have become eligible to receive official script breakdowns (cast descriptions) that had previously gone only to agents (in order to receive them legally, they must be members of the TMA or have written endorsements from three agencies), and they have been quietly submitting their clients—as well as lobbying for them—in informal settings and sometimes even in formal ones: calls, emails, and office visits. Since managers are neither licensed nor franchised by anyone, and since the SAG-ATA franchise agreement has expired, perhaps permanently, the legal boundaries between the two groups have become increasingly murky. While the California Supreme Court unanimously upheld the Talent Agencies Act's prohibition on managers procuring employment for their clients in 2008, the punishment for doing so (withholding of the manager's commission) was essentially removed—with the court holding that an "isolated instance of procurement" would not automatically mean that the manager couldn't be paid for doing it! The Court also begged the California legislature to rewrite the law, so it appears that agents and managers will be overlapping their duties even more in the coming years.

Still, certain distinctions will probably continue. In Los Angeles, the agent (at least) will remain virtually indispensable for *regularly working* actors in TV and film. Managers can be immensely helpful in Hollywood, but they are not as crucial for the entry-level performer as agents are. In New York, it's more of a toss-up. Agents are never essential for live theatre, and even smaller roles on television are often cast without the help of agency submissions. In New York, the most important representative will be the person who is most passionate about you—and about advancing your career—regardless of his or her official title.

> ASIDE FROM JAMES: One actress I know, Allison Layman, got out of grad school without an agent at first, but reached out and managed to get her roles in the old-fashioned way—by making daily contacts with top-ranking casting directors and getting a great reputation reading opposite auditioning actors in CD call-backs. In her first year out of school, she had managed to book a Broadway play as an understudy, get cast on a

new hot TV series, work the regional circuit working steadily, leading her to a top tier talent agent—signed, sealed and delivered.

The bottom line: every serious actor should make a serious effort to get agent representation. You can survive without it, but not for long. Veteran CD Mike Fenton, with the frankness of someone 45 years in his trade, admits that it's "impossible" for an actor to see him without an agency referral. "I don't kid actors and I won't kid you: I can only see you when you are represented by an agent who opens the door." There aren't enough hours in the day, Fenton confesses, for him to even open the envelopes containing the résumés of self-submitting actors.

So, try to get an agent. Then think about getting a manager. The next two sections describe in more detail what these folks can (and can't) do for you.

Agents and agencies

No character in the theatre or film industry arouses such contradictory attitudes as the agent. To the beginning actor, without contacts and without credits, the agent appears as a savior: the ultimate path to fame, fortune, and career. Actors fall all over themselves trying to get an agent to "represent" them, to "submit" them, to demonstrate their brilliance to the casting moguls, to do their hatchet work, spade work, telephoning, and interviewing.

To the established actor, however, the agent is often the devil incarnate, the ubiquitous middleman with no interests—artistic or personal—except the inevitable 10% cut. A famous actor once paid his agency a commission of more than $10,000 in pennies, hauled up in an armored truck. Lawsuits, contract breaking, and both actual and virtual theft ("stealing your money" and "stealing your trust," says author K. Callan) are unfortunately common factors of this volatile relationship.

Most agents are somewhere between saviors and thieves, however. For actors, the agent is at least an invaluable aid, and at most a virtual necessity. Therefore, it's necessary to understand the agent's—and agency's—function.

An agent (the word comes from the Greek *agein*, "to drive") pushes forward (yes, "drives") your career, making his or her own income solely to the extent that he or she helps you make yours. The agent's job is to get you employment and to negotiate the best possible salary for you. In return, the agent earns a percentage of what you earn, ordinarily 10% of what you receive through the agent's overtures. The agent *does not charge a fee*. (If an agent proposes a fee, he or she isn't an agent!) If you don't work, the agent doesn't get paid. This creates a tremendous incentive for the agent to produce on your behalf.

Even the 10% commission doesn't always kick in at lower income levels: in SAG-AFTRA work, the union will require you to be paid at least 10% more than "scale" so that your agent's commission won't drag your fee down below minimum SAG standards, while Equity only permits a 5% commission on salaries less than the lowest off-Broadway contract—$566 per week in 2016. (This is one reason why agents aren't as involved in stage work as they are in film: they don't get paid as much or as often.) As a beginner, then, agent's commissions aren't going to break your back, and you should certainly seek such a valuable business partner.

The role and importance of agents and agencies vary significantly not only between stage and camera actors, but also between New York and Hollywood. For stage work, the agent is an important factor in many casting situations, particularly for leading actors; in films and TV, the agent is *crucial* for just about everybody. Thus, in Los Angeles, you simply *must* have an agent, preferably one with whom you have a signed, exclusive contract, if you hope to get serious work in films or television. In New York, the situation is quite a bit freer, and the relationships between agents and actors are generally less formal; while it is standard to start out with a single agent, you may also be represented by several on an unsigned, freelance basis.

What does an agent do for you? Basically, the agent submits your name, and your materials, to CDs for those roles for which you can't submit yourself electronically—which includes virtually all the main roles in professional theatre, film, and television. Your agent can also arrange private interviews and sometimes "general auditions" for you with CDs and others. Obviously, these interviews will be several steps above the cattle-call situations that you (and everyone else) have read about in the trades.

Why can't you arrange all these auditions and interviews yourself? For three reasons:

1. You don't have the breakdowns, so don't know the parts.
2. You don't have the contacts, so don't know the casting people.
3. You don't have the credentials, so most casting people won't see you without an agent's recommendation.

Therefore, you should do everything you can to get an agent to represent and submit you. How? Ask your actor friends what agents they may know and recommend, and who might consider you—particularly if those pals are not in your age or sex group, and won't worry that you could replace them. Look up agencies in phone books and theatre magazines. And, if you are a member of Actors Equity Association (AEA) but without an agent, contact Agent Access Auditions (AAA—and operated by Actors Equity) to get a free audition.

Generally (always in L.A., and more often than not in New York), you want a formalized agency arrangement, usually with an exclusive contract. You'll then redo your website, résumés, and web postings, listing the agency logo, email address, and phone number as your new point of contact; perhaps get some new photos made. He or she will then search through the breakdowns—and whatever other casting information is available to the agency. (Lots of scripts never turn up in the breakdowns, and lots of parts are written into TV shows at the last minute; a good agent is always hustling for this kind of information.) Then the agent will submit you to the appropriate producers or CD for projects you might have a crack at getting into.

If a casting person bites, he or she will call or email the agent, the agent will call you, and an interview and possibly an audition will be set up—not necessarily at your convenience, of course. You will be given whatever information the agent can get about the part. A SAG rule says you must have 24 hours' lead time to read the script, but this doesn't always happen; occasionally you will get a call on "the day of," and you should be prepared.

The interview and audition both depend on you. If you come through the audition and the inevitable call-backs with flying colors, somebody will call the agent back.

Here's another critical step: your agent and the CD will negotiate your salary. Surprisingly, perhaps, you may have little say in it. If all goes well, your agent will get you the best salary the producer is willing to offer; the agent will then call you and tell you the terms. When you get paid, you will give your agent 10% of your gross payment (your fee before tax deductions). Or, more commonly, the production company will make its payment to your agency, which will take its 10% of the gross and send you the balance.

So, the actor–agent relationship is a good one when it works, and most of the time it *does* work. You are spending your time perfecting your craft, and your agent is hustling up and down Sunset Boulevard or Seventh Avenue looking for your future job.

But, of course, there are the inevitable wrinkles. For example, the agent can ignore you. An agent can take you on with marvelous promises and never call you again. When this happens, you question why the agent took you on in the first place. What may have happened is that the next day the agent may have recommended to producers five of his or her other clients, who were just like you but with more experience, or had thought he or she had found someone just like you but "better." Or the agent had the best intentions in the world but turned out not to be very connected or powerful. There can be *any number* of reasons why an agent takes you on but can't find you any work, and it happens all the time. It takes a lot for the CD to pick up that phone call and agree to see a new client, after all, and it finally comes down to a numbers game where the odds are, well, not always in your favor.

So, if you feel ignored—you may just be out of luck. If you haven't signed a contract, just start looking for somebody else. If you have signed a contract, and your agent is no longer sounding optimistic (or returning your phone calls), know that standard SAG-AFTRA-approved contracts allow you to terminate your representation if you have not received 10 days of work in your first 151 days or in any subsequent 91-day period; for AEA, the stipulation is no work for 90 days. In either case, if the agent isn't working out you can probably negotiate an amicable withdrawal sooner than those policies specify.

Also, the agent can promote you for the wrong roles. Agents are not simply clearing offices; they are second-guessers. They do their own breakdowns, of course; you need to make sure they don't break *you* down. "I admit, we play God," confesses one. Well, they *have* to. An agent can't send 50 clients for a single reading—he or she would never get a call again. Remember, most agents know what they're doing, most are objective about your chances, and most probably know how to market you best. But sometimes they don't. (You may be offended at the terms agents use: you are part of their "stable" of talent, you are "marketed" like a cabbage, you are a "juvenile female" instead of an actress—you will have to learn to live with this, too.)

Another wrinkle is that the agent can be too greedy on your behalf. An actor who sings and plays the guitar was offered a terrific contract at a prestigious New York nightclub, where many celebrities got their starts. He had, however, recently signed with an agent who persuaded him he should get more money. He demanded a higher price, as she had advised, and the offer was immediately withdrawn; he never had a second chance. (Shed no tears; he's now a major TV director.) Other agents go well beyond persuading you to overreach your salary potential; they demand it in your name without even consulting you. No matter that you would work for free to get that first credit, your agent may negotiate you right out of it by demanding an extra $200. You may see this as just the chance you take—after all, the agent is interested in the same thing that you are, right? Not exactly. The agent is interested in your *income*, which is not always the same as your artistic and career growth. The best agents are interested in that too; but the greedy ones want their cut and they want it now. Sympathize with them; they pay big-time rental costs. But be alert. Your best interests and theirs are not always exactly the same. The final option is yours, if you demand it. Gary Shaffer, CD for various movies-of-the-week, advises: "If you want to be an actor, have your agent submit you for everything. Don't worry about pay. Tell him not to turn down *anything.*"

Finally, an agent can simply give you bad advice. In this, the agent is no more guilty than anybody else you may come across, but it hurts more when your agent advises you badly, because you feel obligated to take the advice.

In fact, you probably *are* obligated to take it if you want the agent to help you. But the agent is not always the most objective observer of the industry. Remember, some agents are former (or failed) actors, and sometimes they have their own axes to grind—and they may just grind them on you. Some are savvy business people with sharp acumen but little artistic sense. Heck, they may even be in a bad mood. Understand that, despite their savior status in some aspirants' minds, agents do not live a heavenly life. They spend most of their time nagging casting people, working their way through studio phone trees, bugging receptionists for scraps of information and being put on hold; and sometimes they will take out their frustration on their clients, which means on you. So, in their offices, *they* know all the answers: how you should act, what your pictures should look like, what acting teacher you should study with, how right you are for what role, and how much you should weigh. Now, in all honesty, your agent is *probably* right, but the *degree* of probability is not as great as most agents would have you believe.

That said, we certainly don't want to paint a bad picture of agents. There are many outstanding and expert agents on both coasts. You just have to be lucky enough to land one.

Knowing the wrinkles, should you try to get an agent? Of course you should. The agent is on the inside of the business, and you aren't. Some are more careful, likable, honest, and well known than others, but all franchised agents have access to important contacts and information that you don't. In New York, most important casting is done through agencies; in Hollywood, virtually *all* casting is. Indeed, in Hollywood the agent has virtually become a producer, so involved have the agencies grown in packaging and planning film and television productions. Forget the cigar-chomping, ex-vaudevillian image; Hollywood agents now tend to be college graduates and business people. They are the power brokers of the film world.

Managers

Why should you look for a manager as well as an agent—or instead of an agent—particularly when the manager can't negotiate contracts, can't officially submit you, may not even get breakdowns, and then charges you more? "Manager, agent, manager, agent—What's the difference? Five percent!" says veteran Bernie Brillstein, who's been both.

A talent manager, in theory at least, serves you more individually, more personally, and with a greater interest in your long-term future. That is, in fact, Brillstein's "big difference" if it proves to be the case. An agent and manager we recently spoke to broke it down in these simpler terms: "The manager is the one that will go through your wardrobe and tell you what skirt to wear; the agent—not so much!" Your manager should have far fewer clients and much more time for each of them. He or she is interested not so much in your next job but in the whole arc of your professional career, and may eventually become your long-term counselor, health advisor, personal assistant, loyal backer, and the charter of your unique professional destiny in a complex field of endeavor. He or she may even become your producer. Emily Gerson-Saimes, manager at the time to actress Claire Danes, produced the award-winning movie *Temple Grandin*. Both won Emmys for their work.

So, while your agent may be more focused on "booking" your next job and collecting an immediate commission, your manager is, at least in theory, trying to make that job one that will propel you into bigger and better ones and is trying to steer you away from jobs that will stall your career. Thus, literature from the TMA describes its members as working in conjunction with "your agents, publicists, business managers, attorneys and all others," functioning "as facilitator and coordinator of the efforts and activities of [your] entire team."

And that's indeed what they should be doing. Actors often feel that they need such counsel, perhaps to guard them against their own short-term impulses. Early in her career, the late actress Jill Clayburgh, considering herself a member of "the first generation of feminism and the New Hollywood," turned down the title role of the big Sally Field hit, *Norma Rae*, for a Bernardo Bertolucci art film, and saw her career decline precipitously. "I didn't [then] think very hard about the choices that I made," Clayburgh admitted in a recent *Los Angeles Times* story. "We didn't have managers in those days. My God, what kind of person would have a manager? After all, you have agents and you're paying them 10%!" But after watching the later careers of Julia Roberts, Meg Ryan, and Sandra Bullock take off, Clayburgh believed the subsequent generation of actresses had "better master plans."

Do managers actually help you get work? Well, yes, "that's why they hire us," says the TMA. The best managers are able to help get you work through their personal contacts and influence. If your manager is lunching with producers and attending Dodgers games with TV network executives, you're probably in good hands. Look for great enthusiasm on your behalf, subtle understanding of the entertainment media, personal winsomeness and charisma, and, above all, a whole lot of industry clout if you're looking for a great manager.

Since managers (unlike agents) are not certified or regulated, you need to look very closely at this decision, however. Here are some things to be aware of and watch out for:

- Managers hustle for their clients, but they also hustle *for* clients. There are more than twice as many talent management companies than talent agencies in Los Angeles, for example. This should make you suitably suspicious of unexpected come-ons, particularly since they get half again as much in commissions.
- The TMA includes only a fraction of the management companies now in business, and not necessarily the most important ones: 3Arts, Brillstein Entertainment, Management 360, and so on. The organization, therefore, does not really represent the profession to the extent that the acting unions or ATA do.
- Fringe management companies can simply be scam operations, because no franchising or licensing is required and, indeed, absolutely anyone can hang up a shingle and—legally at least—become a manager. The owner of the now-defunct Beverly Hills Artists Management served actual jail time for criminal conspiracy and grand theft after forcing clients to use photographers who paid him kickbacks, promising work that didn't exist, and inventing a purely fictional professional résumé. (His response to the charges, as reported in *Backstage*: "As far as misrepresentation and kickbacks go, let's not be anal here. I mean, this is Hollywood.")
- A manager may misrepresent his or her professional contacts. Show business, remember, is name-dropper land. You should be prepared to cross-check any prospective manager's credits and abilities with existing clients, agents, and other persons in the profession.
- Above all, be very careful what you sign. ATA members often limit themselves to 15% commission (except for models and musicians, who may be assessed 20%) and three-year maximum contracts. Nonmembers may stretch those figures, which are high to begin with, and may also charge you commissions on non-salaried income (residuals and per diem payments, for example) that agents may not. You should have extremely compelling confidence in any manager with whom you sign for three years; that's 15% of your income for a long time to come, no matter how you find the jobs that bring it in.
- Should a manager get you an agent? This often happens. You might, in that case, make signing with a manager dependent on his or her getting you signed with an agent at the same time.

So, you should think hard about getting a manager *and* an agent. After all, why not have two people working on your behalf instead of one? Why not have them hit the market—on your behalf—from all sides? It's a big investment—you'll be paying them 25% of your income—but, after all, 75% of something is a lot more than 100% of nothing! And a lot more fun, too.

Finding and getting your reps

Literally hundreds of agencies and management companies operate in both L.A. and New York. (Agents and managers outside of these cities are far scarcer.)

These vary enormously in their practical worth—particularly to an actor who's starting out. The difference between having a career and not having one can quite easily depend on which door you knock on first. The first doors should be those of the agencies. And they're not going to be doors, actually, but mailboxes; most often electronic ones.

Getting an agent

Agencies are informally ranked in terms of their clout in the field. The so-called A-list agencies represent the top stars in the business, cover a lot of fields (directors, writers, and musicians as well as actors), and are famous in their own right. The top four of these agencies at the moment are William Morris Endeavor Entertainment (WME), Creative Artists Agency (CAA), United Talent Agency (UTA), and International Creative Management (ICM). Each of these companies has offices in New York and L.A., each with upwards of 50 to 100 agents. And there's a lot of movement among both stars and agents between these agencies; indeed, even the agencies themselves may combine and break apart—as did the historic William Morris Agency (founded in 1898) and Endeavor when they joined forces in 2009 to create WME.

Being contracted by A-list agencies may do your ego good, but you can easily get lost in one: top agents must handle millions of dollars in bookings each year to pay their overhead and make their living, and 10% of Tom Hanks's earnings will go a lot further toward achieving those ends than 10% of yours. Mr. Hanks's agent isn't exactly the sort of person who will spend a lot of time with you, either, even if you were somehow to become a client. Which would be unlikely in any case: star agencies are those you work your way into, not get discovered by. Typically, this level of agency will limit themselves to one or two finds of the season out of graduating showcases. So, you may be in good hands. Just make sure what the expectation and game plan for your budding career might be with them.

And there are plenty of B-list or "boutique" agencies, well known in the profession, which handle lots of clients—some of whom are well-known, constantly working actors, and willing to take on extremely promising new talent in whom they see great potential. And there are C-list and even D-list agencies—some with just one or two agents and one to three dozen clients—that are just starting out. As you descend the alphabet, you will, of course, be looking at agencies with less clout, but you may get much more serious attention in return. And the smaller C- and D-level agencies are often young and hungry agents just ready to help you land that big break.

Of course, you might also get super-lucky and attract the attention of a junior agent at a powerhouse agency who is interested in taking on a few younger clients to nurture and develop as potential stars of tomorrow. ICM agent Joshua Pearl, for example, has a back pocket list of talented youths whom he grooms and looks after when he's not occupied with the superstars that top his agency's client list. His most recent success was Corey Hawkins, one time plucked out of Juilliard but, with years of hard work and hustling, now a break-out star from his turn in the film *Straight out of Compton*.

How do you reach these agencies? There are two basic ways, and you can use both, though at different times. Through *mass mailing*, you can go after every agency in the business. With *focused mailing*, you narrow your search from 50 to 10 agencies. For many reasons, it's almost always better to try the focused approach first: (1) because you can tailor your approach to individual agencies, (2) because you'll also have more to go on when (and if) you get any responses, and (3) because you'll save money and heartache (if you get no response, you still have lots of fish out there to try to catch). But how do you narrow your list?

First, learn the territory. If you're registered with some of the actor-posting services, such as nowcasting.com, you'll have access to a full list of agents on both coasts—as well as most other talent reps in the country.

Lacking that, most major agencies (over 150 of them, with more than 1,000 agents) are members of the ATA—you can reach these with their addresses and contact points at agentsassociation.com—and about 50 (though without addresses) are on the National Association of Talent Representatives (NATR) site at natrmembers.html.

You can also get a free list of—and links to—a substantial number of agents at www.workingactors.com. And for reasonable fees, you can get lists—or even mailing labels—for 120-plus agents in New York or 250-plus agents in Los Angeles from showbizltd.com, though we don't strongly recommend these mailing labels as they may look cheap (and you might look lazy, as if you hadn't done the work or research).

Equally obviously, you should ask any friends or family members about agents and agencies they're connected with or have personal knowledge of. Personal contacts (see Chapter 2) are the single most important way of getting your foot into this particular door. Here's where "friend of a friend" can actually prove quite useful, particularly if the people involved know both the agent and something about your work. Your grad school pal who already has representation might be your way into the office (particularly if you don't compete for his or her roles!). Don't be embarrassed to call your uncle if he works at CAA; he's already expecting your call.

Narrowing further, it is almost certainly best, if you're a beginner, to ignore the bigger agencies (which will ignore you in any event), and instead hunt out those small, aggressive, hungrier operations that look at untried talent and have the time and inclination to develop a genuine interest in your development. Only then will the actor–agent relationship, which is a marriage in many ways, prove truly fruitful.

Then, study up on agencies listed in any number of books on the subject. K. Callan's regularly updated *The New York Agent Book* and *The Los Angeles Agent Book*, mentioned in Chapter 2, contain, in addition to the usual contact information, a half- to full-page description of each major New York and Los Angeles agency and its people, philosophy, and numbers (of agents and clients). Other books that also do this (under the rubrics of *Call Sheet, Acting World Books, Henderson's Guides, Silver Screen Directories,* and others) are available at the drama bookshops on both coasts.

If you research all these materials and talk with everyone you know in the business, you should be able to compile a short list of 10 to 20 smallish agencies that might handle people like yourself (as well as a long list of perhaps 100 that just *might* take you on). It's time to go after them.

You could, of course, begin with a mass mailing—sending a photo-résumé and cover letter—to all those on your long list. It's certainly easy to do. But, as mentioned earlier, we suggest starting with your short list.

Submit a tailor-made proposal to each of them. Check out clearly what each agency requests in *Call Sheet* or another source. Don't send unsolicited materials that the agencies clearly won't accept. Honor their requests not to phone or visit (almost all will say that) and take their stipulations of "SAG only," "Postcards only," or, more grimly, "Not accepting unsolicited submissions" seriously.

For those agencies remaining on your short list, create a *cover letter* that specifically shows why you are exactly the person they are looking for. If they say they're looking for ethnic/foreign types or teens 13–19 and either or both fit you, let them know it in no uncertain terms. If you happen to know someone they already know or represent and that person will vouch for you, make that clear as well.

And if you have a referral from a working producer, or even permission to use the producer's name, make that *abundantly* clear. (Indeed, if you have a referral from a producer or a CD or a star, ask that person to send in your materials!)

Then take your cover letter (no more than one page, most of which is white space), place it in a mailing envelope with your photo-résumé, and send it off. Don't seal it tightly (some agencies say don't seal it at all); if it's too much work to unseal, it might get tossed out unopened.

Apply postage, put it in the mail, and take the rest of the day off. Can you email this? Yes, if the agency suggests or requests it. But not otherwise: thumbing through hard copies is faster than scrolling through email attachments (and much faster than printing them out), and most casting folks still prefer snail mail for such unsolicited submissions. Indeed, we don't recommend emailing unsolicited materials. It can be a real nuisance and invasion of privacy, said one well-known New York CD. And it's very easy to hit the delete button.

The most important lesson of this book

And here comes the most important lesson of this book. If you don't get any response in the first few days, *don't despair*. If you don't get any response in the first few *months*, don't despair. Understand: *you haven't been rejected. You've just been overlooked.*

With a half-second glance per photo, casting people don't have time to say, or even think, "Yechh!" Believe it or not, they don't hate you. They don't hate your picture. They don't think you're a terrible actor. *It's just that you're not precisely what they're looking for at this particular moment.* You haven't lost ground, just postage. It's a lesson you're going to have to teach yourself over and over in the months and years to come—so start now.

And so, this is the time to find some work in your town of choice. The next best way to get an agent interested in your acting potential is to be seen doing it.

Even without an agent

And, of course, you don't even need an agent, or a union card, to audition for a play or film. *Backstage* magazine has a regular site that shows, on the day we're looking at it in 2016, 6,422 acting jobs in 2,124 productions in all locations in the United States. Just go to backstage.com and click on

"Casting Calls," where you can click on any of seven American cities where you'd like to audition: NY, L.A., Miami, Chicago, Las Vegas, Philadelphia, or Atlanta. Or, better yet, go to backstage.com/auditions and you can locate, as at the time of writing this (April 3, 2016), 636 productions around the country—and in what region—that are seeking actors, both professional and otherwise. These plays or films are both union and nonunion, paid and not paid, but they tell you from which cities they are seeking submissions and a few things about what their project is.

Showcases

Getting seen involves getting a fairly good role in a *showcase production*. The name says it all: you may be paid little or nothing (you may even have to pay), but you are "shown" in a "case" where you are put on display for all comers.

Showcases are "small theatre" productions staged in New York under Equity's Showcase Code, and those in Los Angeles (colloquially known as "Equity waiver" productions) under that city's 99-Seat Theatre Plan. Each of these agreements permits Equity members, along with nonmembers, to waive full Equity salaries in lieu of carfare, but with payments between $7 and $15 per performance, plus free parking. Even well-located amateur and community theatre can work as a showcase production, if you're not an Equity member (if you're Equity you can't be in them) and can lure a few casting people to see you there.

Membership companies provide particularly popular showcase production opportunities in Los Angeles. You can join these "Equity waiver" theatre groups (membership is by audition), pay your dues, and then showcase yourself in the company's season of regular performances. Theatre 40 in Beverly Hills, for example, has performed over 100 plays in its 30-year history; its 150 members, all professional actors, now pay $20 a month to participate in the company's schedule of eight productions a year, all cast entirely from the company, plus the group's play readings and seminars. The Pacific Resident Theatre Co-op is another such enterprise; its 91 current members and their predecessors have put on more than 100 plays in parent PRT's second (black box) theatre in the past 17 years and also have priority in casting for PRT main-stage productions. In New York, The Flea Theater Company maintains a "by audition" company of non-Equity actors that lasts for one season. In return for being a member of "the Bats," as it's called, the actor is showcased in new works whose authors range from A. R. Gurney to Christopher Durang. Many other such New York companies exist as well.

Then there are *actor showcases*, which aren't plays at all but simply collections of scenes and monologues put together for an evening strictly to show off the participating actors to an invited audience of casting people. Normally such events include a catered reception—or wine and cheese—following the performance to permit some socializing between showcasing actors and the agents and CDs who attend them. Leading drama schools and departments also present such actor showcases in L.A. and/or New York—sometimes in various consortia of several schools—for their graduates, and if the drama schools are well known as having graduated students into well-known Broadway shows or feature films, agencies may send some of their agents to see them.

Other, strictly commercial showcases (also known as "industry nights" or "agents' nights") have been created for actors who pay to get into them, in L.A. particularly. You pay a fee (usually $200 to $600) in return for promised attendance by casting people, who may be paid an "honorarium" to show up. Commercial showcases have a very mixed reputation, however. Veteran CD Mike Fenton complains that "actors do this ridiculous thing of going out and getting into showcases because they've been told that CDs will come and make them stars. This is nonsense. The showcases I have gone to have been dreadful. The quality of the performer is usually God-awful. They're a waste of time." Rob Kendt, past editor of *Backstage*, has found most L.A. actors dissatisfied with their commercial showcase experience, with some complaining that they "smell of influence peddling" or even kickbacks, and others reporting that few are well attended and that many agents and CDs have stopped attending them or simply send their secretaries (who nonetheless pick up the honoraria). Concludes Kendt, "If a showcase isn't done right, leftover food is about all an actor gets out of it." And the authors of this book have yet to come across an important CD on either coast who would attend such commercial showcases unless he or she had been paid to do so.

You can find your way around to auditions for both showcase productions and actor showcases via the *Backstage* trades in both cities, and in the *Village Voice* (in New York) and *LA Weekly* (in Los Angeles). But always keep in mind that it's the quality of the *entire* showcase—not just your scene in it—that counts, and the New York maxim on this topic is "you're only as good as the worst person in the showcase."

When you get a showcase role, in either a full production or a collection of scenes produced for that purpose, you should do everything you can to attract attention (that's the whole point of doing it). This is the time for your mass mailing to agents and CDs, which can include those who overlooked you the first time. Make your showcase appearance the main feature of your cover letter. You can also print up and mail flyers and postcard invitations to the show, printing your photo on the invitation. You might even solicit RSVPs on postage-paid return cards, offer to arrange limousine transportation for reluctant agents (some showcases provide valet parking and buffet meals), and, if you can swing it, pay for advertisements in the trade papers. Follow-up is crucial.

If, in a full showcase production, you get good trade reviews, you can print up and send around brand-new photo-postcard invitations that highlight your mentions in the press. All showcases should record the industry people who attend (ordinarily a sign-in book is provided in the lobby), and all these people should get a follow-up letter or picture (your picture) postcard from you. If you're terrific in your showcase, and show professional potential, they'll get back to you.

Agents and casting people do see showcases, some as often as three or four a week. Many prefer showcase productions—and the chance to see you perform in a new play or a great classic. But actor showcases from well-known schools draw hundreds of agents and CDs, who can see a dozen or two actors from one or two schools in a tightly run hour of well-directed acting scenes.

Showcases, in either case, are your best first way to get seen at *work*, and paid work and agency/managerial representation may well come out of them if you touch all the right bases. Certainly, the combination of an effective showcase and a related photo-résumé submission gives you a much better chance for an agency response than either does alone. "Let me know when you're in something" is a common turn of phrase in this industry, and if the contact is initiated and then followed up by good work, you are doing what is expected. And you're building the foundation to become a working (or at least auditioning) actor.

Interviewing an agent

Once you have an agent interested in you, you'll probably be asked in for an interview. The interview is crucial; it will determine whether the agent takes you on. Because you will also be interviewing for roles later on, you must treat the interview with the agent as seriously as an interview with a producer or CD. The agent will be trying to see if you interview as well as you act, and it is important that you do.

If you are invited to "come in and talk," set up an appointment and keep it. Arrive on time (even though you will probably be asked to wait) and look your best. Be yourself, but be clean, neat, and striking. "Look like an actor and act like an actor," suggests one agent. Be at ease and be positive.

Casting people aren't necessarily any good at interviewing; they may be awkward and nervous, just like you. *Help* the agent interview you. Don't just wait for questions—describe your career, your desires, your commitment, your training, what you feel you can do, and what sacrifices you are prepared to make. Don't ham it up, but be active and infectious; obviously, an agent will be more interested in you if it appears that you have what it takes to generate a career. Have things to talk about other than your career. Show you have interest in life outside of the stage lights. What turns you on, what inspires you, what is going on in the world today that sparks your interest and joy?

Impress the agent with the fact that you want to become a working professional actor and have a realistic outlook about the business and about your future. Don't presume to know more about show business than the agent does, and don't start talking about what's wrong with your life or career. If it seems appropriate, offer to audition right on the spot. Liven up the place. Offer to come back tomorrow with a scene or monologue—and have a rehearsed scene and scene partner ready in case you get a favorable reply.

Ask some questions. How does the agent see you? How does the agent see using you? You might be surprised. It's crucial that you buy into the agent's plans for you. If you want to play classical tragedy and all the agent wants to market you for is a telenovela, you might be in the wrong office. But realize also that no agent makes a livelihood with an actor playing classical tragedy all the time, so be smart and be open: see what might be possible. No agent will be offended if you simply ask: "How do you see me?" Find out, and give the agent the benefit of the doubt. Amazingly, you might prove to be a lot better in *Days of our Lives* than in *As You Like It*. On the other hand, you may not want to spend the rest of your life in the soaps (if they don't die out entirely—as they now have in New York), so you have some decisions to make. Most important, see if there's a real bond between the agent and you. Mutual trust and excitement are every bit as important—if not more so—than immediate consonance on strategies.

Know when to quit talking, and make your departure before you wear out your welcome. (It's best to be leaving "for a voice lesson" than "for an appointment at the dentist's"). Never betray so much as a trace of desperation.

The agent will probably *not* offer you a contract on the spot. He or she may want to think you over, consult with others, see you do additional work, meet the rest of his or her colleagues and staff. If the agent doesn't grab you on the way out, he or she might well call you later. Your task is simply to hang in there until something happens.

And then it *does* happen: an agent decides to take you on as a client. In L.A., you will normally sign an exclusive contract for your agent to represent you in all *dramatic* camera media. Later, you may sign with another agent for commercials and with yet another for live theatre, although some agents will handle all three. In New York, you *may* be asked to sign an exclusive contract, or your agent may simply take you on as a freelance client, in which case you can work with other agents as well.

Should you sign up or freelance? It's probably best to sign—that way, your agent will be more committed to you, and you to your agent. Also, the agent will probably think of you before going to his or her freelance list. An agent who sends up a freelancer for a role first has to confirm the submission with the actor to make sure the actor hasn't already been submitted by another agent; this takes time, and the agent may not want to bother with the extra phone call. But signing up is also signing away; it's a major career decision, something like a marriage, and you should feel good about it before going ahead. Your initial agency contract will normally be for one year, and subsequent re-signings are typically for three years. When you sign with an agent, you have entered into a partnership that both of you hope will prove beneficial. But *you have by no means "made it."* You are still just beginning.

A good agent will take a serious interest in your career. He or she will seek out casting opportunities via Breakdown Services and other sources. Your agent will also, to some extent, be the manager of your career—even if you have a manager (again, see below). It is vital, therefore, that you establish a trusting relationship. This may take some patience on your part. One agent cautions: "It may take a year or so to establish you in the overall market picture, and another two years to get offers coming in with any regularity. The third year is usually when the payoff comes—if it does." If you are hoping for instant results, you may be frustrated. Actors who impatiently switch agents every six months will only have to begin over and over again and never establish an image in the industry.

If you are lucky enough to find an agent who sees you the way you wish to be seen, an agent in whom you have confidence, sign up and then follow his or her advice. You're pretty much going to have to accept your agent's judgment on what you should wear, how you should do your hair, what you should weigh, and which photographs you should use and which you should toss. Talk things over, of course, but be prepared to trust. Nobody's advice is perfect, but your agent is your partner. The two of you should be working together or not at all.

Don't settle back! Just because you have an agent, you can't afford to become a passive participant in your own career. You are still going to have to make your rounds, get yourself known, get involved, and generate your network of contacts.

You're also going to have to energize your own agent! Get to know the office staff. They're people too, and they'll be more interested in you if they know you're interested in them. "Be part of the agency family," advises Broadway's *Urban Cowboy, High Fidelity*, and *If/Then* star Jenn Colella. "Make an emotional connection. Then they'll want to send you out! They can't help it!"

But it's not all just sweetness and Christmas presents, either. As William Bayer explains, "Hustle your hustler. You're going to have to sell and pressure and hustle just as much with an agent as without one; you're going to have to continue to excite your agent, because the moment he gets bored, there's nothing in it for either of you." Exasperating? Yes, but true. Your agent needs reinforcement when putting your name out there. He or she needs casting people to *glow* at the mention of your name, not stare back blankly in bewilderment. And that means getting known.

Getting a manager

Finding and getting a manager is a little more difficult than finding an agent, but it's not impossible. First, you have to decide that you really *want* one— that you need more than an agent to get you jobs, you need a manager to help you create a brilliant and long-lasting career.

And there are plenty of such managers, good and bad. The website talentmanagers.org lists—without charge—101 talent agents around the country, and almost as many talent agencies that they inhabit.

If you have an agent, you should, of course, ask your agent's advice on how to choose from among these lists. Know going in that, as Bernie Brillstein says, "no agent wants to recommend a manager because that's like admitting he can't do his job." But if you have an agent, he or she will have to work very closely with your manager, so you should seek your agent's advice anyway— and the advice of everyone you know who knows the manager you're considering. you certainly want to find a manager who is demonstrably honest, wise, and available, and who seems to feel that you're the same way.

Of course, if you're getting around town and acting in showcases, managers will probably be finding *you*. And then you can talk. Most of what applies to interviewing an agent will also apply to interviewing a manager, so consider yourself, by this point, appropriately informed.

Keeping your reps

Once you have an agent or a manager, or both, you'll want to be sure to keep them happy having you on their list of clients. So, don't be too quick to pick up the phone and read them the riot act for not sending you out (on auditions) enough—not only might they just drop you from their list, but they might also just stop sending you out *without* dropping you, and you'll be left by the phone wondering what happened. After all, who wants to be yelled at? You don't—and neither do they.

The best way to keep your reps happy, of course, is for you to give great auditions when they do send you out, so that the CDs give them good feedback on you—even if you didn't land the role. Great feedback from CDs lets your reps know you're still in the running for upcoming parts—and makes your reps all the more eager to send you back out there.

Christmas presents aren't a bad idea either. As an anonymous "secret agent man" once wrote in *Backstage*, "At the risk of sounding crass—agents spend the entire year trying to give their clients what they need to advance their careers, so when December rolls around, they're in the mood for a little receiving. ... So remember to give your reps a little something at the end of the year." The secret agent even has gift suggestions: "a bottle of wine (but please, no 'two buck Chuck')" or a gift certificate from a unique shop. But "it doesn't have to be expensive," he cheerfully continues, "any gift from a client ... makes me feel good about my relationship with that actor." But how ethical is this? "I already know what you're thinking," the agent replies, "Why should I spend money on my agents?" My response to that is: "What world are you living in? Acting is a business, and that's how business is done!" Yes, it does indeed sound crass. But in a world where "the gross" is the bottom line, a bit of Christmas crassness is, perhaps, a necessary by-product.

Your team

If you have an agent *and* a manager, they become your team—and they have to work as a team. Remember that you're the captain of the team and that your "teammates" are in fact your employees. It may not seem that way. They may be older and wiser and more experienced than you, but they're working for you, not the other way around. Treat them as the pros they are, but in the final analysis you have to provide the leadership. It's your career, after all. And, of course, if you have both agent and manager you're paying them 25% of your acting income, *before taxes*, which could mean about half of your take-home pay! You deserve the best they have to offer!

In the future, your team might expand to include a lawyer and/or a publicist. But let's leave the future to take care of itself. Now it's time to get some work.

Making the rounds

What do actors do when they are not working? They go on what used to be called "rounds." "Making the rounds" means trying to contact—and when possible meet—everybody and anybody who can help get you a job in the theatre.

In years past, making the rounds meant walking the streets of New York—or driving the avenues and boulevards of Los Angeles—to visit the offices of CDs and dropping off your photo-résumé, with the hope (against hope) of being invited in for a chat. Indeed, at one time there were several geographically organized address books that could guide you on a walking or driving tour from one CD office to the next in the most efficient possible manner—just like a trail guide to climbing the Matterhorn.

Today, however, you "make your rounds" mainly via the internet; uninvited office visits, even to slip your photo-résumé under the door, are strongly discouraged. If you do this, take a friend with you in case you get yelled at. It's easier to shake it off.

But with or without an agent, "making the rounds" means getting your information—and when possible your person—before as many CDs as you can, since they are the ones who actually cast (or, at least, have the largest single role in casting) the first roles you're likely to get.

Casting directors

The CD is a relative late-comer in the entertainment world, brought into existence, among other reasons, by the fact that there are just so many of you (actors) out there that directors and producers don't have the time to find out about you—they're too busy directing and producing. CDs are employed by studios, by individual film and television production companies, by Broadway and off-Broadway producers, and by most regional theatres—certainly all the large ones. Some are part of a permanent staff (as at Universal Studios, South Coast Repertory, or the New York Public Theatre); sometimes they are freelancers, working out of their own New York and L.A. offices and hired for individual projects as independent contractors. Their job is to recommend, out of the nation's 150,000 professional actors, the handful of people the director and producer will want to see. You want to be in that handful, naturally.

It is the CD's goal to find the best talent for the project or company he or she is working for. It's your goal to convince the CD that that's you. But, of course, the CD has to see you first, and that's why you need to get in his or her line of sight one way or another.

CDs *want* to know the work of every excellent actor in the business; it's their *job* to know you if you're any good, and it's also their job to know how to get in touch with you. Therefore, they go to showcases all the time, as well as to screenings and theatre productions (Broadway, off-Broadway, or LORT, depending on where they're located). They also watch films and television—probably more television than anybody in the business.

CDs mainly see actors on the basis of direct agency referrals from their breakdowns, but many find actors in other ways, and we will list a few in the paragraphs that follow.

The first way—generally for smaller roles—is for you to electronically submit yourself for a breakdown you found on actorsaccess.com or now-casting.com as described earlier in this chapter. In that case, a CD may directly solicit your materials for a part that is currently being cast, and may also make that solicitation to a larger group of actors *without representation* (otherwise, the listing would only have been made available to agents and/or managers). In these cases, you can consider yourself *invited* by the CD—even though you are one of the thousands of actors equally invited for the same role—and if your specs match those of the character description, you may get a ring.

The second way is to mail or email your photo-résumés directly to CD offices in the city where you plan to work. (Lists and often mailing labels are available for nominal fees at showbiz.com, backstage.com, and other such sources mentioned above.) It's not that different from writing to an agent, but your letter in this case should indicate quite specifically why you think you should be considered for *the particular project* (a film, a play, a TV show) the CD is casting. Know what you're going for. "Watch TV!" says Jeff Greenberg, CD for 47 stylistically unique network television shows, including *Modern Family*, *Frasier*, *Wings*, and *Cheers*. "Know the style of each show," he says, "because the auditions come up so fast. You can be called to audition and be in rehearsal on the same day." In particular, you should know all the shows that shoot in your city of residence. You should also build up a tape library on your DVR of ongoing TV shows lensed in your town so that, if you get a call from one of them the next day, you can take a look at a recent episode to review the show's style before you read for it.

Your letter to a CD should be brief but tailor-made to the person addressed, and your photo-résumé, of course, should be a knockout. If you have an agent or manager, of course, you will be provided with lots of advice—and your photo-résumé will have a better chance of being looked at—but on occasion a CD may give you a call without representation or even professional credits—perhaps because your photo is fantastic, or you just graduated from the training program he or she thinks is fantastic, or the show you were just in got great reviews. You never know.

But understand that mailings arrive at CD offices daily by the hundreds. Literally. In order to invite an actor in from such a mailing, this book's veteran CD co-author admits, "I have to have met you or seen you in something just to hang onto your photo. And you have to have been not just excellent, but *memorable* in what I saw you do. And I have to have *liked* you ... No, I have to have *loved* you in what you were doing."

So, the odds of your being invited in by a CD simply by mailing your materials to an office address are very, very slim—unless, of course, you're the six-foot-six, Swahili-speaking 19-year-old that the script calls for and the CD has so far been unable to find. But they are not zero!

Taking CD workshops

A third way of getting the attention of a CD is by taking an "audition workshop" or "CD intensive" led by one. This is an area, however, that has raised serious ethical issues—by both the acting unions and some state labor boards—that you should know about. Since they appear to ask would-be actors to "pay to be seen," such workshops have been seen to contravene policies long regulating acting employment, and for that reason were temporarily ordered by the courts to "cease and desist" in the state of California in 2002. A subsequent ruling by the California Department of Labor Standards, however, put such workshops back in business—specifying that they be clearly advertised as "solely educational." Among the specific new provisions—still in effect—are that CDs may not use workshops to audition actors, may not describe character breakdowns or use material or sides from roles they are currently casting, must provide "individual critiques, performance adjustments, and/or feedback" that are "of more than a superficial nature" to each participant, and, while they may ask for and comment on your photo-résumé, are required to return it at the end of the workshop meeting. In short, CDs may not use workshop fees as audition "bribes."

Since such workshops have been declared legal, however, they are now common throughout the entertainment industry on both coasts. Many actors have found them extremely helpful, even invaluable. An actor friend (and a cofounder of nowcasting.com) has told us that "all the acting work I've gotten has come from attending some great CD classes." As a *Backstage* editorial by Michael Kostroff says, "If you're interested in educating yourself and learning more about auditioning and want to take a class to improve that skill, then the very best person you could possibly study with would be a seasoned, established casting director. Someone who has spent years watching actors come in and out of the office to audition may well have a lot to impart on that subject." And, Kostroff adds, "There is no question that actors sometimes get work from these workshops." Indeed, "you *have* to do them," adds a veteran L.A. actress, quite emphatically, "otherwise you're simply wasting your time."

Such workshops connect actors with industry personnel to whom they would otherwise lack access. Many provide excellent classes—particularly when students can work on camera, and with material the CD actually casts and has experience with. And they certainly permit networking when network executives, other CDs, and well-known agents share their secrets in the class setting. You may find specialized workshops as well, for instance, on "daytime intensives" for soap operas on one weekend, with some of the top CDs or their associates from those fields; at other times you'll find top pros doing a one-night seminar on TV commercials, or a "*CSI* intensive" that focuses on the material from that show led by its respective CDs or their associates.

So, CD workshops are something to consider—but there's one strong caveat. As an L.A. actress and acting teacher urges her students, "don't do them until you're ready." CDs basically teach cold-reading skills (which is how they audition actors for their shows; see next section), and you've got to be ready to take their advanced instruction in the workshop and to deliver the goods when the workshop concludes. "If you're not ready to give a brilliant reading when you're done, we'll only remember how bad you were," says one CD.

So, work up your cold reading—and other acting—skills before you sign up for your workshop. First impressions are the best.

Other workshops

There are several CDs in the major theatre cities that host such workshops: some require prescreening for attendees, some are led by well-known teachers and former actors, and all require fees—generally in the range of $50–$100 per class. Most advertise in the pages of *Backstage*; others are available online. Check, for starters, oneononenyc.com, actorsconnection.com, and TVI Actors Studio in both New York and L.A., although your authors cannot give specific recommendations in this area, since the teachers may not be the CDs themselves.

But check them out as closely as you can, and then double-check. "For the class to be worthwhile, the casting director must also be a good instructor," says Kostroff. And you also have to make sure he or she is really a CD! "Casting Associates"—if they are so described—are usually fine as well, as long as they are deeply involved in the actual casting process, but beware of being "taught" by a Casting Associate whose work is mainly opening the envelopes or serving as the office receptionist. Legitimate workshops can prove highly valuable if you go with the intention to learn something—not just to get your face in front of the CD. Then do the best work you can possibly do (that's right, it's a *work* shop). Go with the right expectation, give your best effort, and get as much as you can out of the experience. Then—if you have excelled in your work and were memorable in your self-presentation—you can write the CD with your photo-résumé a week later, and it may indeed get the attention you are hoping for.

The best way

The best way by far for most actors, whether represented or not, is simply scouting out the city that is your home base, seeing theatre at all levels, working in showcases (see below), taking acting classes and workshops (see below), and doing what you can to meet other actors—and directors, playwrights, producers, filmmakers, and theatre people of every variety—around town. Yes, this is "pounding the pavement" in the old-fashioned sense. Hang out with whomever you can find in the acting community or theatre community that is your base—and which ordinarily begins with the people you've studied with, who are taking the same path you are. Build up a network of like-minded colleagues—this will probably become your biggest single power source in these first years of your career search. And you don't have to look far to find others in this community you don't yet know: "Everybody is an actor here" is what most entry-level actors discover when they hit the ground in Manhattan or Hollywood. So, chat up the people you meet in the theatre bookshops, or theatre lobbies, or those you work with in your day job, and get to know the folks on the same road that you're heading down. They can be your access to the next crossroads—and the ones after that.

Meeting a CD

We will talk in the next section about auditioning with a CD, but here let us say a few words about meeting one.

Understand that one of the main goals of CDs is to find new talent. They *want* to hire you. For most, it's a thrill to discover the next Al Pacino or Meryl Streep, but even beyond that, it will please their own bosses—the directors and producers they work for—who are often looking for fresh faces to support their more experienced and celebrated star players.

Understand that CDs are on the line as much as you are. If they don't find the freshest new face, the most stunning new actor, the most perfect "fits" for the producers' shows, they're out of a job. "We are rejected as often as actors, if not more," says Paul Weber, in-house CD for MGM Worldwide Television. "We are turned down by agents, producers, networks, studios. We are gypsies, just like actors. As casting directors, we empathize." So, don't treat CDs as enemies or foreigners. They're in the same industry as you are, and—though it's hard to see it from your side of their desks—they're just as vulnerable.

> ASIDE FROM JAMES: Understand that we are rooting for you. We want you to be great! I have to know that one of those few people I bring in is gonna hit. Otherwise I'm not doing my job.

If a CD has taken an interest in you—having met you at a party or a CD workshop or seen you in a showcase production—write him or her a follow-up postcard or email. Ask if you can arrange a meeting. Ask if you could volunteer as a "reader"—which is what CDs sometimes use to read opposite the actors they are auditioning. Don't be disappointed if you don't hear back. If your contact was with a CD workshop and you enjoyed it and felt you learned something, swallow your pride and take another one from the same CD. "After all," says one working actress in L.A., "$50 to $100 is not a lot to pay for a couple of hours of intense instruction from a top professional in this extremely difficult business to gain a foothold in." Also, sometimes things take time. It may be three months to a year before you hear from the CD. Keep that faith!

The CD may call you in to read for a show, or for a general audition (called simply "a general"), or for a reading and/or an interview. If it's an audition, we have many suggestions for you in the next chapter. If it's just an interview, don't be in the least disappointed. "Quite often a sit down chat can tell just as much if not more than the old traditional monologue for me," says this book's CD/co-author. "In this case we're not asking you to recite your résumé and credits; we have those. No, we want to know how you work in the world. We like to hear your likes and dislikes. I love an actor with a strong point of view—whatever that may be. In the interview, it's your personality that becomes all important—so let yourself shine!"

You should, of course, have some photo-résumés to leave, and this is a great time to bring your demo reel DVD if you have one. Be sure to have your name, address, and phone number on it, and let the CD know that he or she can keep it. You should have plenty of dubs, in fact; they are inexpensive, and you don't want the CD to get irritated by thinking he or she will be expected to return it. Besides, it is doing more good sitting on the CD's desk than on a shelf above your refrigerator.

A final word on reps and CDs

Agents, managers, and CDs can help you only so far. The ultimate initiative on building your career must be yours, and you have to keep at it. "If you stop pushing for one minute, they forget you," says actress Teri Garr. "You're out. Gone, goodbye!" So, don't wait for the phone to ring. Forget about "finding yourself." *Submit* yourself! Check the breakdowns, the trade papers, the actor websites every day. Stay in touch with your industry friends and make new ones. Send out your photo-résumés and postcards. And audition! Get into shows, showcases, student films, CD workshops, anything that will get you before the eyes of those in a position to engage you.

When you meet a rep or a CD—or, for that matter, *anybody* in this business—log his or her name and contact information into a notebook or a well-backed-up computer file, together with the date, time, place, what you discussed, the names of the other people in the office, what the person said of you and of your prospects, and particularly about his or her own future projects. Write down anything you can think of that might prove useful, and look over this logbook from time to time, and particularly when you are invited to see the person the next time—which might be months or years later. "Picking up where you left off" is crucial in this most personal of businesses (what could be more personal, in fact, than auditioning for a role in a play or film, when it is chiefly personalities that are to be performed?). And forgetting what happened the last time you were in that office—particularly when the CD remembers—can be disastrous.

> ASIDE FROM JAMES: I can't tell you how many actors I've cast later come up to me as though we've never met. Nothing annoys me more than an actor that doesn't remember that I gave her a job—and particularly her first one!

When you get representation, you can give him or her a list of those people on your list: your "industry fans," not merely CDs, but playwrights, directors, producers, theatre companies that you've worked with, and so forth. This will make your agent and/or manager even more helpful in arranging the advancement of your acting career.

Got all this down? OK, now it's time to go to the most important chapter. The Casting Room.

5 The Casting Room

The casting room is where it all comes together. The casting process always has three parts, the same ones Aristotle declared essential for a play: a beginning, a middle, and an end. The beginning is when you walk into the room and introduce yourself and perhaps exchange a few words with the casting people. The middle is when you read for the casting director (CD), which is your audition. The end is when you are either dismissed or invited to exchange a few more words—or perhaps many more words, in which case it becomes an interview and call-back. We'll look at these parts in order, but of course, they may not follow this order exactly when you actually experience the process. (Not all plays begin at the beginning either. See Pinter's *Betrayal*, or Jason Robert Brown's *The Last Five Years*.)

The casting room itself is usually part of a large office, or a studio adjacent to one, where you will stand or sit during your audition in front of the CD and his or her assistants and associates. There will also probably be a chair where someone—either the CD or, more likely, an assistant—will "read with you," saying the lines of the other character or characters in the script. If you are lucky, there is "a reader" in which a good actor has been hired or has volunteered to help out that day. In that case, you are in luck and will have a good scene partner for those valuable five minutes or so.

Increasingly, these days, there will also be a video camera and operator, iPad, iPhone, or some sort of taping device and a neutral backdrop behind you, so that your audition can be captured on video and either fed live to CDs and directors elsewhere (in a technology called Skype or teleconferencing, which CD Paul Haber says "has become the next step in this need for speed") or video-recorded to be shown to other casting people and producers, either on a DVD or on a privately shared website such as those provided by Cast It Systems. Such sites allow CDs, directors, and producers in various offices around town, or around the country, to compare your audition side by side with 2 to 50 others for the same role. For the film *Kit Kittredge: American Girl*, for example, CD Nancy Nayor reviewed video-recorded auditions held in Los Angeles, New York, Toronto, and Chicago over a three-month period, which were combined on her privately accessed Cast It site.

So, get to know what the casting room is like. That's where your acting begins.

Introductions

Let's talk preliminaries first. Your name is called. You're nervous, perhaps, but that's OK, it happens all the time, even (sometimes) to veteran actors. Indeed, actors' nervousness is the same thing as excitement. But know that the slightest hint of desperation can spell doom.

There's no real reason to be nervous, much less desperate, however. For the big secret is that the casting people don't hate you! In fact, they *want you to be good*. And sometimes (when they haven't found anyone they like yet) *they* are the desperate ones—they desperately want you to be good. And not just good, but great! Todd Thaler, CD of *Are We There Yet?* and *Heartlock*, reminds us that every actor walking into the room should know there is no play, movie, commercial, or television show without them. We need them. They are essential to the process.

> ASIDE FROM JAMES: I always assume that actors are talented when they walk into the room. I'm sometimes disappointed, of course, but not too often. But beyond the talent, I'm hoping to see a fascinating personality. Something special: a mystique, a unique point of view about life. Equate this to dating: what is it about people that keeps them in your mind? Why would you like to spend more time with one person rather than another? What drives you to ask someone for a "second date?" You want to find out more about them, don't you? Well, that's what I do. Find out more so that can I feel confident that an audience will want to spend two to three hours watching an actor on stage, or in multiple episodes or even whole seasons in a TV series. For film and TV particularly, we are looking primarily for personality. That's why I invited my waitress at EJ's Luncheonette to audition for a prime-time network series, and why I brought in the guy standing next to me on the subway for a feature film. They fascinated me. They seemed special. They had a great perspective on life. And yes, they both booked the jobs.

OK. You walk in the door, script in one hand and photo-résumé in the other. They look at you. And their decision *may already have been made!*

Particularly in television, casting people want to see the *character*—the person as written on the page—walk into the room! Television is much more personality driven than live theatre. So, the *very first impression* may determine which mental box—"yes," "maybe," or "no"—is being checked as you cross the threshold.

And now the door is closed behind you. From this moment on, you are auditioning. You are auditioning as *the character*, and you are also auditioning as *the professional actor*.

And it is *your* audition, not theirs. As CD Mark Brandon (*Lion King*) says, "the minute the actor walks in the door, he or she is the one who should be in control of the audition. The minute the actor lets someone else *take charge* is the minute that the audition is going to be a failure."

But how should you take charge? Here are some opening pointers:

- Don't shake hands unless the casting people extend their own first. It isn't necessary to touch every person behind the table; some CDs, in fact, loathe such contact, keeping a bottle of hand sanitizer on the table, knowing how many germs they might otherwise encounter that day. There is a genuine way to connect with the people behind the table without having to touch. Use your eyes, your smile.
- Take the "psychological temperature" of the room as soon as you come in. You'll get a quick sense of it: are they formal or casual? Are they laughing? Somber? Eating? Funereal?
- Adjust to the room. If the auditioners look tired and exhausted, realize that it's your job to change all that. Let them know they have found the right actor to perk them up! You are the answer to their prayers. If they seem serious and grim, don't cut up and joke with them—just adjust!
- Keep the chitchat to a minimum unless you feel you are prompted otherwise.

Once you have the feel of things (and this should take a second and a half), exchange your hellos, introduce yourself, offer your photo-résumé, and wait for instructions. If the moment allows, say hello to your reader, or connect with him or her with a nod or a smile, for this person will be your life-line for the next five minutes or so. Ordinarily, you will soon hear the magic words, "OK, Joe, whenever you're ready." And you begin.

Eventually, this gets easier. You will quickly learn what to expect from different CDs. Yes, CDs have individual personalities and styles of working too! Soon you will know in an instant how to present yourself when walking into such rooms and meeting such people. Actors love to learn the CDs' personalities as well. It becomes the word on the street who among them is a tiger and who is as kind as a lamb. You, too, will learn who these "keepers of the keys" are! But know now that even the friendliest of auditioners can have a bad day, can be stressed out, overworked, sick, or simply exhausted from seeing several dozen people before you that day. Be sensitive to all this and adjust.

And yes, occasionally you will get a downright unfriendly room. This can happen to the best actors, so when it happens to you don't let it throw you. Do your best work, leave the room, and shake it off. And on to the next…

The audition

Auditions are how you show what you can do. If you are at the beginning of your career, it is absolutely essential that you learn to audition—not just well, but brilliantly.

In the trade, these auditions are generally called "readings," because in most cases, when you're auditioning for a specific play, film, TV show, or commercial role, you are given a script and will be "reading" your lines aloud. But as you'll see later on in this section, you're not really reading at all; certainly not if you can help it. You're *performing*, and performing as though your career depended on it—which, in general, it does.

We'll retain the term "audition" in this book, however, since it covers the entire scope of how you perform for casting people when invited to do so. And also because the term "reading"—besides being somewhat of a misnomer—is also often conflated with the "pre-reading," which, as you will soon see, is sometimes used as an audition to get an audition.

Any audition is, of course, an artificial situation. It's a form of acting, but it's not acting in a play (or a film), and it's not, in most cases, acting with other people (much less with costumes, scenery, and props). It often takes place without an audience or in an empty studio, often in the most depressing of circumstances. It thus is only a fragment of acting, and often you feel fragmented doing it. But you *have* to do it, and you have to be a knockout doing it.

Actors often have hang-ups about auditioning and feel that they audition much more poorly than they perform on stage or before the camera. This may indeed be the case, but there's no use simply lamenting it. Producers with tens of thousands of actors to choose from don't need to bother having faith in you. They will choose someone they *know* can do the role, and they will know it on the basis of his or her audition.

And you will be auditioning throughout your career. Even famous stars audition. Marlon Brando, as big a superstar as existed at the time, auditioned for his title role in *The Godfather*. Renée Elise Goldsberry auditioned for her breakout performance in the 2016 Broadway blockbuster, *Hamilton*. "Even celebrities are being asked to pre-read for smaller roles," said Orion Barnes of L.A.'s Rogers Orion Agency. And Susan Sarandon, auditioning for *Bull Durham* after doing some 45 films and TV series, subsequently admitted: "it was humiliating." But as four-times Tony-nominated and recent star of television's *The Walking Dead* Tovah Feldshuh says, "*everybody* auditions. They may not call it that in New York. It goes under the guise of 'going over the score,' or a 'work session' but it's the same thing. Directors like to see who they are working with."

So, learning how to audition—and to audition brilliantly—is not an asset; it's a necessity.

The (other) most important lesson in this book

There are *two* "most important" lessons in this book. One you've already read. The other one is this, and you may find it shocking: *your audition must be at the absolute, full-on level of a finished performance.* This is the biggest single difference between professional auditions and most of their amateur (including academic) counterparts.

In college, it's usually OK—and in many situations even preferable—to hold back at auditions. Directors in such circumstances may want to have "somewhere left to go" with you; they may not want "to see it all in the audition" because they feel they may then have little room to shape your ultimate performance. This may be as it should be, because in a college the actors are students, the directors are teachers, and the rehearsal hall is a classroom. But professional entertainment is a business, not a curricular activity. And given the opportunity, professional directors will shape their performance in the casting room rather than the rehearsal hall. Which is why you've heard the adage that "directing is 90% casting."

This is much truer in film and TV than in theatre, because the camera media traditionally schedule little or no time for discussion between actors and directors, and amazingly little even for rehearsal. It's not hyperbole to say that film/TV directors, much of the time, don't coach a performance as much as *buy* one. And they buy it because they saw it in the casting room. For television, particularly, is often more a producer's than a director's medium. Directors are typically "guns for hire" on television, with a new director on each episode. So, your audition performance will more often than not be examined by the producer and/or the writer along with the director. And if you don't then deliver the performance on the director's set (perhaps the very next day), he or she will just fire you and hire somebody else. So, when TV CDs say—as they all do—that the one thing they hate is "unpreparedness," what they actually mean is that actors must be *prepared to deliver a final performance when they walk into the audition room.*

Rarely will they explain this in so many words, however. They may not even understand it themselves. But what CDs want is to see you deliver the final performance right there in their office (even while you're holding the script in your hand), then to deliver it again to the director in your call-back, and *then* to deliver it before the rolling cameras the next morning. Statistically, more actors audition off-book. If they are holding their sides (and we recommend it), they are not even using them. They know their lines well enough to be off-book. That is true preparedness!

Before you panic over all this, let us add that this is not as rigid in the legitimate (live) theatre, where there is ample rehearsal time, the directors generally pride themselves on coaching and shaping skills, and being brilliant doesn't mean being absolutely perfect in every detail the first time through. If you're brilliant but miss a couple of things, the director (or CD) might invite you to make "adjustments" that will bring you more into synch with what's being sought. It really depends on whether they have found other great options for the part yet—or not. This can determine how long you might last in the room.

The most important thing to remember in all this is to make choices! Be bold, be specific, and be your best.

> ASIDE FROM JAMES: I'm not a big believer in "leading the horse to water". I think the actor either understands the part *instinctively*, or doesn't. And if you don't, someone coming in right after you will get it. It doesn't necessarily mean that you're a bad actor. Maybe it's just not your role.

Make no mistake: professional acting is a champion business, and there's a ton of money at stake. Even in live theatre, if you're not a known actor, you're going to have to absolutely nail the audition 100%. You're going to have to thrill when the character's thrilling and cry real tears when the character's crying, and, if it's part of the role, you're going to have to make the women swoon and the men melt, or you're not going to get a call-back. When Vadim Perelman met the Iranian actress Shohreh Aghdashloo for *House of Sand and Fog*, little known in the United States, he gave her the script and sides and asked her to return the next day and "make him cry." She did, got the part, and wound up with an Oscar nomination for her efforts.

Well, this is what you've been studying and working toward, and mailing your photos and résumés for, so now go out there and do it. Forget "leaving room for the director" to shape you. *You* take charge. Deliver the goods. Shape your director. You want to be the answers to all his or her hopes and prayers.

Kinds of audition

For a repertory theatre company or an EPA (Equity Principal Audition), and on some (increasingly rare) occasions for an agent or CD, you may be asked to give a *prepared audition,* in which you present either a prepared monologue or a scene for two persons. Such prepared auditions are normally given in the theatre or a casting office or other comparable space. They are often also called *general auditions,* or *generals,* since ordinarily you are not auditioning for a given role, but for a part in a theatre repertory (as with a Shakespeare festival) or perhaps for an understudy part at an Equity call. (More on this later.)

For a specific part in a play, film, TV show, or commercial, however, you will be asked to give a *reading* from the script (though you should try to have this mostly or fully memorized). You may also be asked to discuss the part or script, to sing, to improvise, or to demonstrate specific skills in and after such a reading.

But prior to a reading before the CD, director, and producers, you might be screened with a *pre-read,* more commonly called a *pre-screen,* which is held by the CD or, more often, his or her casting associates. A CD may, for example, ask to pre-read 25 or even 100 to select the best few that will pass through to the reading itself. ("Pre-screen" is a misnomer of sorts, however, as there really is no "pre" to the "screen." It is a first screen before an audition. Hence "pre-read.")

You may even—particularly in the film/TV world—be asked to give a *pre-pre-reading.* The invitation to "pre-pre-read" is a request that you *make a self-tape of yourself reading from the script,* which you can then submit electronically to the casting office. A self-tape may be offered to actors who have electronically self-submitted their materials in response to a cast breakdown they have found on a casting website (see previous chapter) or a request from the CD. Casting offices offering the opportunity to pre-pre-read will then invite some (or even all) submitters who meet the criteria specified in the breakdown to download sides from the script, to digitally record themselves performing them on video, and then to electronically submit their video to the casting office. If your pre-pre-read is close enough to what they want, it may lead to a subsequent invitation to come into the casting office to pre-read, and on a few occasions it may even lead directly to the audition, which will take place before the director and producers as well as the CD. This is super-helpful for the actor out of town—perhaps on a different coast or working the boards regionally. It allows the actor to remain in the game. The self-tape provides the actor with an opportunity, and opportunity is the name of the game here. After that, it's up to you to book the job.

We'll discuss these different kinds of auditions—prepared auditions, readings, pre-readings, and pre-pre-readings—separately. But it is important to remember the many layers involved in getting the job.

Prepared auditions

Prepared auditions (with material you choose and prepare) are almost always *monologues*—which have become standard for stage work, particularly for open calls at regional theatres and equity principal auditions. Prepared two-person *scenes* are, on rare occasions, also requested by agencies calling you in for possible representation. Stage auditions for theatres usually take place in a rehearsal studio and occasionally on a stage; film and TV auditions are most likely to be held in a CD's or producer's office or an audition studio. You must be prepared for any combination of these variables.

In *open call* auditions, as for a regional theatre or Broadway and some off-Broadway contracts, you will generally be offered the opportunity to present one or two monologues, ordinarily with an overall three- to five-minute time limit. Because this time limit is given does not mean you need to reach it! Monologues should be about a minute to a minute and a half—tops. Always leave them wanting more.

For a singing audition, 16 bars is the usual limit (and 32 the maximum). The call will usually state whether you are to sing *a cappella* or bring an accompanist, or whether an accompanist will be provided (in which case you bring your sheet music); sometimes you may accompany yourself on a guitar or piano, depending upon the audition. If this is you, bring in a music book. Despite the 16-bar requirement, the casting office and musical director may ask to hear something else. "Do you have something upbeat? Do you have another ballad with less belt? What rock'n'roll songs do you have? Any Gershwin? How 'bout more intimate where you can sit in the chair there?" These words and more may come your way.

Open call auditions are the "cattle calls" of show business. CDs may see 20 or 30 actors an hour (many more if it's a dance audition), and it's hard not to get depressed at the minimal attention (and maximum competition) you'll be getting. If you've seen *A Chorus Line*, you know what it's all about; that show was created by people who knew professional auditions from the inside out. Still, people do get cast from open calls, and persistence pays off. Elinore O'Connell, newly in Equity at the time she heard about the *Les Misérables* open call in Los Angeles, simply *knew* that Fantine was her role, so she rehearsed her audition daily for months. When 3,000 actors showed up on the appointed date, she didn't even make it into the room on the first day, or on the second. On the third (and final) day, she arrived at the theatre before dawn but still couldn't get in; hundreds were already camped out by the door. Undaunted, she waited outside the theatre until dusk, when, as the sun was setting, a kindly production assistant took pity on her and invited her in. She got the role.

Your job, therefore, is to be the exception by being exceptional. For stage work, your initial audition pieces will almost always be monologues. Most LORT auditions ask for two contrasting monologues, one in verse and one in prose, delivered in no more than four minutes. Oftentimes the season for this theatre is already announced. So, tailor your work appropriately. Do the work of an author whose work is being presented in the current season, thus making sense for what the theatre does these days, and showing that you have done your homework and you have smarts.

Some of these pieces may have been written before the twentieth century, but at least one should usually be contemporary. Graduate auditions through URTA also use a similar format: although it is rarely required that one monologue be from a comedy, it is usually helpful if one is. CDs, who may hear dozens of monologues in a three-hour casting session, are ordinarily quite grateful for something that is genuinely funny, witty, or charming—after all the Medeas and Hamlets.

Every actor should have two or three additional monologues always at the ready. You never know when you might get a chance to use them. The CD, still unsure after your prepared pieces, may turn to you and ask "Got anything else?" or "Got anything funny?" Obviously, you should be ready to oblige.

For your prepared auditions, you might keep the following tips in mind:

Choosing prepared audition material

- The material you choose should show you in a role in which you could be cast *today*. It should be *you*—or something very close to you—something that shows the most exciting aspects of your personality. Particularly if you are auditioning for film or television (or for the agent who wants to book you in these media), choose something close to your age and personality, and in a style close to that of the role (or roles) for which you are auditioning. If you are auditioning at a dinner theatre, it is silly to do a scene from *Othello*. And though you played old ladies in college, you won't be doing them on Broadway for a while—so don't give casting people your Aunt Eller until you are in your forties.
- Stay away from accents and dialects, unless, of course, one is called for by the audition notice and you can do it to perfection. Dialect pieces should be in your "back pocket," to be given as an additional one you can pull out in the blink of an eye if asked for.
- Choose material that is self-explanatory. In no case should you explain (or have to explain) the plot of your scene or the characterization you're trying to convey. At most, you should announce the name of the play and proceed.

- Choose scenes that don't require specific pieces of furniture, properties, or extensive movement, scenes you could present in a variety of locations without bringing a suitcase full of production aids. Indeed, the simpler the better—which will be especially handy if you're trying to pull this off in an office no bigger than a bathroom.
- Choose material that isn't shopworn; find fresh material and steer clear of monologue books. Last year's most popular Broadway play is probably not your best bet; you'll be competing—in the minds of your auditioners—with that year's Tony-winning performances.
- Choose material that you find truly thrilling. It's amazing the amount of great material and superb writing that is out there. Read it, practice it, learn it, and perform it. Stay away from mediocrity.
- *Brevity* is essential, as mentioned. Don't try to fill up the allocated time frame; give yourself some elbow room instead, and deliver a real jolt—theatrical *impact*. Your audition should grab the CD's attention right away, tease and taunt a bit, build to a climax, and then end powerfully—and before your deadline!
- The *grabber* is critically important: if casting people haven't made up their minds about you by "hello" (see above), they will certainly have a good idea by the *first few seconds* of your audition. They want to be dazzled, and right away. Remember, casting people are not educators, looking for flaws and readying "critiques"; they are producers, directors, and CDs, looking for actors who can capture an audience, entertain them, wring them out, and send them home raving about the show.
- Stay away from truly unpleasant material. We can't tell you how many people pull out the "injured animal" stuff. No one wants to hear it. Perhaps in the context of a play it works, but no one wants to hear about the dying dog or the wounded bird.
- It's frequently rewarding to find and extract scenes from contemporary *novels* for audition material; chances are the dialogue is realistic and the scene fresh. You might also consider screenplays and one-act or ten-minute plays that few casting people have seen. Remember, they are judging *you*, not the material, and your scene doesn't have to be a masterpiece for them to love you doing it.
- Choose audition material that is *exciting*, to you and to the people you can get to look at it. "What good is truth if it's dull and boring?" says Michael Shurtleff in his excellent book *Audition.*
- Above all, choose material that shows you at your best—and do your best. As Jon Lovitz says, "Move them: make them laugh, make them cry, scare them." You don't want your audition scenes to be merely good. You want them to be *great*; you want them to be *terrific.* Choose material at

which you excel, even if it means not doing exactly what has been asked for or what has been suggested here. The audition will fail if you do not come off looking better than anybody the CDs have seen that day, and doing a merely competent job with material you don't like is as bad as nothing at all. Have your agent or manager, if you have one, preview your audition pieces and comment on them. If you are doing a full stage audition, by all means get a coach or director to help you.

Preparing your prepared audition

Preparedness is, of course, critical. How much should you prepare? That question has no easy answer. You can be over-rehearsed, but you can never be over-prepared, certainly not for "prepared" auditions.

Preparedness is what gives you confidence and calm, taking your mind off yourself and letting you concentrate on the business at hand. A relaxed preparedness is perhaps the most professional attitude you can bring to an audition. George C. Scott, when in college, got the title role in a campus production of *Richard III* by memorizing the *entire part*, word for word, before the audition. "They were flabbergasted," Scott tells us, and he went on to a fabulous career. All too frequently, amateur actors slight their preparation on the grounds that it will "rob them of spontaneity," but it takes little objective contemplation to realize that spontaneity is the result of careful, not shoddy, preparation. And that sort of preparation is never wasted.

- Prepare your monologues and scenes under the *various circumstances* in which you may have to perform them. Rehearse on large stages and in small offices. Rehearse with a "director" watching you, or try out your audition piece in an acting class, at a party, in your home, and wherever you can get an audience of one or more to see you. Get used to performing amid general inattention and extraneous noise. Ever audition for an agent with three phone lines ringing? Now is the time to prepare for this.
- Rehearse and prepare your introduction to your scene, your transition between one monologue and the next, and even the "thank you" with which you conclude your audition. If you haven't taken the time and energy to work on your audition, how can you demonstrate your willingness to work on your part?
- Keep your scenes *loose* and not dependent on any single planned "effect." Let the environment of your performance, whether it be office or stage, affect what you and your partner do. Preparation does not mean rigidly fixing every movement and gesture of a scene; some actors prefer to prepare their lines only, leaving the physical and emotional actions

free and unrehearsed. This is particularly useful for film and television auditions, and in fact, it more closely duplicates the way these scenes would be shot professionally than would conventional stage rehearsing. Remember, in an audition the producer is looking not for a fully polished performance, but for your ability to act—and react—convincingly and *magnificently.*

- If you are asked to do two scenes, choose two that differ in tone and style rather than in age.
- If you're asked to bring in a two-person scene (which is rare), choose someone you trust for your acting partner. He or she should be willing to give you the focus if it's your audition; you can return the favor when it's your partner who gets the call. *Never select a poor partner in the hope of looking good by comparison;* you'll both look terrible.

Presenting your prepared audition

- Take and claim your space when you audition. If there's a chair, feel free to move or turn it where you want it to be. So, take charge. Take control. Take stage.
- If you're auditioning for a CD and they provide you someone to read with (which is common), make the most of whomever you have. Endow that reader with everything you need in order to pull from yourself your maximum authenticity, emotion, and inspiration. Your "partner" may be another actor or the CD or an inexperienced intern; whoever it is, and however well or poorly he or she reads, make this unknown partner the object of your acting passion! Make the scene work for you!
- Saying a quick "hello" to the reader when checking in can help before you start.
- You may know from experience that you're likely to be interrupted 15 seconds into your monologue or 16 bars into your song, but put that out of your mind. For those 4 minutes or 15 seconds, dominate the stage you are on and make it your own. If you don't trust yourself, why should they? Make it a *stunning* 16 bars, a fantastic 15 seconds. Never look as though you're waiting to be cut off. Want to go on, and on, and on!
- Should you use props? A simple but appropriate prop that you can keep in your pocket and bring out at precisely the right moment can humanize and give a lift to an audition, particularly in a modern piece. One actor reports losing a role in call-backs because of a very cleverly incorporated flash instamatic camera in his competitor's audition. "A brilliant and outrageous idea," our colleague reports, "but I was edged out by a *camera*!" You, too, can do some edging out—but don't haul a

prop bag into the rehearsal hall, and don't use anything that you can't manipulate expertly. (And don't ever smoke or chew gum—unless you are certain it is appropriate to the scene.)

- Don't look directly at the auditioners unless they ask you to. Rather, "place" the characters you're (presumably) speaking to out in the audience, just left or right of those hearing your audition, and focus on them. The auditioners are trying to work, take notes, and read your résumé. They are not there to be your scene partner.

- In group auditions where other actors are waiting their turn (which is rare in the professional world but sometimes happens), you may find that you have a tendency to play to your fellow actors in the wings rather than to the producers out front. We understand this, because while the other actors are your competition, they're also your peers, and you may think them a more comfortable audience. They are, but forget this. Now is the time to turn your back on the competition and take the stage as your own. Cruel? No. You are not auditioning as part of an ensemble (yet, anyway) but as an individual. Your competitors will (or should) be as well.

- Get in the light. Stay in the light. Speak up and be heard.

- Play the room. Adjust to the space—small or large—in which you find yourself.

- *Go all the way*, emotionally, with your audition. As mentioned in discussing "the (other) most important lesson" above, there's absolutely no reason to hold back, waiting for a director to show you the way. Unless you're cast, there will be no director and no "way." Put those emotions into your acting, not just into your thinking. Don't overestimate how well CDs can see into your silences and private reveries; let your feelings and words flow through your entire body, where they can be seen, heard, and *felt*. Excite the listeners. "How strong should the reading be?" asked Gary Shaffer, who cast more than 60 films and TV series during his 25-year career. "The exciting readings get the role," he answered. "The closer you get to performance level in your reading, the better chance you have of getting cast. The person who cries real tears gets the job."

Dress, comportment, and behavior in the audition room

- Your clothes should represent you. They should show a personal style, a point of view.

    ASIDE FROM JAMES: We have a code in our office when an actor has no style or fashion sense. We write 1–800-DRESS, which means the actor's style is so generic and bland that it looks like they chose it only to look like everybody else. Think fashion forward.

- Unless you're auditioning for the role of a corporate executive, steer clear of formal business attire: suits and ties and tailored dresses. You're an actor; dress like one.
- But dress like a *professional* actor, not a college student. Remember that you're auditioning for working professionals—producers, directors, and CDs—who associate mainly with other professionals. Your appearance should let them feel that you live (or want to live) in the same world as they do. Bare feet, stained T-shirts, and deliberate grunge rarely have the same effect in Hollywood, New York, or LORT casting offices as they have in your university's drama class. Unless you're up for the role of a hot young teenager, dress as an adult professional; that is, in clothing that is clean, fresh, well fitted, and appropriate to your age and interests. Jack Falahee, breakout star on ABC's *How to Get Away with Murder*, says: "Especially when living in New York, you're dealing with how crazy the city can be itself, and catching the subway and getting to the audition and removing layers of clothes or putting on layers of clothing based on the weather is a total nightmare. I would always go to auditions as early as possible so I could just sit there and acclimate and change my sweaty T-shirt."
- One final word on clothes: you must be completely *comfortable* in them. If you are comfortable only in tattered campus gear, then that's what you're going to have to wear until and unless you become accustomed to something better. You can't worry about the way you look. Worry, of course, is murder.
- Your *grooming* should leave you clean, neat, and odorless. Makeup for women should be subtle but effective. Hair (including facial hair) is always crucial; it should look terrific *for you*, particularly in film and television, where there is an exceptionally high standard for makeup and hair, especially for women.

> ASIDE FROM JAMES: Be "camera ready." Nine times out of ten, if I'm getting feedback from a network on an actress's audition it is not about her beats or intentions but about her hairstyle, dress, and eyeliner.

- Perfume, says CD Lisa Miller Katz, is "inappropriate." We completely agree. And leave the dangly earrings at home.
- Enjoy yourself. Be likable. "A casting session is like a party," says CD Beverly Long. "It should be festive. You, the actor, are my invited guest. If you throw the lawn furniture into the pool, you don't get invited back.

Remember, your goal is not to see every CD *once*, but to get invited back to these parties over and over again." CD Cindy Tolan (*Avenue Q*, *The Curious Incident of the Dog in the Night Time*) echoes this, advising actors to treat the audition experience as if they were at a cocktail party: "You don't know anybody, so be polite, shake hands when offered, then it's on to 'nice to see you', small chit-chat and then move on. You should have manners."

- Trust your instincts. Trust where they take you. You'll either get the part or not get it based on those instincts—so, don't fret about it. Not getting a part doesn't mean you're a bad actor, just that it wasn't *your* part.

- If invited to chat, this doesn't mean that you start reciting your résumé and acting credits. CDs want to know how you see the *world*. They like to hear your likes and dislikes. They love actors with strong points of view and fresh ideas. Show who *you* are, apart from your acting career. This is your time to shine!

- When you finish your audition, don't apologize for *anything*. Don't give any indication that you aren't proud of everything you just did, even if you blew your lines or tripped on the carpet. How do they know these were mistakes? This is not a time for abject humility (or, on the other hand, for cocky smugness).

- If it seems appropriate, and they aren't giving you "You can leave now" signals, you might ask if there's anything else they want to hear. You should do everything in your power at this point to convince your audience that you love to audition, that you enjoyed doing this audition particularly, and that you'd be happy to do it again if they were interested. But know when to leave a room. The CDs behind the table know what they want, and when they indicate the audition is over, be gracious and get out quickly. If they want more, they know how to ask for it. If you are given three sets of sides but are dismissed after reading the first, don't look defeated or tell them that you stayed up all night working on all three pieces. They got what they needed—they may even be planning on calling you back. Don't make it tough for them to do so!

- Show confidence. Exclusively. Your auditioners are looking at you not only for talent and an appropriateness for the role, but also for personal stamina and a positive, professional attitude. Don't turn them off with grimaces or mutterings that convey your personal discomfort and only show that you're not yet ready for professional work.

- Don't be a pain. "If you're painful in the audition, we have to assume you're going to be painful on the set," says CD Bonnie Gillespie. And don't be a pain in the outer office, either. "Assistants tell us," Gillespie cautions. And you better be sure they only say nice things!

Auditions are *competitions,* and you must understand and treat them as such. You are being examined for your usefulness in an industry that wants to make money through your efforts. There are many competitors for every acting job; each, in effect, is put on a moving treadmill and passed in front of the CDs and producers. It is your task to *stop the treadmill* and make the auditioners notice your individual value to their project. Whatever you can do to accomplish that, within the bounds of your own ability and—yes—ethics, you ought to know how to do and be prepared to do.

After the prepared audition

Your audition over, you smile, say thank you, and, unless told otherwise, head for the door. Let the work speak for itself. If they want to extend your opportunity, they'll stop you on the spot. Don't expect feedback. These people are casting for specific projects; they're concentrating on those projects, and if they don't see you fitting into them, they're—in their heads, anyway—already on to their next candidate. Don't blame them; giving you acting counsel is not their job. They're not paid for it, don't have time for it, possibly don't even have the skill for it, and in any case they aren't your teachers. The only feedback you may glean from them is the look in their eyes and the warmth (or speediness) of their thank-you-very-muches when you're finished.

Keep an audition diary. It can be a five and dime notepad or the Notes app on your iPhone. Whatever you do, record your visits and appointments. Just get into the habit of keeping records. For each audition, create a one-page entry. The basics get recorded: the project, the CD, the assistant, who was in the room, notes on the part, any adjustments given, the sides, and any other specifics like location and what you wore, what you read or sang. Then write down your feelings about the audition—how it went and what response you might have gotten. Do it right after, while it's all uppermost and clear minded. Don't be that person who can't recall if they ever auditioned for that CD before. And do note when certain things come up again and again. Maybe the same notes about rushing keep coming up, or you have strong feelings about how you worked with this particular accompanist. Help fine tune your work—and your chances of being hired—with the help of a diary that tracks your career.

The 45-second prepared audition

Casting people in the film/TV industry don't ask for prepared auditions nearly as much as they did in past generations. Perhaps it's because there's simply more time pressure than ever before—more films, more TV shows, and more networks broadcasting 24/7. Perhaps the advent of internet technology—which allows the instant transmission of scripts to actors and performance videos to CDs—has made it much more possible to arrange readings of actual roles than was previously the case. Whatever the reason, script "readings" are now the main form of audition in film and television, and increasingly on the stage as well.

Before moving to readings, however, we'd like to suggest an exercise called "the 45-second audition." It's just what it says, a 45-second long (maximum!) monologue, with the additional limitations that it be done entirely while seated, in the actor's normal voice, with no introduction, no props, and absolutely no hype—no shouting, no screaming, no surprising stage business, no histrionics. Movement is limited to perhaps leaning forward in the chair and perhaps leaning backward—once only for each! Everything else in the way of "acting" is done in the eyes, the voice, the feelings, and, above all, the unsaid and unexpressed. Intense intimacy, not bluster, is the key. The material should not be from anything familiar; perhaps you can find it in a novel, short story, or little-known drama, or even something you've written yourself.

This is a monologue you might give on occasions when you're across the desk (or lunch table) from a casting person—an agent, a CD, or a director, generally in the film/TV world—who asks if by chance you have a monologue. You simply say "Sure" and begin it with no further ado. There should be no introduction and no change between the voice saying "Sure" and the voice saying the first word of the monologue; your eyes, by moving from the casting person's gaze to the imaginary character to whom your character is speaking, makes the entire segue. You are now inhabiting another world entirely.

You may not be asked to deliver such a monologue in the next ten years. But if you are, and if you have prepared this (usually with some feedback, generated within a group of actors preparing their own 45-second pieces), you might find it the perfect vehicle for moving on to the next step.

A final word about monologues: except in Shakespeare festivals, no one gets cast simply from doing one. What you are seeking with your monologue is to be taken to the next step, which is reading for a specific role in a production. But the monologue tells the viewer something about you; it represents your "thing." You should wear your monologue like a good set of clothes: good fit, great style, not too loud and crazy. It works for you—and for your work.

Readings, pre-readings, pre-pre-readings

All readings are for a specific job. The name is a little misleading, however, because if you really want the part, you aren't just going to be "reading" it—you're going to be acting it.

As mentioned earlier, the invitation to "pre-read" is to attend a screening audition for the final reading. But this is nothing you need think about—it's really only a distinction for the CD, and you probably won't even know whether it's a read or a pre-read—and in fact, the CD may not even know at that time, and only decide after he or she sees what the first batch of readings provides. So, forget about it: in any reading you're asked to do, treat it like a final audition.

In a professional situation, when you're asked to read for a part, you are supposed to be able to get a copy of the script—at least the portion to be used at the reading—at least 24 hours in advance of your reading in film and TV, and 48 hours in live theatre. (Exceptions are made when the part hasn't been written yet, as in TV, where this is not all that unusual; in such cases you may get the script when you show up for the reading itself!)

The internet has long since replaced the fax as the means of script transmission: you can check the biggest companies carrying these (mainly for film and TV roles), among which currently are Sides Express, Showfax, Now Casting, and Actors Access. Note, however, that membership or a charge is involved for securing such scripts. Your part will normally come in what is called a "side," which once meant a script with just your character's lines and cues but now mainly refers simply to the section of text that includes your part.

When you come in, you're asked to "read" the part for the CD, usually with a reader or the CD's assistant reading opposite you—or, for stage work, you may be reading with a stage manager, or even with the director or other actors. Readings can take place over a period of days, or even months; the casting of the 2008 Broadway revival of *South Pacific* took a full year. Television works much faster: ordinarily, a TV CD will ask to "pre-read" up to a dozen actors for each of the smaller and nonrecurring "day-player" roles in that show, from whom perhaps two or three will be selected to show to the producers the following day. Your goal, of course, is to be so *terrific* that you are selected as one of the two or three, and then the one.

But as you now know, you don't "read" your lines; you have to act them. The 24 hours between your invitation to "read" and actually doing it is to give you time to *memorize your part*, since the goal of such a "reading" is to *act the daylights* out of the role while still, largely as a gesture to tradition, holding the script in one hand and referring to it (or pretending to do so) every now and then.

That means you must *prepare* the daylights out of that script as well. "The actor who best understands the role and is securely off-book will land the role," says *Backstage* editorialist Tom Mills. "If you expect to wing it at the audition, your results will almost always be dismal." So, *learn the part* before you go off to "read it" to the CDs or producers.

Should you go in "off-book" then; that is, without your script? No, never, and for two reasons: first, holding your script will give you more confidence than going in bare, and you won't worry about forgetting your lines; second, holding the script tells them you're not quite at full performance level, even if you are. Mike Fenton again: "It is your obligation as a professional actor to be off-book, but don't let the director know it, because you don't want the director to think he or she is seeing a finished performance." Don Scardino, producer of *30 Rock* and director of many TV episodics, agrees, saying he doesn't expect you to *fully* memorize the part unless you are going to get paid for doing it. "But get close to it. You want to be the one we pay!"

Being 99% off-book will allow you to fully *interact*—emotionally, physically, gesturally, and romantically—with your (temporary) acting partner, no matter how uninterested your partner in the office reading might prove to be. You'll be able to get angry, sad, hot, or excited, or fall in love. You're not going to be able to do *any* of that if you're simply reading words off a page, nor will anybody be able to see your eyes if they're buried in the page.

So, hold the script, glance at the script, gesture with the script, but don't—for even a moment—become *absorbed* by the script. This may not be the most important lesson in this book, but it's the most important lesson in this section. If you are asked to read for a part, get the script, learn it, and make it fly off the page.

Some "reading techniques" will help you interact powerfully while still holding on to the pages, even when you haven't been able to memorize the part perfectly. (And sometimes you just can't, as, for example, when you have multiple auditions in a single day.) "Learn how to use your pages," advises Jeff Greenberg. "Recopy them if necessary." Actor Bob Gunton pastes his pages on pieces of cardboard so they won't flop around when he holds them. Highlight them, write notes, undo the staples, whatever works for you to make it your own. Specifically, learn to *spot-review* your semi-memorized lines, one at a time, while the other character is speaking. Keeping your script about chest-high (though not covering your face!), try marking your "place" with your thumb opposite the lines as they're spoken. When you have a moment during the other character's line, steal a glance at your words—without tilting your head if possible. This isn't easy at first, but it's something you can—and should—learn and practice. (It helps to do this with a few friends.)

Cold readings

You should also learn to do a *cold reading*, that is, to act from a script you've never seen before in your life. It doesn't happen too often these days, with sides readily available on the internet, but it's not unheard of, particularly when parts are suddenly added to films and TV shows already in production.

> ASIDE FROM JAMES: We do many "morning of" auditions, calling people in the morning and having them show up to audition in the afternoon. It's the nature of television; it's not ideal but you make the best of it. But understand that the producers don't care when you were called or how little time you had to look over the script—they *still* want to see a great performance.

You can develop your cold-reading technique either in the privacy of your home or in classes that specialize in it.

Tony Barr, onetime CBS producer and founder of the Film Actors' Workshop, advises that "you should work your tail off learning to become a good cold reader. Take a speed reading course. At the very least, read aloud from any source whatsoever for at least fifteen minutes a day, taking your eyes off the page as much as you can without interrupting the flow of your reading." This will prove useful to you not only in cold readings, should they come your way, but also in readings where you only have the time to half-memorize and spot-review.

The more you practice acting full-out with a script in your hand, the more comfortable you'll be when you find yourself in a casting room two years from now.

Most of the suggestions for prepared auditions (above) apply to readings and cold readings as well; a few other tips apply to readings even more specifically, particularly in film and television:

- *Prepare bold emotional choices* for the characters you're playing, even if you know little about the material other than the few pages you're given. Make these choices in terms of the "characters" you're reading with. Love them, hate them, envy them, worship them, but don't just stare blankly at them. Raise the stakes. Then raise them higher. Don't let indecisiveness get the best of you. You will have to make bold decisions based on little information. Don't let that stymie you: decide—and conquer!
- In his book *Audition*, Michael Shurtleff recommends that you always look for a "love interest" in your characters, even if this is not specifically indicated in your particular scene. This is a first-rate idea. Such an awareness creates a human electricity between actors and enlivens their relationship—whatever else might be going on—in the eyes of CDs (and, subsequently, audiences). It's rarely out of place. Lacking a

love interest, incarnate hatred or jealousy can work as well. But prepare *something* to do with your character and the person he or she is speaking to, and then do it.

- Intensity, persuasiveness, sexual longing, passion, madcap inventiveness—these are all wonderful qualities to show in a reading where appropriate to the material (and perhaps even where they are *not* appropriate). Blandness and passivity are the only true crimes in this medium. However, it is best to avoid broad external characterizations unless you are certain that this is precisely what is wanted—and you can do them extremely well. Read the character as your most intense, exciting self, and let the director see your deepest personal qualities—your lusts and your longings and your winsome charm—emerge.

- If the role requires a dialect and you can do it perfectly, then do it. If you can only fake it, don't even try. In general, don't try *anything* in a professional audition that will make you look less than fabulous.

- Be simple. Be connected and move through the piece moment to moment.

- Be flexible. Be ready to take direction and change things. If you are given "an adjustment," be ready to shift immediately. And don't take such an adjustment as a criticism; it's actually a good sign—it means they're interested in you and they are already starting to "rehearse" you in the role! If they weren't interested, they'd hardly waste their time trying to refine your performance.

- Don't talk about yourself unless they ask you to. You might think they're interested in your Shakespeare festival performance, but you're wrong: they are there to cast their specific project. What they want to see and hear is the work you do in front of them. All else—keep it for the wrap party.

- Accentuate the positive. Eliminate the negative. Find the reason why you want to stay in the room with that other person in the scene. Keep saying yes. You will find more open doors and undiscovered pathways with one "yes" than with 20 "no"s.

- Feel free to ask a quick and specific question before the reading, particularly if the character seems unclear. Asking "Hey, is this guy supposed to be a wimp, or is all this innocence just a pretense?" might get you a little closer, in your reading, to what the CD and the producers have in mind, and they probably won't mind taking the time to answer you. However, don't ask a long-winded question, don't try to follow up, and certainly don't start telling the CD why you disagree with his or her answer! Most importantly, however: remember to trust your instincts. Self-doubt is the enemy. It will undermine your greatest of choices.

- But don't ask a broad general question such as "Is there anything you want to tell me before I begin?" They want to see what your instincts are. If there's anything they want to tell you before you begin, they won't need your prompting. CDs are not shy. They will speak up if it's necessary!

- Don't waste anybody's time. "Never walk in the room and start doing breathing exercises," CD Jeff Greenberg advises. If you need a warm-up, do it on your own time, not the CD's. The halls outside most casting rooms are filled with actors stretching, huh-buh-buh-bubbing and doing their yoga exercises; join the crowd if you want or need to, but don't make a show of it.

- Particularly for comedy, be *precise* with the language you're given. "Don't change a *syllable*," Greenberg advised actors auditioning for the long-running *Frasier.* "Adding an 'um' or a 'well' can kill the joke, or destroy the rhythm or meaning." Remember that the producers of most comedy shows on television are the writers and that hell hath no fury like a writer misquoted.

- *Dress* for the part you're reading for. It isn't necessary, and is probably even harmful, to costume yourself in full detail, but you should do your best to *look the part* by drawing on clothing from your own wardrobe or finding clothes that you would wear in daily activities. If it's a Western show, by all means dig out your Arizona gear; if the scene takes place in a law office, grab your pinstripe suit. But don't go so far as to look silly on the street, and don't go all the way into period dress—it may make you feel uncomfortable and will almost certainly make you look desperate. Simply look the part without looking as if you're trying to look the part. Look as if you *are* the part. Tony-winning actress Nina Arianda came in with a full bag of costume pieces for her initial audition for *Venus in Fur.* She knew what was required to embody the part of Vanda. And clothes were a very important and first part of that. Most CDs like nothing better than to cast the real thing, if the real thing also comes in with a credible acting résumé. Jonathan Schaech, who played the John Lennon-type character in *That Thing You Do,* came to his audition dressed as a rock musician from the early 1960s, complete with a black skinny tie and a 1960s haircut. Admired one interviewer, "It wasn't like somebody costumed you; it was your own choice and your own ability to distill the character for the purposes of the audition." Schaech replied, "I was there to get the job, and to show that I knew Jimmy better than anybody else."

- Don't worry overmuch if you muff a line. While you're supposed to nail the part, everybody knows it's still a reading, and few directors will be troubled if you blow one or two details while you're still (in their minds, at least) on-book. If you do it a few times. however, that's a red flag.

- If asked to "do it again," simply do it again. Don't try to show them new tricks: if they like what they saw, they probably just want to see if you can repeat it. This shows that you will be able to repeat yourself when you get on the set. Unless you're given an adjustment, the opportunity to do it again is exactly that; don't go standing on your head to show what else you can do.

- Likewise, if they say "Great! Try something else," do it! Make clear you are not a one-hit wonder and can switch to whatever you want—and think they might want! Are you game for anything? Can you be playful? And do you have lots of options to give the creative team? Go for it!

- Finally, what they *must* see is the essential character coming through you, and your innate *honesty and theatricality* in the role. Do you understand the part? Are you sympathetic? Exciting? Sexy? Entertaining? Charming? Scary? Wonderful to look at? Will your presence *improve* the part, flesh it out from what lies silently on the page? Will you inspire the writers and producers to write well for you? Finally, are you going to be fun to work with?

> ASIDE FROM JAMES: "If a television show runs six seasons, will the producers want to hang out with you this long? Will the writing team be inspired enough by who you are to write story upon story for you? Will the viewers want to invite you into their homes each week and each season like an old friend?" This helps put things into perspective for me while I'm casting a recurring or series regular on a television show.

Self-tapes

You may also want to create *self-tapes*, as they may become more and more common throughout the shelf life of this book—and of your career.

Self-tapes make physical distance a non-issue during the early rounds of the audition game these days. You'll need a video camera, possibly on your iPad or iPhone or any new digital gizmo that comes into play, of course, and a friend to operate it—or you can mount it on a tripod and do your thing in front of it. Self-tapes have advantages, of course: you don't have to drive to a studio, you don't have to wait around until you're called, and, more to the point, you can shoot your reading as many times as you want until it looks like you want it to. The quality won't be professional, of course, but nor will anyone else's.

Quality is important, especially for film and television auditions, which can be offered and cast straight from a tape. For musical theatre and straight plays, it is often crucial to still see the actor live. But it can lead to work. Co-author Calleri's most recent recurring role on Hulu's *The Path* was initiated by a self-tape. Chris Gattelli, choreographer of *Newsies*, was wowed by a young talent via video clips before the show was even looking for replacements. CD Bernard Telsey, however, says that tapes will never replace live sessions. And "nothing can beat having the actor in the room auditioning for you in a live situation," says veteran Broadway director Jerry Mitchell, who adds, "I'm looking at how quickly they learn, how they take adjustments, how they adapt to different styles. For that you need to be in the room." So, the self-tape is often the important first step, but rarely, if ever, the final one.

Our advice on preparing a self-tape, in addition to everything on the previous pages about readings, is the following:

- Put yourself in front of a neutral background. Scenery is utterly unimportant. Many actor friends we know paint a blue wall just for this purpose. Or they go out and buy a portable blue fold-up screen. B&H Photo in New York is the actor's touchstone for all things involving video, lighting, sound, and the like. Simon's Camera and Samy's Camera are equivalents in Los Angeles. The people who work at all these shops are very knowledgeable about the latest and most up-to-date technology.
- CD Maribeth Fox's (*Carol*) advice is to invest in good background paper for self-tapes, recommending blue paper for blue eyes and gray for everyone in general, a camera with a chip that is capable of creating compressed videos on a computer so CDs don't need to spend a long time downloading footage, and a lightbox (image presenter) that can do wonders for your physical presence on camera. Fox says, "if a self-tape takes me 10 minutes to download, you're out!"
- Wear something from your wardrobe reasonably like what the character would be wearing, but don't go for a full-bore costume.
- Keep the camera steady, and don't get tricky with the photography. Again, tripods are key for this. And they even have the smallest of smartphones that can hook up now to the largest of tripods.
- Stay in camera range, but express yourself physically as you perform. Work in medium close-up to close-up shot range. It's difficult to see facial expression and range working in full-body shots.
- Light yourself evenly so that the clip is easy to watch and not overly "theatrical." This is crucial. We can't tell you the number of self-tapes we have witnessed with bad lighting that's too dark or overshadowed.

- Slate yourself (say your name) at the beginning, give the name of the show you're reading for, and give your name and contact phone number at the end, finishing with a quick "thank you" and blackout. There are easy video editing programs nowadays to make a professional slate in writing if you don't want to say it on-camera. These "video written" slates look fantastic, and you can put much needed information on a three-second clip, such as your name, contact phone, agency or manager contact if you have one, and the role played along with the project.
- View your video and shoot it as many times as you want until you have something you're proud of.
- Submit it before the deadline—and as far before as you can. Submitting this kind of self-tape is relatively simple nowadays. Sites like Vimeo or a private YouTube account can be shared by invitation, and there are now countless other sites available that can do the trick—easily and cheaply.

Call-backs

If your reading has been as thrilling, scary, sexy, and/or charming as you hoped, you might be invited to any number of call-backs. These sometimes take place before an expanded audience: normally the director, and often a lot of other people (consider them producers) as well. Generally, at least three to five of you will be called back, maybe more—and maybe (for a series lead, say) a lot more.

Hang onto your copy of the script! You may not hear about the call-back for days or even weeks. With the script by your bedside, you'll be able to have the part fully memorized when you go in again—and this time you won't have to hide the fact. Keep a journal with all its pertinent information from the first audition—who was in the room, what notes were given. And keep the sides as well for safekeeping if you have the good fortune and talent to book a call-back.

When you're called back, you have to once again deliver the goods—over and over. You may be given "adjustments" to make, and you'll be judged on how (apparently) effortlessly and effectively you make them. Call-backs are mainly about acting, not talking, so avoid the temptation to "discuss" the part or the project unless they engage first. Try to find out what they want and give it to them. Unless told (or "adjusted") otherwise, do it the same way you did it for the CD. That's what got you there in the first place, so don't abandon it. Perfect it, of course, but don't decide it's time to show your other side. Avoid the temptation to try out a new outfit or suddenly curl your hair when you always wear it straight. They want you only for one role, and you're already close to it. So, don't jump ship! Nail it.

Nudity at auditions

There may be times in an audition when you will be asked to take off your clothes. This is a gray area. The *Backstage* casting notices include the statement: "No nudity should be required during an audition even if the role requires nudity." Note the word *should*; it's not illegal. Equity does not permit nudity during interviews or at an initial audition, and permits it at callbacks only when an Equity stage manager or other representative is present and the "professional artistic position" of the director and producers has been verified. The SAG contract assures that film/filmed TV performers must receive prior notification of any interview or audition requiring nudity "and shall have the absolute right to have a person of the performer's choice present at that audition." But know that nudity is a common feature in contemporary theatre and film; if you're going to be auditioning for *Puppetry of the Penis* (a show consisting of genital contortionists), you're going to be dropping your drawers shortly after the preliminary handshake. The unions (even if you are not a member) will protect you from unscrupulous voyeurs who happen to be producing films and plays, but if you plan to do the broadest spectrum of contemporary films or plays, you should expect that this might come up. More than likely, it might at first involve only the men stripping off their shirts or both sexes being told to wear tight or revealing clothing for an audition. It's only after you book the job that the real fun begins.

Audition attitude

You will have to adopt a pretty stable audition attitude. Like everything else in the life of a beginning (or even a lifetime) professional actor, auditions are high-stress exercises and can lead to paranoia. Even if everybody from the producer on down is extremely polite, you are unceremoniously directed to perform when they ask you to and to leave when they tell you to. It's hard to take charge of such a situation. It's discouraging to the strong and ruinous to the weak, and you better be prepared for it. You must develop a rock-solid professional attitude to weather the inevitable storms.

You didn't get called back? This doesn't mean you don't have talent, looks, or personality—only that you weren't what they were looking for on this occasion. There could be a million reasons why, and "talent" is only one of them.

After the call-back that doesn't come, remember your first "most important" lesson: *you weren't rejected, just overlooked*. Laura Linney didn't score a single agent interview after her Juilliard showcase. An unknown Michael Richards thought he had totally failed his audition with Marc Hirschfeld for *Married with Children*, but Hirschfeld remembered him and some time afterward brought him in to read for the part of Kramer in a new show called *Seinfeld*. You know the rest.

So, remember: you're not there just to get the part. You're also there to be *remembered* and called again. Leave the room happy for the opportunity to show your work.

Interviews

Interviews now tend to follow auditions rather than precede them. (Note that SAG contracts never refer to auditions, only "interviews"—interviews in which you audition.) Interviews can be more important than auditions, particularly in commercial casting. Commercial CD Adrienne Berg reports, "We don't ask anyone to come in and read a monologue or give us a scene. We give great meetings!"

Interviews are a stumbling block for many actors, and "I don't interview well" is unfortunately a common complaint. Actors capable of playing characters with strength, compassion, and subtlety may fall to pieces when they are asked to play themselves. "So, the audition was fine," a CD might say. "Now tell me about yourself." Gulp. For that's what you do in an interview—you play yourself. You must not think for a moment that an interview is simply a casual, obligatory windup to an audition. For a beginning actor, the interview is the producer's chance to find out if the terrific performance you've just delivered is something you can summon up again and again, in performance after performance or take after take. In short, do you have the maturity, commitment, and psychological balance to be a professional in a high-stakes business?

Interviews let casting people know just what kind of person you are, which is why they're particularly important. Esteemed theatre director Andrei Serban loves to meet the actor in an intimate atmosphere to make them feel at ease in the attempt to get some sort of true and sincere response from the actor. He equates it to looking for an organic impulse in an acting exercise, rather that the cliché or false pretense usually portrayed in a "politely correct answer." Indeed, film and television directors may rely more on your personal "quality" than on your acting. They want you to be a *person*—and specifically the person *they are looking for*—when the door opens and you walk into the room. Of course, they will have acting questions they want answered as well: do you hit your moments, capture the humor, drive the scene? But that's basically gravy: they're most concerned with seeing your sense of self—who you are in the world and how you relate to it. In short, your "personality" (see Chapter 2). Alexa Fogel, award-winning CD of such shows as *The Wire*, *Treme*, and *True Detective*, knows whether a certain actor might not be served best with an interview situation for her creative team. She is aware of which actors may read better compared with the ones who only present a great meeting. And while some actors articulate their characters with the written dialogue rather than a thoughtful character discussion, Alexa adjusts audition circumstances depending on her impression of the actor auditioning.

Play yourself, and play yourself boldly, but *select* those aspects of yourself you want to display. Be yourself, but be your *best* self. You are an actor. Look like it and act like it. You are a *professional*. Let them know that too. Arrive well ahead of time, armed with extra copies of your photo-résumé (even though you've sent one ahead), and a reel if you have one. Relax and let your salable qualities shine.

Don't just sit back and wait for something to happen, however. *Make it happen.* Be vivacious, not retiring. Be friendly but not self-effacing. Be funny, if you feel like it, but not at your own (or their) expense. Be polite, but don't *rely* on being polite. Don't simply wait for questions and then meekly answer them; an interview is not a criminal investigation. Ask questions yourself, and start the conversation when it seems appropriate. You are not a butterfly mounted on a pin or a patient etherized upon a table; you have to *live* during your interview.

So, tell them about yourself. Be positive and infectious. If you begin by telling them your problems, the interview is over before it begins. "Well, I suppose you want to know about my credits. I don't have any." Only a psychologist can explain why so many actors destroy themselves by offering such remarks. How about "I want to do this show because I love kids" or "I played Coriolanus at Ashland last summer" or "I write features for *Hot Rod* magazine?" Actress and longtime CD from South Coast Repertory Martha McFarland says, "Tell them three things they'll remember tomorrow morning."

Of course you're insecure, but don't let it show. Tell them things you would like them to know, and avoid things you would rather they didn't. Nobody has asked you to present both sides of the case, after all. They have every reason in the world *not* to cast you. Don't make that decision any easier for them. *Never* be desperate. As *Backstage* former editor Thomas Mills advises, "Nobody gets a job because they need it. Indeed, it's much better to look like you *don't* need it."

A positive personality, not repetition of facts, provides the content of the good interview. Richard Dreyfuss says of his successful first interviews: "I would try to take over in the sense of going beyond [their] questions. I would ask questions about the script. I would give them my opinion about the script. I would let them see as much of Rick Dreyfuss as possible, rather than just the information of my history."

You have to be memorable. CDs and producers see a great many people when they are casting, so you have to stand out in their memory—one way or another. If you can look memorable, say something memorable, or do something memorable, it helps. Mere politeness (which, after all, you must practice) is not enough to stimulate anybody's interest; *everybody* is polite. A downright hostile attitude, though not recommended, is better than stolid numbness. Be attractively unique, a little (or a lot, if you can swing it) dangerous. Find an *exciting* way to be different. Show them that beneath your nice exterior, and your professional calm, lies the fire of passion and charisma. It's acting, and that's what you're good at, isn't it? So, get together with a few friends (or, if you're still in school, classmates) and *rehearse* an interview. It's a lot easier when you've practiced.

> ASIDE FROM JAMES: Mock interviews are one of the staples I do with my third year graduate actors at Columbia. It teaches them to think on their toes and to expect the unexpected. Interviews will vary and be as different as the strange and fascinating people you will meet in the industry.

And while casting-couch sex is almost always out of bounds these days, carefully sharing your sex appeal is certainly not. Longtime producer Lynda Obst reports that nobody sleeps his or her way to the top anymore, but she also considers flirting an "essential tool." Obst is speaking of "tactical flirting... walking the line between virtual and actual seduction." The casting couch, it seems, has become the "casting gaze." As Obst explains, "With eyes focused on her prey, she makes the other the most interesting person in the world, as though the person were a real date. His interests interest her. His past movies are among her favorites. The point is to make him see that she is fun to work with because she *likes* him and that she's not looking to find fault or to judge him." Whether this is flirting or simply agreeability may be a matter of semantics. Of one thing Obst is sure: "No clothing is ever removed ... because nobody really [goes all the way]."

Interviewing takes practice. You should go to every interview you can, because with each you will acquire not only valuable know-how, but also an unfaked confidence. It may take 10 to 15 interviews before you really start to "come out," because the tendency of most sensitive people (and most actors *are* sensitive people) is to sit docilely and be inoffensive. Face it: that's largely just nerves. If you leave your interview breathing a sigh of relief, you've probably blown it. Conversely, if you leave feeling excited—feeling that you've met some interesting people—they probably feel the same way about you, and you've probably done very well.

So, go in there and have a good time. Be yourself. And get to know the secretaries and receptionists. This is where you can be nice, because you need all the friends you can find in this business. Indeed, one of director Adrian Hall's assistants told me that Hall used to pop into the outside office after interviews and ask his staff, "OK, who was an asshole outside?" You certainly wouldn't want to be named on such an occasion! CDs typically ask their intern or assistant who caused trouble in the waiting room hallway. Who gave attitude or grief to the assistants outside the rehearsal hall? Also remember that today's secretary is tomorrow's CD, and next month's producer.

The screen test

Screen tests are used in film and television to see how you act and look on camera. The screen test may be a very simple affair during which you turn your face from left to right in front of a camera and "slate yourself" (speak your name) or improvise a conversation, or it may be as involved as a complete scene that you rehearse with a studio director and perform with sets and costumes. A "chemistry test" involves reading with another actor in order to test just that—your chemistry or "spark" with the other actor. This can be useful for new recurring roles (like a new love interest for a main character) or new series regulars. For major roles in films and television, the screen test is usually the last stage of the audition, and the finalists for a certain role may screen-test opposite each other. Such formal screen tests are universal for actors on the verge of "booking a series" (becoming a regular on a TV show), by which time they will have already received—and signed—a pre-negotiated agreement that dictates the terms under which they will be contracted if the "roomful of suits" (the TV executives with final authority) give their "thumbs up" to the test.

Getting to the point where you are actually working on a set involving multiple auditions and extensive negotiations. "Testing" is a good thing. It means you are in the mix. And one test often leads to others. Execs love to focus on who is testing and therefore "who is hot" at any given moment. The momentum can lead to interest on other projects—and also, it's fantastic confidence building. It's a sign that they like you and that you are doing all the right things. The "test" is to television what the "final call-back" is to theatre. Even if you do not get the role, testing on series regulars and seeing how they all work is great preparation toward screen success.

But you may have been "screen tested" from your initial visit to a CD's office, since the digital *videotaping of auditions* has now become routine in network television and film, is all but universal in the casting of commercials, and is often now used in stage casting as well. Such taped auditions are uploaded onto network-hosted internet sites so that many casting people—CDs, directors, producers, and network executives—can view auditions for the entire project, which may include simultaneous auditions in, say, New York, Hollywood, London, Chicago, and Bangkok. Such videotape and/or digital files allow casting people to retain your "electronic audition" indefinitely, to show it to others after you've left their office, and to examine your work closely and repeatedly against other contenders for the same role. It is wise, therefore, to study camera acting during your training, and become comfortable working in front of taping crews and equipment, as part of your career preparation. Many commercial schools, advertising regularly in the trades, offer both instruction and facilities for taping auditions and scenes, and you should explore these opportunities. Even some of the finest MFA and BFA programs are now starting to add this full time to their curricula, knowing this is the new reality of the business. It is, indeed, a necessary survivor skill if you really want to be a working actor of today.

Pilot season

Pilot season—you hear about it all the time. But what is it exactly? Over recent years it has become less and less clear, but typically, pilot season begins in January and runs through the spring. How do you get in on pilot season? Easier said than done. Networks and studios are putting together their most prized ensembles to create a show. Some of these roles have names—others might be just starting out. After the CD sees a wide range of roles for every series regular on their pilot, the producers and network/studio will decide to test a small handful, usually between three and five actors. This means you will final audition in front of the studio execs and show creators. If you are in New York, they may fly you (on their dime) to studio in a matter of 24–48 hours. This can be an incredibly challenging and stressful scenario for even the oldest pro. With your deal pre-negotiated beforehand, the stakes are high. Typically, for a newcomer, you may receive a weekly $20,000 and up if you get cast in a pilot. In addition, you may virtually sign your life away for the series' run, if you are so fortunate that the pilot ends up running for six to ten years. If it "goes," you then make a considerable sum per episode—with salary bumps along the way for each year it stays on. So, it is fully understandable that these jobs are very sought after. And in recent years, even the biggest of names have flocked to television for the paychecks, and often for great writing as well. Most network series get a 22-episode season each year until they die out. Streaming and cable content shows generally run less often—typically 10–13 episodes a year—but this makes them more desirable if you are eager to work on other projects or do a play in the off season.

So, what are the types of orders when talking about pilots, and how does this pertain to you, the actor? Typically, there are three types of orders a project can receive from a network or studio that are good to know about.

Type 1. Pilot order—A network has committed to production of a pilot. All the pieces are in order and the pilot is shot. Then it's a waiting game to see if the network likes the finished project enough to move forward with the other episodes. Worst case scenario—you shoot the pilot over a couple weeks and walk home with a large chunk of change to get you throughout the next dry spell. Best case—the pilot is a success and it is ordered to series. You are employed for a season and well compensated to boot.

Type 2. Cast-contingent order—When the project is required to find the right actors of whom the network approves before it is given a green light to open. This happens when finding the perfect lead—or the famous star—is required to make the show a success. The producers can't find the right star to play the first female President of the United States, or the bright new undiscovered talent that will attract millions of viewers—the show doesn't go on.

Type 3. Straight to series order—The network/studio is so confident about the project that the producers skip the pilot altogether. Multiple episodes are ordered. This has become more common of late, particularly with streaming and cable content. It's the best of situations, as it means steady and guaranteed employment for a set time.

Some other options

Thus far, we've looked at acting in the "big three" of commercial stage, screen, and television. Several acting options that you might consider fall a bit outside of that basic triangle. These include performing in TV commercials (a big moneymaker), in web series or web-episodes, in industrial shows, on a cruise ship, in CD-ROMs, on voiceovers, in student films, and as an extra.

TV commercials

Commercials mean staple income for many actors between their dramatic roles; some actors work in the commercial field exclusively. The top pay is outstanding when it comes. As a successful New York stage and TV actress reports on her sideline career, "my best commercials make about $25,000 to $30,000 a year, maybe $35,000 for a really good one (before the 10% of agent's commission and taxes are deducted, of course). That's about average for strong national spots. Of course, there are the spots that start strong and fail: I did a spot for a new product that tanked, so they pulled all of the spots and I only made about $3,000. Then there are the national spots you book that never run; those really suck! The fun thing is when a spot gets renegotiated after its standard 18 month run, or runs in a foreign market. One commercial earned me $23,000 for its year-long U.S. run, then made an additional $12,000 when it ran in Europe!" Commercials, therefore, are a major source of income for professional SAG actors, earning more money for union members than film work, and almost as much as TV appearances.

Most national commercials—the true moneymakers—are cast and produced in New York or Los Angeles, with New York still slightly ahead in volume of production. In recent years, Chicago has proved an up-and-coming "third city" in this field and now accounts for about 10% of the national action. Local commercials are shot in cities all around the country, however. Specialized agencies handle most of the casting and production for this mini-art form.

Rounds, interviews, and auditions for commercial work follow pretty much the same pattern as their counterparts in film and television work, except that there is more of everything—more rounds, more interviews, more photos, and more pavement pounding. Commercial actors are always "on the street," attending "go-sees" (an instruction to go and see someone else) and auditions, often with garment bags in their back seat or over their shoulder, because the work is rarely for more than a day at a time and there's tremendous competition for each little part. A union card is essential for commercial work, but you can get on the street without one, armed with a *Call Sheet* (in New York) or with one of several studio guides (in Los Angeles).

Commercials don't always use all of you. There are specialists in this field—"hand" people, for example, who are never seen except from the wrist outward, usually holding the product in a provocative manner. Honey-tongued speakers can "audition" by making *audio* demo tapes for voiceovers; these are the voices that speak off-camera, narrating or bringing home the message of the commercial. Many professional studios will make such demos for you (they advertise in the trades), and agencies will listen to them. "The most successful people in this business," says a commercial producer, "knock on doors and send tapes. They apply themselves. With talent and application you've got to make it in this town [Los Angeles] because this town soaks up talent."

Everyone should realize that acting in commercials is unlike acting in most other forms. Some of it, in fact, is "deliberately bad" so as to, in the advertising term, "burn in" the sponsor's message all the more forcefully. "Head-On, Apply directly to the (fill in your own body part)!" You might feel better about acting in commercials by thinking of them as 30-second Bertolt Brecht "theatre of alienation" plays, where your goal is not to create a convincing character but to convey an idea (OK, to sell a product) to the audience. It's an alienating role, for sure. "We have no names," laments one commercial actor; "we're just the 'talent.' " "It's demeaning," says Linda Kelsey (a commercial actress who has graduated to starring roles in prime-time TV). "It's kind of plastic acting—instead of selling the truth of a character you're playing, you sell the fantasy of the product."

But it's also honest and lucrative work, and you can meet a lot of people on their way up; today's commercial director is very likely tomorrow's film director. And commercials can often become a great laboratory for the young actor; they will get your face on the screen, often in L.A. and New York, where this really counts. Brad Pitt's career got a big boost in an early Pringles TV commercial, and Matt LeBlanc got his start dousing a hot dog with Heinz ketchup. And that's just for starters: Morgan Freeman once touted Listerine atop a telephone pole, Seth Green showed his skills with a Nerf slingshot, and Bruce Willis sang the praises (literally) of Seagram's Golden Wine Coolers before they made the really big time as well.

If you go for commercial work, go for it fully, and respect the work for what it is. "Never, for a minute, feel superior to it or treat it with disdain," writes Cortland Jessup. "Don't waste your time passing judgments or getting caught up in the 'is it acting or not' debate." Commercial work requires bright spontaneity, strong discipline, and improvisational skills. "I use the same technique to learn a sixty-second spot as [to do] Neil Simon," says Beverly Sanders, one of the finest performers in the field. "The key to me in commercials is to listen. You must be a quick study, and you must pay attention to the director, to *everyone*. It really takes a good actor to do a good job." It took Sanders 18 months of pavement pounding to get her first commercial, but now she has done hundreds of them and has made it her career.

And auditioning for these can be a surprising pleasure for the working actor. It often requires very little prep time, great improvisation skills, and low stakes in terms of booking the job. You may want to try it only part time, but if you do, go into it with a full commitment.

More than any other format, commercial acting is interesting because once you break the glass ceiling and "book" your first job, your odds of booking others increase substantially. CDs love to book their favorites. There are lots of cooks in this kitchen, however: the director, ad agency, and product placement executive are all typically on hand for call-backs—and a single call-back can typically be an eight-hour day. It is also very common to be put "on hold" during this process, meaning that the CD may require you to remain available (you're "avail" in trade lingo) for one to several days for the specific shoot. You are not the only actor on hold, however: several others may be "held" for the same role while decisions are being made. You then are either booked or "released" for the one-day job.

You may also fail to get a commercial booking if you have a "conflict"— that is, you can't do a Tylenol ad if you've done one for Bayer, or for Coca Cola if you've made a Pepsi commercial. That's why actors who do commercials only write "Commercials available upon request" on their résumés— so as not to scare off future commercial opportunities.

There are many classes in both New York and Hollywood–Los Angeles on commercial acting technique (they advertise in the trades); and a couple of worthwhile books on the subject can be found in the Drama bookstores on both coasts.

Industrial shows

Industrial shows (sometimes known as "business theatre") consist of stage productions mounted by corporations or industries that are, more or less, the "commercials" of live theatre—though a great deal less frequent. Over 100 producers across the country produce these shows, which are presented at dealers' conventions, buyers' conventions, and other in-house gatherings of corporations or national groups of various kinds. The industrial show can be based around a theme or used to introduce a new product or even to sing the praises of the corporation's management and history. Many of these shows are splashy mini-epics, produced with great professional skill and with big budgets. The annual "Toy Fair" that hits New York each winter happily employs hundreds of actors each season to show off the latest trend for children. It's good, fast, and well-paying work.

Performing in industrials usually demands first-class musical skills (singing and dancing); good stage credits are also highly desirable, if not mandatory. The pay is excellent (it's Equity's highest minimum salary), the working conditions are sometimes spectacular (you may perform in the Caribbean or Hawaii), and the duration is short, putting you back on the street before you know it, a little more tanned and a lot richer. Almost all business theatre is packaged in New York; you can get the names of producers from the occasional listings in *Backstage*. The days of business theatre are clearly waning, however. In 2007–08, actor workweeks in industrial productions had declined to less than a third (254) of what they had been a decade before. Indeed, business theatre income now consists of less than one tenth of 1% of overall Equity actor earnings. Business theatre is clearly turning from being show business to no business.

Performing on shipboard

Cruise ships have become a relatively new performance venue since this book was first written. Mainly for singer/dancers, shipboard performance is increasingly remunerative at the financial level (the salaries include room and board, and you'll have virtually no other expenses). Plus, it pays the added dividends of foreign travel and possible oceanic adventure for those capable of hitting their high Cs on the high seas.

Most shipboard contracts are for six months and, though nonunion, pay at approximately LORT A wage levels (roughly $840 per week). You will, of course, have to both dance and probably sing (though lip-synching is increasingly customary when riding the waves). And you'll also be expected to "have a presence on the ship" and entertain the clientele during the day: running bingo tournaments, teaching ballroom dancing, and hosting "What's Your Line?" games after dinner. Outgoing and unattached young performers are particularly recruited for these spots, which feature an intense learning experience—playing before large (if semi-captive) audiences night after night—often on state-of-the-art stages that are comparable to top Vegas showrooms. More and more of the latest from Broadway are licensed and adapted for the sea, so you can find *Chicago*, *Mamma Mia*, or *Rock of Ages* or the like as your musical opportunity. And non-musicals appear as well: on the Queen Mary Cruise Line you can see Shakespeare's *Romeo and Juliet* and *A Midsummer Night's Dream*. These may not be Broadway shows, but they're a start. Of course, there is the occasional seasickness, shared (and cramped) cabins (unless you are the lead singer), and nightly parades of baba au rhums and baked Alaskas to put up with in the dining room.

And you must also realize that the life of leisure can be the devil's playground. As actor and dancer—now CD—Paul Davis explains, "We would finish a show at 11, go to the midnight buffet, have cocktails till dawn, and sleep to one in the afternoon the next day. And this was every night!" But once you get on land, the adjustment can be challenging—a shipboard lifestyle doesn't fit into the N.Y./L.A. marketplace. Davis recommends taking every opportunity at ports of call to take a dance class. And to keep up with your training: lead singers often offer private voice coaching between sessions and can provide great training while sailing the seas. So, keep in shape, and take advantage of the gym time so that once you hit land you will be in top form.

Cruise ship auditions, if you're interested, are held regularly in New York and Los Angeles (they're widely advertised in the trades), often for casts of 50 to 75 at a time. Don't think you'll get cast in *The Lion King* just because you dance on a Disney cruise ship, but you will have taken at least a half-step in the right direction and saved up some money in the meantime.

New media: the digital-interactive market

There is an increasing acting market for new media: video games, webisodes, streaming, and made-for-new-media entertainment. Indeed, one of the main sticking points in the 2008 Screen Actors Guild's extended negotiations with the AMPTP (Alliance of Motion Picture and Television Producers) was how its actors should properly be compensated for their online and electronically produced—and/or reproduced—performances.

Video games

Actors have been making six-figure salaries in the CD-ROM market for more than two decades. Stars are particularly sought, of course: Christopher Walken, Burgess Meredith, and Karen Allen starred in *Ripper* by Take 2 Interactive Software in 1996; between them, the actors received well over $1 million of the CD-ROM's total $4 million budget. "I wouldn't want to make a living doing it. But I would do it again. They paid well, and they were very jovial, and it was all a lot of fun," said Meredith. More recent stars have subsequently (and profitably) entered the field: Bruce Willis landed a supersalary for *Apocalypse* with PlayStation in 1998, Jennifer Garner reprised her Golden Globe-winning *Alien* TV role in the 3-D game of that name for Acclaim Entertainment in 2004, and Mark Hamill (Luke Skywalker in *Star Wars*) has made a major career in the game market in recent years, playing the main character in *Wing Commander* for Origin Systems, the Joker in various *Batman* games, and, more recently, Goro Jamina in the celebrated *Yakuza* series begun in 2005 by Sony's PlayStation 2. But video game acting is not particularly remunerative for non-stars, as royalties and residuals are not part of the package, and the standard pay in this field is only the basic, SAG-negotiated fee (currently $730) for each day on the shoot.

Webisodes

Webisodes are videos made for internet distribution, either by television networks (in which case they are usually rebroadcasts of previously aired shows, or short linking episodes not in the original production) or on internet sites such as YouTube or Vimeo. The greatest success story to date—*High Maintenance*—is a web series created by husband and wife team Ben Sinclair and Katja Blichfeld. The show follows a nameless marijuana deliveryman called The Guy (played by Sinclair) as he delivers his product to clients in New York City. Each episode is between 5 and 12 minutes in length. "Freed of the constraints of thirty-minute or one-hour formulas, the episodes are luxurious and twisty and humane, radiating new ideas about storytelling," wrote television critic Emily Nussbaum in an article for *The New Yorker*. Sinclair said that the TV shows Six Feet Under and Party Down were inspirations for the web series. And the talent pool in New York City is rich—and familiar to Blichfeld, who was an Emmy award–winning CD of 30 Rock. Each episode cost less than $1,000 to make. In 2014, Vimeo announced that the website would provide financial backing for upcoming episodes of original programming via its Vimeo on Demand platform. And in 2015, HBO announced that it had ordered six television episodes, to premiere in 2016. Talk about a success story!

Voiceovers

A voiceover is an off-camera voice; you hear voiceovers all the time in radio and TV commercials, in some TV shows, film, and new media, and, of course, in animated films, where the voiceover performer may have star status. Voiceovers are also employed in films that are made in the United States and, before being shipped abroad, dubbed into foreign languages. Voiceovers—both English and foreign—are also used in the diversified corporate video/CD-ROM field, which in recent years has expanded the voiceover field throughout the country. While you're not necessarily likely to be the voice of AT&T, a lot of voiceover work goes to relative unknowns who have mastered this particularly challenging art.

The techniques of voiceover performance are daunting but, for most actors, learnable. You have to be able to speak with great clarity, particularly in the CD-ROM field, where audio quality is not up to broadcast standards. You also have to be able to speak rapidly and with high energy, especially in animated films, where you have to make emotional transitions (for example, from furious to terrified) at, well, Donald Duck speed. You should be able to do a variety of voices, from wacky cartoon characters to persuasive advertising pitches and inspiring public service announcements. Some people in this business do up to a hundred different voices, making them very desirable for film voiceovers, where producers may want to hire one unseen actor to perform a whole repertory of voiced-over roles. Above all, as with all acting, you have to be terrific. "You have to convey the belief that this is the greatest product on earth," says Ted Kryszco, a Grammy-winning Disney voiceover artist and producer. He adds, "And to do that you must really commit to the copy." Learn mike technique and vocal timing.

Voiceover work can be a major source of income—and creative opportunities—for veteran and beginning actors alike. Broadway/West End vet Jim Dale became so recognized and beloved as the voice on the Harry Potter books-on-tape series that producer Bryan Fuller tapped him for the voiceover narration for TV's *Pushing Daisies*. Veterans Jon Hamm's and Morgan Freeman's mellifluous vocals have now become synonymous with car commercials. And young actress Jennifer Ikeda found voiceover work after her training at Juilliard, which provided her with significant income before she gained star status in the 2008 Broadway revival of *Top Girls*.

You can train for voiceover work at several specialized schools in the Los Angeles and New York areas; the schools should also aim you toward the best current career tracks in this field. While training, you should also learn dubbing ability, the skill of reading your script while looking at the screen and blending your words with the character's lips. If you want to do foreign language dubbing—a burgeoning field as the film world grows increasingly global—you must in most cases be a genuine native speaker of the language, and sometimes even of the character's regional dialect.

Lots of agents and casting offices specialize in voiceovers. Your calling card to them is not a photo but a high-quality, professionally produced demo tape, about three minutes long, with 10 to 12 different voice samples. While union actors (SAG/AFTRA) will get the bulk of production studio work, most corporate and foreign production companies employ nonunion performers. The pay—which is usually by the day or the hour—depends on many factors: your union status, the depth of the producer's pockets, the specific supply/demand ratio of voiceover artists in your area (French language dubbers get paid more than Spanish ones in Los Angeles, for example), and, for TV commercials, the length of time your voiceover is on the air—voiceover artists in TV get residuals along with the other actors. Voiceover pros may earn from $500 to $1,000 a day in this field, though rarely with clockwork regularity.

Student films

You don't want to act in a student film, do you? Heck, you've *been* a student; that's all behind you now. Well, you might be passing up a great opportunity. While it won't get you any money, acting in a student film at one of the nation's top film schools—such as the acronymic pantheon of NYU, Columbia, UCLA, and USC—can provide, in addition to a terrific on-camera learning experience, some solid (if semi-professional) résumé credits, great clips for your demo reel, and real industry contacts—particularly if your director or cinematographer goes on to bigger and (commercially) better things. You might even be making great cinema art. That, after all, is usually the intention. Dustin Hoffman, Bridget Fonda, and Alec Baldwin all acted in student films. Robert DeNiro's first film role, in fact, was in *The Wedding Party*, a comedy that took four years to complete and two more years to release, and received disastrous reviews. But it was directed by Brian de Palma, then at Sarah Lawrence, and the rest—as we suppose you know—is history. Indeed, a great many American directors went to film school and made such films, and they remember the actors who toiled in them for nothing.

Student films are advertised in the trades, and the roles are sometimes put out by Breakdown Services. Often they are technically quite sophisticated; some even get national distribution. You're rarely paid anything for participating in a student film, but you'll be offered "CCM" — Copy (a DVD), Credit (billing), and Meals (usually Domino's Pizza). Your copy, of course, depends on the film's being completed, which only about half are (many run out of funds or energy, or the student graduates or drops out). Indeed, many aren't even started; they're just ideas that get cast and then fizzle— sometimes without anyone even calling you to say it's off. If it is completed, you still might not get any film: make certain it's going to be produced, and get assurances in writing that you'll receive any clips in which you appear. (If they don't show up, write the dean of the film school!) And you might get paid after all. Many student films (about 40 a year) are produced under a SAG experimental contract that provides for deferred compensation (at least to the SAG actors), which kicks in if the film ends up being distributed commercially. Even if you're nonunion, you'll probably be able to negotiate for some of those proceeds.

Be an extra

Everything has changed in the past few years with "atmosphere players," or extras as they're commonly called. Standard advice in the past was to steer clear of this work, which means playing nonspeaking parts in feature films and TV, on the grounds that being an extra forever typed you as a non-actor. 'Tain't so anymore, and for one main reason: the disappearance of the Screen Extras Guild (SEG). Extras now come under the jurisdiction of SAG, if they come under union jurisdiction at all. Needless to say, this has gone a long way toward removing any stigma that might have adhered to being an extra. Performing as an extra—for which you do not need to be in any union—may even get you into SAG via the voucher system, which, while complicated, is becoming a favored route to SAG carding (see method four under "Unions" in Chapter 4).

To work as an extra, you register with a specialized extra-casting agency, of which by far the largest and most famous is Central Casting, which has offices in both New York and Los Angeles. Registration is inexpensive (it's currently $25—which goes toward a "photographic/electronic image fee"), and you need no union card (fully half of its clients are nonunion) or experience. Registration is somewhat complex, however, and includes a required appearance in person at one of its offices—at 31st and 6th Avenue in Manhattan, or on Flower Street in Burbank, CA. For complete information, go to Central Casting's website at www.centralcasting.org, click on "Background Actors," specify either New York or Los Angeles, and then go to the site's comprehensive FAQs, which will guide you through the process.

There are other extra-casting agencies in both L.A. and New York; all are listed in *Call Sheet*. There is also coverage of the L.A. extra scene in an occasional trade magazine, *Extra's Extra*, and in other literature available from Back To One Entertainment (www.backtoone.net).

Why should you consider extra work? Not to support your family, certainly, unless you work into the wee hours. Union extras were making $148 a day in early 2013, but nonunion extras will be making quite a bit less—not enough, in fact, to get them up to the minimum wage. But everyone receives time and a half during the first four hours of overtime plus double pay for the next four hours, and extras receive their *daily* rate *per hour* during what's known as "golden time" after that. You can also get "bumps" of from $14 to $50 for supplements: wearing your own formal garb, using your car, operating firearms, standing in for a star when the crew is setting the lights, and so forth. SAG often imposes fines on producers who cast non-union actors, but such fines are waived under many circumstances; being registered with Central Casting is one of those circumstances. Making the producer happier will likely make you happier as well.

If money or getting into a union isn't enough reason for doing extra work, getting some on-set experience might be: there's no better way—apart from getting an actual acting job—to learn your way around a Hollywood studio or film location. Moreover, you can—if you're not so brazen about it as to get kicked off the set—meet some of the people there too. As a drama student, Edmond Stoops signed on as an extra for the film *Meteor*, which was being filmed on his college campus, and spent most of his down time chatting with the star (and his idol), Peter O'Toole. When in one scene O'Toole needed to address a line to someone, he turned and said it to Stoops. The director, taken by surprise, indicated that Stoops should respond, which he did (his line was "OK!"); he was upgraded to a day performer and landed his SAG card—as well as lunch with Lawrence of Arabia.

Extras can go on to become actors. Sissy Spacek's first role was as an extra in Andy Warhol's *Trash*; she had one second of screen time. Mel Gibson earned all of $20 for his first film, *Summer City*; he earns $25 million per picture now. Sylvester Stallone's first part was as a hooded gangster in Woody Allen's *Bananas*; he had no lines and wasn't listed in the cast—a small start for a giant career. The occasional actor often gets "bumped up" from being an extra on set to a few speaking lines. Being in the right place at the right time occurs from time to time and can lead to a great fortune. But it takes dedication and lots of luck.

But don't think of being an extra as an acting career. It's only an extra career. And don't even *dream* of listing extra credits on your acting résumé!

Write your own

Of course, with the right talent, application, and persistence, you can write your own play or screenplay and write yourself into it as well. Indeed, sometimes you can win the double jackpot. The most famous—nay, legendary—example of writing oneself into a starring role is surely Sylvester Stallone, who wrote the screenplay for *Rocky* when he had played only two small roles in Hollywood. Stallone offered his screenplay with the proviso that he play the title role; producers, though admiring the script, insisted on a named star for the lead. Though broke at the time, Stallone held firm, turning down offers of up to $200,000 for the script until United Artists agreed to his terms. You probably know the rest. And now, some 40 years later, he has received an Oscar nomination for *Creed*. Hard-plugging Hollywood actor Jon Favreau wrote a script about himself and his actor friends between supporting-role engagements, and eventually produced it as an independent film, *Swingers*, with himself and his buddies in the leads. Mindy Kaling started her career from a downtown comedy piece she wrote with partner Brenda Withers about Ben Affleck and Matt Damon, in which she played Ben! The cast of the sleeper TV hit, *It's Always Sunny in Philadelphia*, got their break after writing and producing their own half-hour TV show and getting it seen. Nothing in this should suggest that it's easier to break into show business by writing than by acting—and it is said that everybody in Hollywood is working on one or more screenplays—but writing your own show can surely put one more iron in the fire. More and more actors of today are self produced–self written. Look at the stunning work from NYC theatre companies Pig Iron and The Debate Society as lead examples of this.

The job offer

If you have played all your cards right, if you are as good as you think you are, and if your contacts, interviews, auditions, and readings have gone brilliantly, you may be offered a part. You now have to decide whether you will take it. For most actors, this is the easiest decision of their lives. There are some jobs, however, that you might want to think twice about taking, even if they are the first thing that comes your way.

Things to consider

The job could be a *nonunion* job. Many theatres and independent film companies skirt union regulations and jurisdiction. Even though they may pay you a union-scale wage, they do not operate according to certain procedures that the union requires. Check with the union. If the producer is operating in frank violation of union regulations, you may find yourself blackballed from future employment. This is rare, but it pays to investigate. If it happens to you, you may never live it down.

The job could be *quasi-union*. That is, it could be a workshop or experimental production (some student films come under this category) that operates under a special waiver or dispensation from the union. In such a case you may not be paid, or you may be given "deferred payment," which means you will not get any money until the project is successfully marketed (which, sadly, rarely happens). If the project is nonunion but is operated in accordance with the union, you have nothing to fear, but you might not get any more out of it than the work itself.

The job could be *non-jurisdictional*. That is, the union chooses to have nothing to do with it, or decides it is simply out of its jurisdiction. *Fuerza Bruta* and *De La Guarda* are now longtime running off-Broadway spectaculars, interactive but nonunion, with performers 40 feet about your head; they are in this category along with numerous others. Be on the lookout, however, for fair wages, insurance issues, and long and unrestricted hours if seeking non-jurisdictional acting opportunities.

The job could be union but far from the city (*any* city), keeping you from auditioning for bigger things during your time on the job. For example, you could be hired at a summertime Equity dinner theatre in the mountains and, while hoofing for tourists, miss auditions for the next Broadway season.

The job could require *nudity* or *pornography*. Don't confuse the two. It's long been the case that acting in full-on pornography won't help your long-term career; count on it only for modest income (and a possible immodest infection). The days when careers could be ruined by the exposure of past pornographic dalliances are over, but we haven't reached the point at which your future will be enhanced by being in a skin flick. The advice from here is to stay clear.

However, there is a great deal of nudity in current theatre and film, even in the mainstream. This may mean revealing quite a bit more of you than you're prepared for. Distinguished Broadway stage shows such as *Spring Awakening*, *Take Me Out*, *The Full Monty*, and revivals of *Hair*, *Les Liaisons Dangereuses*, and *Equus*, plus dozens of recent off-Broadway shows (*Intimacy*, *Sleep No More*), have included scenes of full or partial nudity, following over 25 Broadway and off-Broadway productions featuring full frontal nudity (mostly male) since the 1960s. And the majority of R- and NC-rated feature films, and cable TV programming, employ nudity and/or simulated sex acts. Semi-bared breasts and buttocks are now even seen on occasional network TV. As an auditioning actor, you may say that you will perform such a scene only if it is "tastefully done"—but you can be sure that everyone will assure you that "*of course* it will be tastefully done." The real problem is that there is no way to tell what is meant by "tastefully" until the final cut or dress rehearsal. You simply will have no idea, unless you've signed a contract that rigorously specifies what body areas are involved and for how long, and just what parts of you your mother will see when she goes to see you in it. At any rate, don't hold out hope that "if they want me badly enough, they'll get a double for the nude scenes." They won't want you that badly.

Doing nude scenes may also be harder than you think. On stage, it will mean facing crowds of often leering strangers. On film, it might mean hours of takes and retakes in the altogether, with fully dressed technicians, pub-licists, cast members, extras, and people you've never seen before milling around. Of course, Equity and SAG rules do what they can (SAG requires a closed set) to contain your nudity in a professional environment, but actresses who've considered themselves utterly uninhibited have often been reduced to quivering tears by the process, which, after all, is exactly how torturers humiliate their prisoners. Tovah Feldshuh turned down half a million dollars to star in the film *Exquisite Beauty* after finding that she was to be in the nude for *40 pages* of the script. When, in 2005, Lee Eun-Ju, one of South Korea's leading film actresses, committed suicide at 24, her family blamed her action on "severe bouts of depression and insomnia" brought on by the many nude scenes she had done in *The Scarlet Letter*. "I wanted to make money," Lee's suicide note said. There are some things that money cannot and should not buy, and you might want to seriously consider your own psychological stamina before signing on to a role that requires nudity. (Your agent can help you if you do, however; which body parts—and how much of them—will be exposed can be negotiated into your contract with fine-tooth-comb detail.)

The job could be in a *daytime drama* if you are in (or willing to be in) Los Angeles (*The Bold and the Beautiful, Days of Our Lives, General Hospital, The Young and the Restless*). But "What, *me* in a *soap opera*?" actors have sometimes moaned. Why not? Daytime TV is, at minimum, a great training ground for on-camera acting. "It's like being shot out of a can-non," says Jennifer Roszell (formerly Eleni on *Guiding Light*), for whom the soaps proved a great starting point to a flourishing New York prime-time and stage career. Says Leann Hunley of *Days of Our Lives*, "You're getting paid to learn, you're thinking on your feet every day, and you do every range of emotion possible. It's like being in an acting class day after day, with not a week apart." A high school dropout named Demi Moore says that her best training came from playing Jackie Templeton on *General Hospital* in 1982. The list of now-famous actors who've been on soaps will stagger you: Meg Ryan, Alec Baldwin, Robin Wright, Josh Duhamel, Charles Dutton, Brad Pitt, Keli Ripa, Robert DeNiro, James Earl Jones, Cicely Tyson, Ted Danson, Kathleen Turner, Ryan Phillippe, Mor-gan Freeman, Julianne Moore, Christian Slater, Ellen Burstyn, Warren Beatty, Marisa Tomei, Kevin Bacon, Sigourney Weaver, Susan Sarandon, Eva Longoria. A recent trend is for soap stars to go into Broadway leads: Jacob Young (*All My Children*) recently moved into the role of Lumière in *Beauty and the Beast*, and, from the cast of *As The World Turns*, Tamara Tunie stepped into the role of Calpurnia in the Broadway revival of Shake-speare's *Julius Caesar*, while Tonya Pinkins won a Tony nomination for the 2004 *Caroline, or Change* and played Mame Wilks in the 2007 *Radio Golf*. Of course, these actors were trained for more than soap operas (Pinkins has played roles on Broadway since 1981), but it was their visibility on daytime TV that made them more bankable for 8 p.m. curtains on the Great White Way. The Guiding Light from here: don't turn your nose up at daytime drama.

You may of course find the role *too small*, the contract *too long* (soap operas ask you to sign for three years), or the play *too offensive* or involving a dialect you find ethnically degrading. Perhaps it's a commercial for a product you find personally disgusting, or you're being asked to work with actors or directors you don't respect or to be in a television show you loathe. But just how picky can you afford to be?

Take the job!

While there are a number of reasons why you might not choose to accept every job that comes your way, preferring to wait until the "right one" comes along, you can hardly decline your way into an acting career. Listen to the veterans. Lucille (*I Love Lucy*) Ball acknowledged that she reached the top of her profession by taking "absolutely every job" she could get. Tony Curtis advised *Variety* that "anybody in this business should take any job he can get." Jason Robards said, "The only advice I have for young people is, no matter how you do it, do it in front of people who pay." So, unless you sense an utter and absolute catastrophe ahead, *take the job!*

There is more than just an immediate reason for this: one job will lead to another; power begets power. One fine actor worked steadily for ten years, at which time he looked back and realized that *every single job* he had gotten, beyond the first, had evolved from a previous one. A beginning actor, therefore, should refuse a paying acting job only for extraordinarily compelling reasons.

How much will you make?

You have a job. Now that you have struggled, humbled yourself, and suffered financial hardships by the carload, you are ready to cash in your chips, right? What will the job pay? A survey by salary.com indicates that the median annual actor/performer salary in the United States is $53,535 as of September 21, 2016, which sounds like a pretty good deal until you realize that they are only surveying working professional actors who are already in the unions and have been hired for some length of time. Most actors, even those in the unions, are *not* working at any given time.

But the top 10% of those who are will earn an average of $76,133; the bottom 10% $35,541. Still, you will have to get a job first, and then get into a union, and then hold *onto* the job—or get another one—at which point you will begin to earn some real money.

So, as we've made clear so far, the income of an actor is not great. According to HigherEd Jobs, which has scientifically surveyed the field, the starting salary for a "New Assistant Professor" in the United States is $65,372, which is more than $12,000 higher than the salary of the average professional actor who has been working for 25 years.

But if you work you get paid, and you should know how much you will make. All the unions have negotiated contracts on your behalf; these contracts specify, among other things, the minimum salaries you will receive. These salary "scales" are written in astonishing detail; for example, the Codified Basic Agreement negotiated between SAG and the various motion picture producers is a 172-page book. Contracts for stage actors, film actors, and TV actors are different, even since the SAG-AFTRA consolidation. And all the actor contracts are renegotiated continuously upon expiration, so the following information, which is accurate as of this printing, is subject to regular change.

Stage roles

If you land a part in a Broadway play, or in a Broadway National Tour, you are covered by Equity's Production Contract. Your minimum weekly salary under that contract will be $2,034 a week in mid-2017. For a role on a 2017 Broadway show on tour, you will have a minimum salary of $1,325 but will also receive a daily sum for road expenses. (On the road, however, lower scales may apply for chorus members in large-cast musicals.)

If you get a part in off-Broadway's American Nonprofit Theatre Companies group (ANTC), which is comprised of certain Manhattan theatres of 199 seats or less outside the "Broadway Box"—currently the Atlantic Theater, Classic Stage, MCC Theater, New Group, Primary Stages, Signature Theatre, Vineyard Theatre, Keen Company, Playwrights Horizons, and Second Stage—you will earn a minimum of $337 to $558 in 2016, and almost certainly more by the time you read this book. If you get into a commercial off-Broadway show, you'll be making a bit more: a minimum of $525 per week on the smallest stages and upward of $927 on the larger ones. America's regional theatres are classed by Equity in five salary groups according to size and potential gross income. LORT A theatres—such as Minneapolis's Guthrie Theatre, Los Angeles's Center Theater Group, and San Francisco's American Conservatory Theatre—paid a minimum weekly salary of $963 through 2016, while B+ companies like Princeton's McCarter paid $909; B companies like Atlanta's Alliance, $836; and C and D companies (which are often smaller stages in the larger companies) $776 and $608, respectively. Small Professional Theatres (SPTs), naturally, pay less due to their "developing" status; their minimums in 2016 ranged from $229 to $689 per week, though Equity may negotiate different agreements above that for larger SPTs. Yet smaller theatres, while overseen by Equity in New York and L.A., pay stipends (they cannot call these "salaries") that barely cover more than "minimum public transportation" for each performance.

Can you argue for more than the minimum? Well, obviously well-known and audience-attracting Broadway stars draw the big bucks: $30,000 to $50,000 weeks are in the ballpark, and the original title stars of *The Producers* were said to have taken home $70,000 every Monday morning when their show opened, and more than $100,000 when they returned to their roles later in the run. But who knows? Most star actors keep their salaries under wraps. One magazine reported that Julia Roberts raked in $150,000 a week to perform in *Three Days of Rain*, but another reported a "mere" $35,000. But the average Production Contract salary is usually only a little above the scale cited above, and for most off-Broadway and many regional stages, the scale minimum is in fact the universal wage. So-called "favored nations contracts," common in those situations, provide that everyone gets the same scale pay and the same billing, but *same* translates as "rock bottom." It's fair, all right, but fairly bleak.

If you are nonunion, of course, minimums don't apply. Apprentice actors can get $100 a week, less, more, or even nothing; it's really up to the theatre and the actor. Shakespeare festivals pay nonunion actors $2,500 or more for the summer, which might run for 12 to 14 weeks. But housing is often provided, and additional money may be paid for leading theatre tours and teaching classes after the shows open.

The fact is that few actors can truly earn a living from stage work alone. Don't count on salary.com to predict your salary: fewer than half of Equity's members work at all in any given year, meaning that the real median income for professional *stage* actors is $0. That's right: zero. Paul Hecht, who has won Tony nominations and critical praise for his many Broadway and off-Broadway roles but earns his living doing TV commercial voiceovers, says:

> The situation for an actor in New York these days is that one can't afford to be an actor. I don't even know what other job it's comparable to. And we're talking about people who are high up in their profession, not people just out of school. You're looking at a middle-aged man at the height

of his artistic powers who has to treat [stage] experiences as if they were artistic sabbaticals. But I'm an actor, and I love the theatre, and I'm stuck.

We're sorry to report this, but it's close to the truth. However, it's not *totally* the truth, and that's why thousands of college students are drama majors—and then become film and theatre aspirants!

ASIDE FROM ROBERT: I have been teaching acting on my campus, the University of California, Irvine, for 50 years. As I write this in 2016, *ten* of my former acting students are performing on Broadway, with seven playing starring or supporting roles, and one has earned a Tony nomination. Dozens more are performing off-Broadway and on tour or in cities around our country, and by now several hundreds have performed in over 1,000 professional and union-funded stage, film, and TV shows throughout the United States and abroad—several, by now, having reached close to lifetime careers in their chosen fields.

Film/TV roles

If you find employment in films or television, higher minimums prevail. Basically, in films, you will be paid either by the day (as a "day player") or by the week; in television, you can be paid by the day or the week or for a three-day half-week.

The most recent television contract for SAG-AFTRA will give you a minimum ("scale") salary of $933 for a day's work in 2016; the weekly rate is set at $3,239. If you are hired for a "major" role in a SAG-AFTRA TV show (these are roles either credited at the top of the show or where you are billed as a "guest star"), you'll get more: $5,132 for a half-hour show and $8,210 for an hour show. And there's a special "three-day" SAG rate for TV shows ($2,363 for either a half-hour or an hour show in 2016). You'll also get your agent's commission on top of this, "scale plus ten" in industry parlance, though of course you won't ever see it.

For most shows, "scale" is not only the minimum, but also at or close to the "top of show" salary for non-regular performers, although well-known actors may receive a "breakage" fee (one "breaking" the favored nations concept of equal pay), which may give them "double-top" (twice the show's normal salary limit)—or, if they are stars, higher fees, perhaps in the $20,000 to $50,000 range.

Salaries (though not scale minimums) are, of course, much higher for series regulars and stars, and these can be renegotiated when the show is renewed. Starting performers can expect to be offered $15,000 to $20,000 per episode on a network or cable series, says the *Hollywood Reporter*. Big-time actors soar with their salaries: *The Big Bang Theory*'s three stars, Jim Parsons, Johnny Galecki, and Kaley Cuoco, each received a million dollars per episode in 2015–16, an amount that began when James Gandolfini hit the same jackpot on HBO's *The Sopranos* in its final 2006–07 season. Ashton Kutcher and Jon Cryer collectively brought in $35 million in 2013–14, and the top four actors in *Modern Family* made, between them, $45.5 million dollars the season following.

For commercials, the minimum SAG session (video-shoot) fee was $627.75 per shooting session in 2016, to which additional fees are added with additional showings. Commercial and regular TV actors also pick up payments, popularly called "residuals," for subsequent airings of both their show and replayed commercials. Calculating these residuals, however, is an accountant's nightmare; payments begin with an additional 100% of the actor's original base fee for its first prime-time network rerun and continue on a diminishing scale (from 50% down to 5% of initial compensation) in 13-week blocks for their subsequent non-prime-time network and syndicated reruns. These performers also receive compensation for foreign telecasts, though at greatly reduced levels. Actors in TV commercials, therefore, tend to live off their residual checks, which account for far more of SAG members' income than do session fees: a single commercial, shot in a single day, can pay residual income for years and may eventually mount well into the five figures.

The potential for big salaries in film, of course, is huge—for recognized movie stars. We mentioned the "$25 million club" at the beginning of the book, and some stars can earn that sum in these days with a single role, such as Leonardo DiCaprio, who earned his $25 million in *The Wolf of Wall Street*. The other five between $15 million and $25 million were Angelina Jolie (*Maleficent*), Matt Damon (the *Bourne* franchise), Bradley Cooper (*American Sniper*), and Sandra Bullock (*Gravity*). Indeed, star salaries and incomes have skyrocketed in recent years and are now 40 times what they were when the first edition of this book appeared in 1972.

Non-stars, however, have not enjoyed such a boom time. In fact, the giant salaries paid to those "bankable" performers at the top have led to decreased incomes right below—and then all the way down the line. According to one agent, actor "quotes"—the fee actors received in their past engagement and expect to use as a stepping-stone for their next one—have declined from 25% to 50% in the past few years. Indeed, scale plus commission is increasingly considered close to the "top of the show" salary for guest-star or guest-costar TV roles, even for veteran pros. This situation is becoming increasingly common in film as well: Golden Globe awardee and Oscar nominee Sally Kirkland, though "a millionaire for a while" from her 150 films and TV series since 1960 (and continuing through 2017 and almost certainly beyond), admits: "I am now offered scale plus ten all the time." (Kirkland gamely makes clear that she never accepts such a fee: "I just have to be really creative in negotiations.")

The bottom line is that, according to the *Hollywood Reporter*, the "vast majority" of SAG members "take home less than $1,000 a year from acting jobs." Gulp.

And so, the great preponderance of SAG-AFTRA members, as with Equity members, still have their day jobs. It's hard to make a living as an actor, even as a very good and very well-known actor, and even in films and TV. The work is uneven, unsteady, and unsure—for just about everybody. Neither a Tony nor an Emmy nor an Oscar means there's a job for you next month or next year. Jeffrey Wright, who won a Tony for *Angels in America*, was shocked when he was unemployed for a full year afterward. Mercedes Ruehl didn't work for a year after winning an Oscar for her role in *The Fisher King*. "Somebody had told me," she recalled, " 'You've won best supporting actress. That means you're not going to work for another year.' And I went, 'hah, hah, hah'—and then I *didn't*!" Even established stars have to hustle. Toward the end of his storied career, Henry Fonda said that getting work was his "operative problem." How could that be? "You have no idea what your next job is, you think, 'Well, that's it! I won't work again!' " he explained. And if Fonda felt that way, how do the rest of them feel? That's why acting is more a club than a profession.

Getting the *second* job

This book has focused on getting your first job, getting the "big break." Most young actors believe that the first foot in the door pries it wide open. Unfortunately, this isn't so. The door can slam shut all over again and be even harder to open a second time.

Do you think this isn't true? Shakespeare festivals, which typically rehire two-thirds to three-quarters of their designers and technicians for the following season, rarely take back more than one-third of their actors. Why? We don't always know. Maybe their audiences want to see fresh faces on stage. Maybe the non-rehired actors didn't deliver on all of their artistic promise—not night after night, anyway. Maybe some of those actors were seen, by the season's end, as simply a pain in the ass.

Listen to veteran stage/film actor-director Charles Grodin: "It's amazing to me how actors don't seem to realize that being troublesome will impact their careers. Working on the other side of it as a producer, director, or writer, I can say that the first question that comes up when people are interested in hiring someone is, 'What's he like to work with?' And word gets around quickly. Employers call each other, and you definitely can get hurt if you cause people grief." Your behavior on the set, in fact, is your second most important asset in getting rehired. The first is delivering a knockout performance, of course, but the second is hardly less important—at least when there are others around who can also deliver knockout performances. And there always are. Jeff Greenberg says, "I want to hire wonderful people to take to a set filled with wonderful people. I don't want an inkling of an attitude. There are enough people out there that if there's someone we feel might be troublesome, we just don't want to go down that road."

I think it's necessary to carry this a bit further than to just say "Behave yourself and don't be troublesome." What you really must do is actively, vigorously, and even rapturously support—heart and soul and then some—the production and production team that's been smart enough to hire you: without reservation, moodiness, alienation, or the slightest hint of carping.

You think that's easy? It's not. There will surely be things to criticize or complain about if you're the type to do so. That's fine in the academic theatre. Indeed, it's expected; it's what *academic* means (the term comes from Plato's original teaching gymnasium). But it can spell disaster for a beginner in the professional theatre. Remember, Plato never had to deal with opening nights, howling investors, or union regulations. You've been hired as a professional, so be professional. Recall the words of screenwriter James Agate: "A professional is a man who can do his job when he doesn't feel like it." There will be times you might not feel like it; transcend them. "Acting professionally," the title of this book, has a double meaning. Think about it.

Prepare fully, and then even more fully, for your first day in the rehearsal hall or on the set. "Hit the ground running," advised Noah Wyle to guest performers on *ER*. "Be fully prepared and integrated into our style, our mode: move fast, don't take any moments for yourself." Make decisions about your character's goals, tactics, and expectations. Do everything you've learned to be outstanding from the first moment of rehearsal. If you can, learn your lines solidly, and then more solidly, even before rehearsals start, particularly for work in film or television. "The single most startling principle to grasp for the theatre actor entering the world of film for the first time," says Michael Caine, "is that not only have you got to know your lines on day one, you will also have directed yourself to play them in a certain way. And all this accomplished *without* necessarily discussing the role with the director, *without* meeting the other people in the cast, *without* rehearsal on the set." While stage actors normally have the opportunity of learning lines during, rather than before, rehearsal, don't take advantage of that. Rather, use line-learning to your advantage, and get to work on it immediately. In any event, you're not going to have the luxury of casual preparation you might have enjoyed in school. Broadway director Jerry Zaks expects a full-out, word-perfect run-through two weeks into rehearsal. You (the beginner, presumably with a small part) should be ready in two *days*—if you really want a second job, that is.

Then, in the studio or on the set, deliver. Share. Be alert, ready, eager, capable, and professional. Don't waste people's time asking for special favors, but make the most of every opportunity you have. Work for the success of the whole production, not just your little part in it. Help the other actors in any way you can. Michael Caine again: "Almost without exception, actors help each other. In the movie business, the list of people whose careers suddenly ground to a halt is the same as the list of actors who tried to make enemies or pull tricks." Be positive and courageous.

Finally, be healthy! Acting, unfortunately, is not a business where you can simply call in sick, even when you *are* sick. As noted earlier, no note from your mother—or your doctor—can repay the production company for the lost hours of rehearsal or shooting caused by your absence. A missed rehearsal—for whatever reason—can seriously jeopardize a stage production; a missed day on the film set could cost tens or even hundreds of thousands of dollars, even if you're not the star of the show. A reputation for chronic ailments is particularly deadly: no production company can mortgage the schedule to your migraine headaches or chronic fatigue syndrome, and actors with known illnesses may not be insurable—and hence not castable. That's why Teri Garr (*Tootsie, Close Encounters of the Third Kind*) kept her symptoms of multiple sclerosis secret for 19 years. "I was afraid I wouldn't get work," she revealed in 2002. And it's not just the money; there's a psychological factor as well. "In Hollywood, illness is equated with decrepitude," screenwriter Chris Thompson has remarked. Kathleen Turner, suffering from rheumatoid arthritis, said that "it seemed wiser to let people think I was drinking too much [which she wasn't], rather than let them know I was ill." If you suffer from such medical problems, you'll have to figure out how to work through them at maximum capacity when you need to—or seriously consider another line of work, one where you are more easily replaceable on a day-to-day basis. "The show must go on" is more than a cliché; it's an economic necessity.

Do I really *have* to do all this? You might ask. No, you don't have to, and nobody will make you. But you should. Not because we say so or because anybody says so (and few people *will* say so, because nobody in this business wants to come off as a scold). Do it because you want to be seen not only as a *great* actor but also as an actor who has a *great attitude*—not just a good one, not just an acceptable one, but a truly great one. You want to be me.

6 Other Opportunities

If you've come this far, where are you?

You have talent, personality, contacts, training, a home base, a photo-résumé, a demo reel, an agent, some knockout auditions, great interview and reading techniques, a union card, and now a first paying job. You are at the beginning of your career—and you know where to find out what you need from here on.

A career is not merely begun, however; it must be sustained. That will require your constant attention, your every effort. Nothing comes easy to an actor, and nothing *stays* easy. As two-time Golden Globe nominee Lee Pace recalls, "I remember leaving school debating whether I wanted to do TV, theater, or film. It never occurred to me that it would be so hard to get *any* job. Then you have to do it well—and that's even harder."

The steps of the ladder are irregular, with long gaps in-between. Maybe when you get half-way up, you may find the ladder isn't going where you wanted to go. "Clients will go through periods where they may not book anything for years," says longtime casting director (CD) Lindsay Jenkins. "They'll audition, they'll get out, they'll get callbacks, they'll get put on 'avail,' the avails are repeatedly released. They may go three or four years and not book a job, then all of a sudden for some reason they'll book, and then they may book three in a row. Why? Who knows? It's a wacky business."

In this final section, you can take a look at some possibilities for acting professionally *outside* the wacky business.

Outside the industry

Everything in this book, so far, is about how actors accommodate them-selves to the existing theatre, film, and television industries—which, of course, have their own rules and procedures, some of which may not thrill you as you get closer to them. "You've got to really be *sick* to want to be an actor here," says a well-known Hollywood agent. To be an industry actor means to stand, sit, smile, and squat on command, and often the command comes down from a source that you are hard pressed to respect.

Industry acting means schlepping about at your own expense, from office to office and from CD to CD, and being emotionally and financially subject to a ruling elite which you may have no personal interest in or sympathy with.

Industry acting means spending most of your life looking for work, even when you are well into middle age. And most of your professional concentration will be not on developing the work itself, but, rather, on developing your network of contacts, improving your self-marketing skills, and figuring out where your next job is coming from. That's exciting, to be sure, but will it still be so in the coming years and decades? And how will you feel at 40 years old being asked "So, tell me about yourself, Charley" by a CD half your age? How will you feel at 60?

When you must audition and interview regularly for work and when that work is rarely won—and is transitory when it does come—you may begin to develop psychological problems. After all, it is *you* that you are putting up there on the stage, and it is you getting knocked down over and over. When rejection is piled atop rejection, no matter how many successes come in-between, something happens in the pit of your stomach. Insecurity nibbles at your psyche; anxiety saps your nerve. Every job you lose must mean a personal flaw. You may retreat into a shell and self-destruct, or you may stuff yourself with bluster and become a parody of your former self. Actors who defensively overinflate their egos, promoting their talents and sounding their trumpets at the slightest occasion, become the most pathetic sights in New York and Hollywood. As the fine actor and director Austin Pendleton points out,

> Nothing bothers casting people more than the neurotic oversell, and that is because an actor who oversells himself is an actor who does not trust himself and nothing, *nothing* disturbs show business professionals more than that. Self-mistrust is, after all, the ultimate buried nightmare for anybody in the business, as it is for bullfighters and tightrope-walkers.

Are you a bullfighter or a tightrope-walker? Most actors fight contrary desires at war within them: a desire for security versus a lust for fame; a desire for personal happiness versus a need for artistic and emotional freedom. Many industry actors, even successful ones, find themselves virtual slaves to their profession and are unable to make a personal decision without first consulting their agents, their producers, and their managers. Others enslave themselves to a set of industry conventions that are brutally dehumanizing. The vast majority are poor almost to the point of starvation. You can see why your parents paled when you told them you wanted to be an actor.

More and more people today are seeking, and finding, acting careers outside the acting industries. These careers must be deemed compromising for those who seek solely to act for a living—they ordinarily require additional tasks and tangential skills—and they don't ordinarily offer even the distant hope of super-stardom or superwealth. If you are utterly committed to being a professional actor, you will probably find these quasi-acting careers unacceptable, and for the truly committed actor they probably *are* unacceptable. But you should take the opportunity to think about them, and about yourself as well, before heading off into the industry.

Comedy and solo performance

Stand-up comedy was one of the growth industries of the 1980s: the beginning of that decade saw only a handful of professional comics, mainly filling spots on the *Tonight Show* and working the occasional Las Vegas or New York nightclub gig; by the decade's end, more than 2,000 pros were working in 370 full-time comedy clubs around the country and appearing on dozens of talk/interview TV shows and a 24-hour comedy cable network—and, for that matter, teaching most of the driving-safety programs authorized by California's Department of Motor Vehicles. By the 1990s, many of those club comics had become actors, mostly in TV sitcoms, but also in films—even serious films. A partial list of ex-comics now acting professionally includes Steve Martin, Amy Schumer, Dane Cook, Ellen DeGeneres, Eddie Murphy, Drew Carey, Garry Shandling, Kathy Griffin, Jon Lovitz, Roseanne, Tina Fey, Amy PoehlerDavi, Tim Allen, Jon Stewart, Margaret Cho, Paul Reiser, Richard Lewis, Ray Romano, and Kevin Pollak.

Let's add to comedy the art of *solo performance* (the "one-man" or "one-woman" show), which today includes some of the most brilliant theatre artists of our time: Eric Bogosian, Billy Crystal, Danny Hoch, Claudia Shear, John Leguizamo, Lily Tomlin, and Laurie Anderson. This genre, which often cross-lists with performance art, normally does not begin in any wing of the worldwide entertainment industry, but arises strictly in the imagination of the artist. Often it moves into the realm of off-Broadway theatre (Lisa Kron's *2.5 Minute Ride*) or Broadway theatre (Chazz Palminteri's *A Bronx Tale*) and sometimes into film acting (Bogosian's casting in *Under Siege*). But solo performance—like comedy—is an art in itself, not merely a break-in opportunity for the industry. It may appeal to you strictly for its own considerable rewards.

Comedy and solo performance can be an outstanding way to develop stage presence, make friends in the world of entertainment, and pay the bills. It is also, as we've seen, a great stepping-stone to the stage or studio, if that's your ultimate goal. Of course, you will need an inventive wit, an original style, a uniquely perceptive view of the world around you, and gigantic quantities of self-motivation and ambition. Neither comedy nor solo performance gives you a playwright or director who might offer guidance or encouragement. But if you have (and can deliver) the goods—and that's a big "if"—put together a knockout act. Comedy, in particular, is a relatively easy field to break into, and you don't need scenery, a partner, or a role to audition for a comedy club. Most such clubs find time to look at new talent occasionally (some have an "amateur night" or an "open mike" night), and at these you can often get seen without much ado. First-class places such as the Upright Citizens Brigade Theatre (in both New York and Los Angeles, with each one also hosting a comedy Training Center) or the Second City (in Chicago, Hollywood, and Toronto) are always scouted by TV CDs looking for budding late-night talent. And the historic *Saturday Night Live* (its "life" began in 1975) has probably launched more film box office stars than any university theatre program. This is not a coincidence, however; these venues are chock-full of talent. Getting seen by talent scouts, however, requires more exposure than a single shot at your local club, so you will have to build up a repertoire of routines—and a repertoire of clubs you perform in—in order to move up the ladder.

Academic theatre

A second alternative is academic theatre. America doesn't yet have a national theatre, but we do have a series of publicly supported theatre and film-producing units in the nation's colleges and universities. These theatre, drama, video, and film departments began as academic branches of English, speech, and communications before (and shortly after) the Second World War. They have since become producing organizations that, within their obvious limitations, advance live theatre, as well as film and video art, in exciting ways. Hundreds of professional theatre artists now associate themselves, both part time and full time, with academic drama and film programs, partly for the financial security and prestige such positions can bring, and partly to have the freedom to work without commercial limitations.

A position with a university drama or film department will generally require you to *teach* acting-and/or perhaps directing, playwriting, filmmaking, dramatic literature, or theatre technique—usually for a nine-month academic year. This can leave you free to act professionally at summer theatres, and some institutions may offer some of the contacts to help bring this about. You may also be in a position to direct plays with students, and

perhaps to act in student productions as well. And, depending on the institution, you may have a high degree of freedom to teach and direct material
you choose, and in a manner you choose, as well as take occasional leaves
of absence to perform professionally in regional theatres or theatre festivals. Academic employment in this form provides a reasonable annual salary and, at most institutions, a position with eventual job security (tenure)
if you make the grade. And professors who excel in their profession may
earn quite sizable salaries, move in interesting theatre and film circles, and
enjoy even greater professional opportunities.

Academic life also provides an intellectual fervor, a great measure of
artistic freedom, the excitement of working with young people, and, at
some institutions, occasional sabbatical leaves (in addition to summers
off) with full pay. Some institutions also run professional theatres, with faculty artists hired as the situation provides, giving you a chance to enjoy the
best of both worlds.

But make no mistake: university theatres and film schools are academic, not professional, arts institutions, and any academic position
entails at least some compromise of the highest professional standards.
An academic position, as you would expect, requires far more in the
way of intellectual and pedagogical preparation than does the ordinary
Broadway or Hollywood or LORT career. University jobs are *not* easy
to come by, nor are they easy to sustain. Many universities expect their
drama faculties to publish books or articles in their areas of specialty (the
well-known "publish or perish" mandate), and all serious academic theatre departments require their staff members to develop and maintain
active careers, either as scholars (as evidenced by publication) or as pro-
fessional-level theatre artists (as evidenced by successful artistic works
both on and off campus). The best institutions also demand excellent
teaching, evidenced by sound and innovative pedagogies (teaching plans
and theories), students who look good on stage and get work when they
graduate, and outstanding teaching evaluations. And if you don't really
love teaching, you probably won't be an outstanding teacher—and won't
be able to build or sustain an academic career.

A successful academic career, therefore, is every bit as professional
and as demanding as the acting careers we have been discussing. If you
are interested in pursuing such a career, you should *at minimum* earn an
MFA degree from a highly reputable institution—the best that you can
get into. And while an MFA is considered a "terminal degree" (i.e., all you
need) for most positions in the acting/directing area, a PhD or DFA is
often helpful, even in these practical fields. Such a doctoral degree would
be a major undertaking, to be sure (a book-length dissertation is almost

always required), but it can prove immensely worthwhile and will almost certainly be necessary if your faculty position expects you to do research, initiate historical or theoretical investigations, and publish scholarly books and articles.

Whichever degree or degrees you go for, choose fields of interest and read everything you can about them; by all means, you should try to develop new ideas of your own. Learn one or two foreign languages; academic theatre is increasingly seen as a global art. Attend scholarly conventions (ATHA—the Association for Theatre in Higher Education—is the umbrella organization in this area, covering practical theatre as well as scholarship, while ASTR—the American Society for Theatre Research—dominates the areas of dramatic literature, theatre history, and theatre/performance theory) and find out how you can make an artistic or intellectual contribution to future conventions.

You will make your strongest job application by developing a professional reputation along with your academic one. Establish yourself as an actor or director or virtually anything else with a summer theatre, LORT theatre, off-Broadway theatre, or other professional group. Write and publish play reviews or scholarly essays. Write actual plays, or translate plays in the public domain (those not requiring copyright permissions), and see if you can get them produced. Make a name for yourself *somewhere*, for there are literally hundreds of applications for every drama faculty opening, even at institutions of modest repute, and your application needs the cachet of something special besides your academic degree and your splendid faculty recommendations.

The job market for drama faculty aspirants is year-round, but most positions will begin in September, with their application periods beginning a full year earlier. Openings are widely advertised by law, however (how refreshing for readers of this book!), and most campuses are scrupulous about strictly employing fair employment practices. You can find weekly or monthly job listings in Academic Keys, or HigherEdjobs, or the Association for Theatre in Higher Education (ATHE) Job Bank, or TCG's ARTSEARCH, although modest subscription rates are often required.

Finally, the truly successful university drama and film instructors are invariably people who have a love for teaching, academic freedom, and university life. Teaching, on the other hand, may be a very unhappy alternative for the person who is captivated by the desire to act professionally or who is intellectually insecure. A university instructor is not simply a professional actor or director, but a professional educator; would-be actors who go on to graduate school only to get a degree "to fall back on" may never find much satisfaction on a college campus. Essentially, an academic program is one of scrutiny and analysis as much as production and performance. Academic life is fascinating to anyone driven by curiosity and a desire for knowledge, but it is a supreme bore for someone looking for the thrill of the follow-spot or the film studio. Because it involves as much effort to become a successful professor as to be a successful actor, a budding actor should not expect to "fall back" on the profession of teaching. You will probably only fall back on your back.

Your own company

For the performer who wants to create and perform but has little or no interest in academia, there is a third alternative between the industries and the campus—the private, nonunion theatre company. Some of the most exciting and artistic work in America and abroad has, in the past, been done by such semi-professional companies, under the leadership of such near-legendary figures as the European directors Konstantin Stanislavsky, André Antoine, Jacques Copeau, and Jerzy Grotowski, and modern Americans such as Ronnie Davis, Robert Wilson, Paul Sills, Joseph Chaikin, Charles Ludlam, Julian Beck, and Andre Gregory. Such work proliferates today: in the La Mama and Labyrinth Theatre Companies in New York, for example, and the Fountain Theatre and Theatre 40 in Los Angeles. You may already know of a theatre collective or an experimental group in or near your own town.

Such amateur works often flower into full-blown professional operations, if that's what their directors wish. David Emmes and Martin Benson, together with several fellow graduates of San Francisco State University, created a tiny amateur theatre in an abandoned dockside warehouse in 1964. As we write this more than 50 years later, their South Coast Repertory Theatre, with Emmes and Benson still directing plays there, and some of their original actors still acting in them, has won the Tony Award for regional theatre and ushered dozens of new plays into the current national American repertoire. Graduates of your co-authors' university have graduated and gone out over the same period to perform on Broadway and around the world, create and administer regional theatre companies and Shakespeare festivals throughout America, and produce independent theatre and film projects that have made their mark throughout America and a wide range of countries abroad. Talented and dedicated enthusiasts can not only create theatre, but also create the theatres in which to do it.

Amateur and semi-professional theatres begin and operate outside the established acting unions or industry. Some such groups may have a short life, to be sure, but some develop an enviable measure of security. Many are communal in both art and living arrangements. Most of these groups try to make ends meet at the box office, while some survive with local or foundation grants; some thrive for a generation or more without ever going under union auspices. Some—let's go all the way here—tour the world and create theatrical history. That's certainly true of Julian Beck and Judith Malina's Living Theatre, Ronnie Davis's San Francisco Mime Troupe, and the Chicago Steppenwolf Company. And the semi-professional and all-but-wordless *Sleep No More*, which at the time of writing has been running with full houses for more than five years on 27th Street in New York City (in what they call the McKittrick Hotel, although it's not a hotel at all), has been one of the greatest hit shows in America, and has won both Drama Desk and Obie Awards.

There's nothing to prevent you from looking up and joining one of these groups, if it will take you, and there's nothing to prevent you from starting up your own. All it takes is a building, some friends, some paint and ply-wood, and some energy and ideas—and ideals. True, you will have to work in the daytime at "regular" jobs to be free to rehearse at night, but if you are doing what makes you happy, you will be well rewarded. For most people, the urge to perform need not be satisfied by working on Broadway, in Hollywood, or on the Yale Drama School stage; it can be quite satisfactorily fulfilled by acting with friends before a small audience in your own home-town. You should certainly consider this option before you pack your bags for either coast. Some of the most genuinely artistic work in the country is done at theatres like these.

What is true of the theatre is also true of film. The rapid growth of inde-pendent filmmaking in America in recent decades has been extraordinary, and a large group of nonunion amateur filmmakers is growing nation-wide. These filmmakers have a literature, a character, and an opportunity to exchange presentations. Student and amateur films are being commer-cially marketed, too, so a venture into independent filmmaking does not necessarily cut off all professional possibilities.

The video arts—and other new media—are entering a new age of decen-tralization that, at this point, holds even greater promise of diversified development. Digital camcorders, home editing studios, cable and satellite redistribution systems, interactive gaming, YouTube, and the proliferation of new forms of broadband webcasting: all these new media augur an inter-national flow of digitized transmissions of various forms that, while prob-ably not the sort of thing you learned in drama school, have already become overwhelming in their social—and sometimes aesthetic—impact. Newer and newer media, indeed, are being created every day—often by people you are now in school with, often by people very much like yourself. There are few, if any, CDs or agents who deal with these as yet uncreated formats, and you're not likely to see casting notices for them in *Backstage*—so, the advice from here is to, well, plunge in yourself!

What does all this mean in terms of "acting professionally," the title of this book? No one knows for sure, but this profession is clearly heading toward a major expansion of local, specialized, and innovative performance technologies, which will open up wholly new potentials for close-to-home training, employment, and creative artistry in the mediated-acting arts. The Hollywood connection is no longer your only track to a professional career in film/video performance—your camcorder and a few friends might just replace the roles that movie moguls had only a decade ago.

Other theatre jobs

Finally, you should be aware of the tremendous number of jobs in the theatre that are less visible than acting but more widely available. Some of them you are probably quite familiar with: director, designer, technician, playwright, and stage manager. Others were described in previous pages: agent, CD, producer, production assistant, and publicist. Chances are you haven't studied these professions—few courses exist for them in most colleges and universities. But they are, in fact, significant career options for thousands of persons trained in drama. Far more jobs are available in these areas than for actors, and far fewer people are clamoring to break in. There are even areas where the demand for talent exceeds the supply.

Such employment, of course, can lead to professional acting further on if you're still game to get on stage. It may also lead to things you find you like even better than acting. Even very successful actors—Ron Howard, Helen Hunt, Peter Berg, Clint Eastwood, Tom Hanks, Kevin Costner, Cher, Richard Benjamin, Robert Redford, Rob Reiner, and Barbra Streisand are good examples—have found a career change to directing inestimably rewarding at a certain point. Writing, casting, and producing are also where a number of ex-actors wind up, and they're usually very happy to be there. Some actors happily sit out the "middle years" of their adult lives in such positions and then return to acting in their senior years. CD Burt Remsen, acting teacher Lee Strasberg, and director/educator John Houseman enjoyed stunning success as *actors* long after establishing themselves as masters in other midlife career positions. Acting is one of only two professions in which you can start out—and then rise to the very top—during your later life. (The other is to become President of the United States, as ex-actor Ronald Reagan proved.)

Appendix

Being an actor means looking for work on a day-to-day, and increasingly an hour-by-hour, schedule. Work periods are extremely short—often just one day. And the territory in which you must find that work is exceptionally fluid—offices, studios, agents, casting directors, and producers are mostly on the move.

Digging up desirable offices is quite difficult, however, since simply looking up "acting agencies" in Google would have you find over *one million* such places, many of which are entirely bogus. And looking up "casting directors" will bring you well over *15 million* such individuals.

Trade papers—both weekly and daily—have long been the traditional source for reliable and up-to-date casting notices and actor information, but outside of New York and Los Angeles they are hard to locate on a day-to-day basis. And so, the web, when properly used (as detailed in Chapter 4), has become the main point of contact. It is lightning fast; able in an instant to transmit photos, résumés, audio clips, videos, and teleconferences. Indeed, the web now dominates the casting business.

But the web comes with a drawback: you have to know where to look, and how to sift through the millions of listings to find those few that are truly reliable. This appendix, therefore, includes only sites and publications—most mentioned in the previous pages—that are considered authoritative, have been available for a decent period, and should still be in business through the shelf life of this book.

Where to buy published information

In New York, you can find virtually any material published about acting (or the theatre)—including plays, books, journals, and trade papers—by dropping into the legendary Drama Book Shop at 250 West 40th Street, at the southern end of the Broadway theatre district. The DBS was nearly destroyed in an overnight water-pipe burst in early 2016, but since the Tony-winning actor-composer- lyricist Lin-Manuel Miranda appealed to the New York theatre population to restore it, the store has almost doubled its clientele. It's open seven days a week, and if you're not in New York you can order books from the store—and find out its current bookshop hours—at www.dramabookshop.com.

In Los Angeles, the Samuel French Theatre Bookshop at 7623 Sunset Boulevard (at the corner of Stanley) is open seven days a week and has everything published about theatre that you can imagine. In addition to being the West Coast outlet for the Samuel French catalogue of plays, it has virtually every theatre book and magazine in print, as well as a huge collection of books and magazines on film. You can find out more—including current hours—at www.samuelfrench.com.

Drop by these stores when you hit either town. In addition to books and trade papers, they also sell agent and casting director listings that you won't find anywhere else, post what's happening in local theatres, provide two-for-one discount coupons to local plays, host free talks, lectures, or book-signings by professional actors or important scholars, and sometimes share notices of rooms for rent. And the personable employees in these shops are usually theatre buffs themselves—and often actors to boot—and will be happy to offer you advice on the latest and best books on their shelves. You'll also quite possibly run into someone you know—and almost certainly someone you will soon know. If actors constitute a family, these drama bookstores tend to be its kitchen table.

Libraries

Maybe you want to sit in a comfortable library and read from a great collection of acting books. If so, there are two wonderful places for you. In New York, it's the Library of the Performing Arts (LPA) and Dorothy and Lewis B. Cullman Center at 40 Lincoln Center Plaza (www.nypl.org/research/lpa); upstairs is the magnificent Billy Rose Theatre Collection, which has clippings from America's earliest theatre days, and thousands of original donated letters about theatre that were sent to, from, and between major playwrights, actors, and directors. In Los Angeles, it's the Margaret Herrick Library at the Academy of Motion Picture Arts and Sciences (333 South La Cienega Boulevard, Beverly Hills; www.oscars.org/library). Both libraries are free. The LPA is open daily except Sunday, and is mainly devoted to stage work, and the Herrick is open Monday, Tuesday, Thursday, and Friday (but check the appropriate website for current schedules). The LPA mainly emphasizes films (as you see from the URL, this is the Academy that gives out Academy Awards), but each of these great libraries has plenty of materials on all acting media.

The two great trade papers for actors

"Trades" are available in the theatre bookshops mentioned above and at selected newsstands throughout midtown Manhattan and Hollywood/Beverly Hills. Their online sites are often as good as their print versions—and they're free.

By far the most important trade paper for actors on both coasts is *Backstage*, which in 2008 consolidated with its sister publication, the now-discontinued *Backstage West*. *Backstage* is published weekly, and contains literally thousands of casting opportunities and stage reviews on both coasts, plus regular essays on the actor's craft, training, and even how actors can save on their taxes: www.backstage.com.

Show Business, which prides itself as "The Original Actors Guide," was published in New York, weekly from 1941 to 2011, but monthly since 2011. It also lists casting opportunities along with news items and show reviews—mainly in the Big Apple: www.showbusinessweekly.com.

Two famous trades for producers

Variety. Founded as a weekly magazine in 1905 in New York, it became a daily in Los Angeles in 1933 and ended as a printed edition in 2013 when it moved online at Variety.com. Parts—though mainly intended for filmmakers rather than actors or would-be actors—are daily available free of charge. *Variety* continues to carry an international coverage of all media, focusing in particular on film and TV.

Hollywood Reporter. Published weekdays in Los Angeles, mainly covering film and TV but also (under "Culture") New York theatre. As with *Variety*, there are free online stories (with advertisements!) daily, and annually subscribed issues for cost, mostly for those "in the business." See www.hollywoodreporter.com.

Directories—office listings

At the time of writing, directories of most agency, management services, and casting directory offices on the coasts are available online at www.nycasting.com for the New York area and at www.lacasting.com for Los Angeles. More comprehensive published and (increasingly) online websites are currently (as of 2016) available for purchase at the sites listed below, as either single copies or online subscriptions. Each will provide you with current addresses and phone numbers at which theatres, studios, unions, agents, managers, and casting directors within their covered area may be located and contacted. The most reliable directories-for-purchase we know may be found via the following URLs:

www.callsheet.com *or* www.backstage.com, either of which will access the bi-monthly Call Sheet (formerly *Ross Reports*) published by *Backstage*. The most authoritative directory of agents, managers, casting directors, film studios, theatre companies, and acting schools and coaches, mostly in New York and California. Single Call Sheet copies are also available—currently for $20—at drama book stores on both coasts.

www/breakdownservices.com, which accesses Breakdown's *Agency Guide* and *CD Directory* (each covering the L.A. market), and their *New York Casting Directors and Talent Agencies*. Each of these is in a print edition (three per year) with emailed updates.

And for New York theatre information, the bible has to be the super-authoritative *Theatrical Index*, published weekly since 1964, with exhaustive coverage of—as they put it—"the who, where and what of theatre." It's expensive, though: a single print issue can be had for $15.95 at the Drama Book Shop in New York, an online subscription is $19.95, and a year-long online and print subscription will set you back $425. See www.theatricalindex.com.

Sites and books where you list

At the sites listed below you can not only find information, but send out information (résumés, photos, videos) of your own—for a fee, of course, though some initial services may be available without charge. See Chapter 4 for a full discussion of how this all works.

Actors Access, at www.actorsaccess.com.
Now Casting, at www.nowcasting.com.
NY Castings, at www.nycastings.com.
L.A. Casting, at www.lacasting.com.
Casting About, at castingabout.com—which is a division of Breakdown Services and updated daily.
The *Players Directory*, the historic L.A.- and film-based book created in 1937, and which now appears in both a print edition ($75) and an online eBook ($50). You can find both at playersdirectory.com.

Finally, institutional websites that may prove helpful include:

Performers' Unions

Screen Actors Guild (SAG), www.sag.org
American Federation of Television and Radio Artists (AFTRA), www.aftra.com
Actors Equity Association (AEA), www.actorsequity.org

Professional Associations

Association of Talent Agents (ATA), www.agentassociation.com
Casting Society of America (CSA), www.castingsociety.com
Talent Managers Association (TMA), www.talentmanagers.org

Schools and academic organizations

University/Resident Theatre Association, www.urta.com
Association for Theatre in Higher Education (ATHE), www.athe.org

Other important databases, theatre news sources, and actor services

Playbill Online, www.playbill.com
International Movie Data Base, www.imdb.com
Internet Broadway Data Base, www.ibdb.com
Internet Off-Broadway Data Base (also Lortel Archives), www.iobdb.com
Breakdown Services, Inc., www.breakdownservices.com
Central Casting, www.centralcasting.com
Showfax, www.showfax.com
Alliance for Inclusion in the Arts, www.inclusioninthearts.com

Index